D1369971

TOWARD A
EUROPEAN ARMY

TOWARD A EUROPEAN ARMY

A Military Power in the Making?

Trevor C. Salmon
Alistair J. K. Shepherd

LYNNE
RIENNER
PUBLISHERS

BOULDER
LONDON

Published in the United States of America in 2003 by
Lynne Rienner Publishers, Inc.
1800 30th Street, Boulder, Colorado 80301
www.rienner.com

and in the United Kingdom by
Lynne Rienner Publishers, Inc.
3 Henrietta Street, Covent Garden, London WC2E 8LU

Library of Congress Cataloging-in-Publication Data
Salmon, Trevor C.
   Toward a European army : a military power in the making? / Trevor C. Salmon and
Alistair J.K. Shepherd.
      p.   cm.
   Includes bibliographical references and index.
   ISBN 1-58826-236-7 (alk. paper)
   1. Europe—Defenses.   2. Europe—Military policy.   3. European Union.   4. Europe—
Armed Forces.   I. Shepherd, Alistair J.K.   II. Title.
UA646.S24   2003
355'.03354—dc21

                                                                        2003046725

British Cataloguing in Publication Data
A Cataloguing in Publication record for this book
is available from the British Library.

Printed and bound in the United States of America

   The paper used in this publication meets the requirements
∞ of the American National Standard for Permanence of
   Paper for Printed Library Materials Z39.48-1992.

   5   4   3   2   1

Contents

Tables and Figures

Tables

Figures

Preface

In 1951–1952, six Western European states created the European Coal and Steel Community in what was literally a journey to an unknown destination. Fifty years later, there are still doubts about the destination. But the six are now fifteen, and soon to be twenty-five. It is no longer just coal and steel, but a European Union that encompasses a range of competencies, including the Single Market, the Economic and Monetary Union, the Common Foreign and Security Policy, and now the European Security and Defense Policy (ESDP), which for more than a decade has tried to come to terms with the sardonic comment of Mark Eyskens: "L'Europe est un géant économique, un nain politique et, pire encore, un ver de terre lorsqu'il s'agit d'élablorer une capacité de défenses" (Europe is an economic giant, a political dwarf and, even worse, a worm until it concerns itself with elaborating a defense capability).

In 1998–2000, however, it looked as if ESDP was making real progress with "elaborating a defense capability." Since that time, some of the momentum seems to have gone out of the project, which is why this book's subtitle ends with a question mark. It may well be that, sooner or later, the EU will have an autonomous defense capability. However, while the EU often does manage to meet the targets it sets, frequently the end result, like defense contracts, takes longer than expected and emerges in a form different from what was originally intended.

*　*　*

We would like to thank the students and staff at Aberdeen University's Department of Politics and International Relations who have helped with this book. We are especially grateful for the comments, advice, and patience of David Brown, a friend and currently senior lecturer at RMAS Sandhurst, and Richard Shepherd. More personally, we would like to thank Judith, June, and Jenny for their encouragement, support, and forbearance.

—Trevor Salmon and Alistair Shepherd

TOWARD A
EUROPEAN ARMY

1

The EU Security and Defense Policy: Why It Is Important

F or many years, even decades, the European Community/European Union (EC/EU) has strived for a role on the international stage. The Union has successfully become an economic giant on a par with the United States and Japan, able to wield a great deal of influence in global economic, financial, trade, and aid issues. Yet this economic influence has never been matched by political or diplomatic influence, despite several efforts to develop an international political role. Even after the EU established its Common Foreign and Security Policy (CFSP) in 1993, it wielded such little real influence that its resulting declarations and resolutions went largely unheeded. However, as the EU enters the twenty-first century this may be about to change with the development of the European Security and Defense Policy (ESDP).

With the development of ESDP it appears that the EU states, which have consistently argued that they have a significant role to play in security affairs, are finally admitting that they need improved military capabilities to support their political declarations if they are to be taken seriously in international security affairs. As Kofi Annan stated on his return from Iraq, "You can do a lot with diplomacy but, of course, you can do a lot more with diplomacy backed up with firmness and force."[1] The EU states are beginning to put the political and institutional instruments in place, namely CFSP and ESDP, coupled with the agreements being negotiated between the EU and the North Atlantic Treaty Organization (NATO) regarding use of assets and capabilities. However, the military capabilities needed to make ESDP effective have been less quickly developed and are in danger of remaining unfulfilled aspirations.

At the December 2001 European Council summit in Laeken, just three years after the ESDP idea was relaunched, the EU announced that its ESDP had become partially operational. This is a significant step in the evolution of the EU, signaling its intent to play a crucial role in European and international security. The announcement made ESDP, with the proposed European Rapid Reaction Force (ERRF) at its core, a more permanent part of the EU. Yet development of ESDP is by no means complete and it will still require determined leadership, cooperation, innovative thinking, and additional resources to reach its full operating capability.

ESDP has been conceived, partly, as a way of bolstering the hitherto lackluster CFSP. It aims to give CFSP the military backbone it needs to be an effective policy, providing the EU with the influence in international affairs that it already has in the international economy. As will be discussed in subsequent chapters, ESDP is not a new idea, but recent events have brought the EU a little bit closer to achieving a coherent security and defense policy than ever before. The military dimension brought to the EU provides it with an instrument that it has never possessed before and should allow it to influence international events to a much greater extent than it could previously.

The need for a military dimension to CFSP was made painfully clear as the EU tried in vain to broker a peaceful resolution throughout the violent disintegration of Yugoslavia in the 1990s. Without the ability to threaten or undertake military action, the EU was unable to exert sufficient influence on the major parties and powerless to alter the course of events. Eventually, NATO air strikes, led primarily by the United States, forced a settlement in Bosnia in late 1995 and the peace was enforced by NATO's Implementation Force (IFOR). The EU had been forced to rely on the United States to bring a European conflict to an end. This scenario was repeated in Kosovo in 1999, when a much larger NATO air campaign was again required to change events on the ground. During this campaign the United States was again the dominant power, providing the majority of combat aircraft, precision-guided munitions, and intelligence capabilities during Operation Allied Force (OAF). The EU states partially redeemed themselves by providing the bulk of the ground forces needed for the Kosovo Force (KFOR), the subsequent peacekeeping operation. However, even then there were numerous problems in getting the troops and equipment into the theater, which is just on the edges of the EU's external border, and the operation was still run by NATO, using its planning and command structures. Even when the Eurocorps took over command of KFOR, it had to be heavily supported by NATO assets and personnel.

It is therefore apparent that ESDP is of great importance to the EU. It is a new policy that should create the impetus and develop the mechanisms to overcome the problems with the military capability of the EU states. Yet it is also important in a number of broader ways. First, it may reduce the perception of a unipolar international relations system dominated by a single superpower. In the post–September 11, 2001, environment this may seem optimistic, as the United States has acted almost unilaterally in Afghanistan and elsewhere, informing its allies more than consulting them. However, an enhanced EU capability in security and defense could provide alternative or complementary solutions to U.S. proposals and perhaps act as a more neutral power broker in conflicts where the United States may be seen as favoring one side over another. Difficulties may arise for the EU in certain parts of the world due to the colonial past of many of its member states; nevertheless, several former colonies have actually requested help from EU member states during crises (e.g., Sierra Leone in 2001). The EU, through its ESDP, does not desire to rival the United States in international security affairs, something that it could never do militarily, but to complement it and provide the United States with the effective support it claims to want from the Europeans. The problem here is that the United States does not always utilize the assistance offered by EU and other European states, sidelining them, such as in Afghanistan, to ensure that U.S. operations are run with no outside interference that may alter or hinder their style and tempo. Such actions risk the development of a serious rift in the transatlantic relationship.

Second, as suggested earlier, ESDP could complement the already strong economic and diplomatic instruments of the EU and its member states. This will enable the EU to provide a comprehensive range of crisis management capabilities including humanitarian aid, conflict prevention, conflict resolution, peacemaking, and postconflict reconstruction. With the ability to threaten the use of force to support its political and diplomatic statements, coupled with its economic carrots and sticks, the EU may have a better chance of influencing international events, preventing conflict, and, if necessary, intervening to restore peace and stability.

Third, given its enhanced crisis management capabilities, ESDP may reduce the burden on the United States to maintain peace and stability in and around Europe. This will go a long way toward resolving the burden-sharing debate that has dogged the transatlantic relationship for the past fifty years. In turn, this could mean that the United States, if circumstances require, could withdraw from Europe to concentrate its efforts elsewhere in the world. Allowing the United States to focus its efforts elsewhere could in fact strengthen the transatlantic relationship. In a time of serious crisis for the EU, or the rest of Europe, it would remain in the interest of the United States to help. Nevertheless, the United States will simply become more and more disillusioned with the EU if it must continue to resolve crises within Europe and, from the U.S. standpoint, relatively minor conflicts elsewhere on behalf of the EU and other European states. This sentiment is even more pronounced, and is likely to continue to grow, given the new priorities of the United States following the terrorist attacks of September 11,

2001. The EU should not need the United States to continue to provide the security under which it has developed for the past fifty years; it is unfair to the United States and damages the credibility of the EU in international security affairs. This point was made clear by the U.S. ambassador to NATO in February 2002 when he said: "The European allies need to do more, invest more money, raise their defence spending—particularly as a percentage of gross domestic product—in order to invest in new technologies. If this does not happen . . . the United States will have to shoulder a greater share of the responsibility for resolving crises here in Europe and beyond Europe."[2]

Having flourished under the U.S. security blanket for the previous fifty years, Europe is now strong and wealthy enough to provide for its own security in the new international environment, which probably does not indicate the risk of all-out war in the foreseeable future but rather a climate of instability and turmoil. If ESDP does become fully operational, and given international events since the terrorist attacks against New York and Washington on September 11, 2001, it could be that the security and stability of Europe will be left to Europeans for the first time in over fifty years.

Fourth, in light of the new strategic environment, ESDP could give a new impetus to the drive toward making the capability improvements to the armed forces of the EU member states. That impetus now appears to have declined as the momentum of 1998–1999 diminishes. If the impetus returns, the improvements should allow the EU to act independently in the international security arena while ensuring that these EU members remain compatible with the United States, enabling them to undertake joint operations where and when necessary and possibly resulting in an increased influence in decisionmaking. The United States does not rely on EU members for specific capabilities, but it does prefer to undertake military operations with the political support and military contribution of other states, especially Western-oriented states.

The EU is better prepared for those peacekeeping and reconstruction operations that the United States prefers not to undertake at the tail-end of a military campaign. By improving these skills the EU states may gain further influence. This was alluded to in May 2002 by UK foreign minister Jack Straw (echoing U.S. national security adviser Condoleezza Rice) when he talked of a "division of labor" between the United States and the European Union. He hinted that the United States was better at the tough military action and the EU at stabilizing and rebuilding regions and states.[3] Such a division may appear useful, but is in fact unhelpful to both the European Union and the United States. It will reduce the credibility of the former and increase resentment in the latter. However, it must be stressed that the principal beneficiary of improved military capabilities will be the EU. By improving the military element of its capabilities, the EU will be able to operate throughout the spectrum of conflict prevention, crisis management, and conflict resolution within and beyond Europe, improving its credibility on the international stage. As no single EU state itself could hope to have the full range of military capabilities, collaboration and cooperation between EU members appear the logical and effective solution to the tightening of defense resources.

Fifth, the ERRF may provide an additional source of conflict prevention and crisis management capability for the somewhat stagnated and underresourced UN. A rejuvenated and reinforced UN peacekeeping capability could facilitate the quicker and more effective resolution of disputes and conflicts, while reducing the perception of a Western-imposed settlement. A stronger UN should also reduce the reliance on U.S.-dominated ad hoc coalitions to intervene in regional crises, again lessening the burden on the United States to act as the "reluctant sheriff."[4] It would also mean that an effective crisis management operation could take place in parts of the world where a U.S.-dominated coalition may simply exacerbate the situation.

However, with the growing unilateralism of U.S. action in the post–September 11, 2001, environment, these may be rather optimistic objectives. The United States may be moving away from its "reluctant sheriff" role toward a more "unilateralist sheriff" character, intervening in regions of the world it chooses and using its preferred military method, including the possibility of preemptive action. At the same time, it is undertaking this role with little consultation and while reducing its involvement and interest in other parts of the world.

Sixth, although there has been little threat of all-out war within or involving EU states, there has been a continuing presence of instability, disintegration of states, and armed conflict across the world and especially in the regions close to the external borders of the EU. It is these types of crises that the EU will need to be able to handle more comprehensively than it did in the 1990s. To do so it needs an effective and fully operational ESDP. Many of the force projection capabilities necessary for ESDP will also be useful for some operations aimed at preventing the most recent danger—large-scale terrorist attacks. In particular, in operations that aim to preempt terrorist strikes and in operations where military support for the U.S. would provide a united front, an EU capability will be extremely beneficial to its standing in international affairs. The capabilities being discussed for the ERRF could be well suited to both these sorts of antiterrorist operations and the types of disputes that have broken out across the world as states break up.

In the Balkans there is a continuing need for peacekeeping forces in both Bosnia and Kosovo, and the violence of summer 2001 in the Former Yugoslav Republic of Macedonia (FYROM) suggests that there is an equally important role for the EU to play in maintaining the stability of that region. The worst of the disintegration is hopefully in the past, but there are still high tensions in several areas of the Balkans, including Montenegro, FYROM, Albania, and, further afield, Moldova. Moreover, the settlements reached in Bosnia and Kosovo will still require a peacekeeping force for many years to ensure continued stability. The violence of summer 2001 highlights the need for a military element to the proposed role of the EU in FYROM, at least in the immediate future, and then, gradually, a more civilian style operation to strengthen the internal stability of the state through political and economic assistance.

Despite the lack of an external military threat to the territorial integrity of the EU member states, the types of crisis mentioned might require a military dimension to resolve them, and throughout the 1990s the EU states were overly dependent on the United States for military action. The military dimension is a critical supporting factor for the civilian elements of the EU's conflict prevention policy. Without an EU ability to threaten the use of force, the more belligerent personalities within crisis regions will ignore the other instruments at the EU's disposal.

Finally, now that the EU has raised expectations and set out the objectives of ESDP, it cannot afford to fall short. Hence ESDP is important to the EU for the simple but crucial reason that, if it does not become an effective and credible policy, the credibility of the EU as a whole in international affairs will be jeopardized.

However, for the security of Europe to be left to the EU and its partner states, the EU will have to overcome several challenges, which revolve primarily around the military aspect of ESDP, namely the proposed ERRF. As long as these problems persist, and the EU is absorbed in attempting to resolve them, it will have little time, at least in the near future, to develop and define a coherent and effective policy. Nevertheless, these military aspects will have to be overcome, as without a credible military element to ESDP, in support of CFSP, the EU will lack the full range of capabilities for a fully operational security and defense policy.

Current Status of ESDP

The EU has traveled a long way in a short period of time in its desire to play a prominent role in European and international security. Since the latest push for a security and defense element to the EU's policy competencies began, at St. Malo in December 1998, the EU has established functioning institutional mechanisms and a military framework for ESDP.

The institutional mechanisms are intergovernmental in nature, based within the Council secretariat. There are three new bodies, the Political and Security Committee (PSC) (also known by its French acronym, COPS [Comité Politique et de Sécurité]), the European Union Military Committee (EUMC), and the European Union Military Staff (EUMS). These are in addition to the Policy Planning and Early Warning Unit (PPEWU), headed by the Secretary-General of the Council, who also acts as the High Representative for CFSP. These bodies are responsible for strategic planning, managing operations, and directing the development of ESDP and the ERRF. Decisions are taken unanimously within the PSC and the EUMC, and each state has the option to contribute, or not contribute, troops in any particular operation. It is the national governments that decide whether to send troops. The EU has also taken over the Western European Union's (WEU) satellite center and security studies institute to bolster their capabilities.

The addition of the former WEU satellite center at Torrejon in Spain will provide the EU with the ability to independently analyze and draw conclusions from various satellite intelligence sources, both commercial and military, that the center currently receives. It also provides the EU with an established capability should it wish to further develop its satellite intelligence-gathering capabilities, a crucial capability if it wants the ability to undertake fully autonomous military operations. Meanwhile, the Institute for Security Studies will be able to provide a valuable role by contributing ideas, analysis, and recommendations to the new military bodies, the General Affairs Council (GAC) and, if it is introduced, the Defense Ministers Council (DMC). In addition, it will put some of these ideas and developments into the public domain and into the wider research and academic community within Europe and across the Atlantic, generating the debate that benefits new policy developments.

The institutional situation outlined above (and elaborated on later in this book) may not be the final form the management and representation of CFSP and ESDP take. First, some institutional rationalization is necessary to reduce overlap and enhance clarity. For example, three different bodies are currently preparing work for and advising the GAC. Second, some institutional adjustments are being suggested in the context of the Convention on Europe, which reported its findings in June 2003.[5]

The military framework was agreed at the Helsinki European Council in December 1999. It put forward the plan for an ERRF consisting of 60,000 troops (15 brigades) and the necessary support and aerial and naval assets to be fully deployable within sixty days, although some units would be on almost immediate readiness levels.[6] Almost a year later the fourteen states participating in ESDP (Denmark having obtained an opt-out in 1992) pledged over 100,000 troops, 400 aircraft, and 100 naval vessels toward a pool of forces from which the EU could request assets in times of crisis.[7] At the same time, a number of capability shortfalls were identified and the states pledged to work toward rectifying these.

In November 2001 it was announced that ten shortfalls had been resolved and another forty remained, for which an action plan was developed whereby a state or a group of states would offer to remedy a particular shortfall.[8] The most critical shortfalls are in aerial and naval strategic transport, command, control, and communications (C3); intelligence, surveillance, target acquisition, and reconnaissance (ISTAR); precision-strike munitions; and force protection. In addition, a number of qualitative assessments have to be made of existing capabilities, and the readiness levels and mobility of personnel and equipment will have to be improved.

Now, the EU must further build upon the military framework to develop and acquire the military capabilities necessary to make ESDP an effective and credible policy capable of influencing international security affairs as profoundly as the EU can influence economic affairs. The EU member states today stand at a crossroads. They must either invest in certain military capabilities that will be required by the EU to enable it to undertake the full range of Petersberg tasks, or continue to stall in taking the difficult decisions and allow their own, and the EU's, credibility in international security to fall still further.

After the poor showing of European military capability in the Balkans, and especially in Operation Allied Force (OAF), it appeared that the EU states had learned their lesson and would improve and transform their militaries. Today, as the years since that crisis slip by, the impetus for reform and improvements appears to be declining rapidly.

Currently, very few of the capability acquisitions have been undertaken, though significant structural reform of the armed forces of several EU states has taken place. These reforms were first in response to the collapse of the Soviet Union and the end of the Cold War, experiences in the Gulf War of 1991, and more recently experiences in the Balkans. All states have made some adjustments, while many have undergone wholesale transformation. The Netherlands, Belgium, France, Italy, and Spain are just some of the states to have undertaken major structural reforms of their armed forces in response to the new strategic environment. They have all abolished or suspended conscription and, together with most of the other EU members, have downsized their militaries, making them more responsive, flexible, and deployable. How the militaries will restructure in light of the events of September 11, 2001, is still not fully decided, but reviews are under way to provide new roles and capabilities for the armed services. For example, in the UK the Ministry of Defense published a discussion document on developing the reserve forces for a role in "home defence and security" in support of civil agencies such as the police. In particular, support would be provided through a 500-strong reaction force from within the Volunteer Reserves in each army region.[9] In light of the national reforms that have taken place, and those that are continuing, the EU has the potential to become an effective organization for maintaining stability and security in and around Europe. However, these reforms must be followed through and supported by equipment improvements. If the reforms do produce the required force structures and capabilities, they will add a military capability to the EU's well-developed civilian capability in the field of crisis management.

The problem for the EU, and the member states that support ESDP, is twofold. First, since the end of the Kosovo conflict, many commentators, and the general public, find it difficult to identify a threat that requires the EU to have a military dimension. Second, they argue that NATO is there to cover any potential threat that does emerge. However, there are threats, if not to the national survival of the EU member states, then to the beliefs and values that these states, and the EU as a whole, advocate, and NATO appears less comfortable as a crisis management tool than it appears.

Foremost, there are a number of threats to stability and security in and around the borders of Europe that may need military action, or at least the threat of military action, to resolve. This has already occurred in FYROM in summer 2001 and may occur in a number of other areas: North Africa, Moldova, and elsewhere in the EU's near abroad. This arc of primary interest for the EU runs along North Africa, up through parts of the Middle East, and into the Caucasus and Eastern Europe (primarily parts of the former Soviet Union). In addition, the lack of military capabilities has hampered the role of the EU and its member states in the campaign in Afghanistan and thereby reduced the influence that the EU and its member states may have had on the nature, direction, and objectives of the operation. The crises of state collapse and disintegration, ethnic atrocities, terrorism, and regional instability all require the EU to have at its disposal the full range of foreign and security policy instruments, including a military option.

Second, although NATO expanded its remit from collective defense during the Cold War to include crisis management and peace enforcement during the 1990s, the United States, which dominates the organization, has been reluctant to become embroiled in European crises via NATO and has bypassed NATO for operations in Afghanistan. Indeed, the U.S. military has looked poorly upon the coalition it had with European forces in the Balkans, seeing it as "dysfunctional and never to be repeated."[10] Thus, despite being the main proponent of NATO, the United States appears to have an official line on NATO, which is different from the views of some EU states, and a different line when it comes to NATO taking action. This is partly due to the U.S. preference to further reduce its forces in Europe to free up resources for operations and contingencies where there is greater urgency in the eyes of those managing U.S. national security (e.g., Central and Southern Asia, Afghanistan, the Middle East, the Far East, Colombia). Europe is now seen as far less important, and when tough decisions are made Europe is now simply politely consulted and never given any decisionmaking role.[11]

Even the core of the U.S.-Europe relationship and NATO's most important attribute, its collective defense role, as laid out in Article 5, despite being invoked in September 2001, has become less relevant in recent years. More relevant are the types of operations envisaged by the Petersberg tasks, operations that the United States does not particularly want to become involved in. This is especially the case in and around Europe, where the United States believes that the Europeans should be carrying a greater share of the burden for maintaining stability, while it maintains stability elsewhere in the world.

As a significant percentage of NATO's planning and headquarters staff are U.S. personnel, it will be difficult to exclude them from NATO operations. Even using the concept of Combined Joint Task Forces (CJTFs), devised to allow Europeans to undertake operations on behalf of NATO without U.S. participation, there will be a U.S. element. It is also the United States, not NATO, that has the critical military capabilities and assets that the EU states lack, and the United States is unlikely to lend its assets without its personnel, thus negating the idea of the CJTF. Hence if ESDP is to encompass the Petersberg tasks, this could be the best tool to use. NATO has been reforming primarily to sustain a role for itself; though it has been quite capable in crisis management operations, it has not always been very comfortable undertaking them. It has enlarged once since the transformation of Europe in the late 1980s and early 1990s and in November 2002 announced a further enlargement of NATO bringing seven more states into the alliance. As it enlarges, it moves further from its original rationale and closer to a political organization. As the EU is also enlarging, and has invited some of the same states to join, it is creating further stability and security in a broader and more comprehensive manner than NATO could. The EU's engagement with Russia on the critical issues of political and economic reform and its aid to this stricken state is another stabilizing factor the EU brings to the continent of Europe.

So NATO, despite its attempts to reform, may be becoming a less prominent institution for managing crises within the European and international security arena. Even NATO's core role of collective defense appears less pertinent in light of the unilateralist way the United States handled the military campaign in Afghanistan. The offers of assistance from numerous NATO and EU states, in addition to Article 5 being invoked, appeared to have little military utility for the United States and were seen largely as a token of political solidarity by the European NATO members. Article 5 is not particularly relevant to the United States, as the Europeans cannot contribute much in the way of added value to a U.S. military campaign. It is also perhaps less relevant to most of the European members of NATO, for whom an external threat to their territorial integrity and survival is now perceived as unlikely in the foreseeable future. Nonetheless, NATO is an organization from which the EU could learn many lessons in the planning and conduct of military operations. If NATO were to reduce its role, or even disappear, this would not mean the end of a U.S. role in Europe. It would simply mean a much reduced role except during a serious military threat to U.S. allies in the region.

However, the success of ESDP is entirely dependent on whether the EU can develop a full operational capability for crisis management operations by learning the lessons of the Kosovo campaign. If it does not, the EU states may be left with a NATO that is reluctant or unable to engage in crisis management because of the views and concerns of its dominant member state, and an EU capability unable to fulfill the expectations created by ESDP. This would result in an underachieving EU in the international security arena and in the credibility of the EU being severely damaged.

The crisis management operations for which the EU declared itself operational at the Laeken European Council are the low-end Petersberg tasks. These include humanitarian assistance, national evacuation, and possibly traditional peacekeeping operations in less volatile situations. In essence these were operations that EU member states were capable of undertaking prior to the ESDP project being initiated. Hence, ESDP has not yet created any additional capability for the EU, though it has, through the new committees, improved the opportunities for coordination and cooperation when a crisis does occur. The agreement on a European Capability Action Plan (ECAP) in November 2001 holds out hope that some of the capability shortfalls will be overcome, but ultimately these will need extra as well as reallocated funding.

The amount of new funding required depends on the extent of the military capability the EU and its member states would like to develop, and this decision is based on the nature of the threat. On the basis of the EU's previous statements referring to a *fully* autonomous capability, the EU, and/or its member states, will have to acquire highly expensive assets such as intelligence and reconnaissance satellites and precision-guided munitions. It will also have to develop an operational planning capability and some form of permanent operational headquarters based on a core staff that can be supplemented in crises. These are developments that, apart from France, few EU states are in favor of and to which NATO, as an institution, and the United States are opposed. One of the principal reasons for opposition to developing such capabilities is the cost. These sorts of capabilities are very expensive. The *Helios 1* satellite program cost an estimated $1 billion, while a single cruise missile can cost between $500,000 and $1 million, making the decision to procure them a high-profile and large-scale commitment. Currently, defense spending across the EU states is flat and is showing no signs of significant increase after a decade of decline. Yet without an increase in defense spending, and not just a reprioritization of spending, the Helsinki Headline Goal cannot be met and full autonomy will not be achieved. If the EU, or the national defense ministries, cannot justify spending increases in terms of the threat and the utility of these newer capabilities, it will be almost impossible to acquire the funding.

The threat is harder to define now than it was fifteen years ago; its nature and impact are very different, impacting on specific targets and values as opposed to entire states and territories. The threat of terrorism has obviously risen in profile since 2001 and the means for tackling it are beginning to shift too, with discussions on preemptive action and defensive intervention. These sorts of actions require high-capability intelligence resources, both human and technological, and these require greater funding. The continuing tensions in the Balkans, South Asia, and the Middle East also all require high levels of intelligence. Without reliable and detailed intelligence, political and diplomatic action will be less effective, thereby strengthening the need to resort to military options. To be a credible actor, the EU needs to have all the intelligence it can possibly gather. If diplomacy cannot avert a crisis, such as in the Balkans in the 1990s, and intervention is required to halt the belligerent parties, then precision-guided munitions are one method to incapacitate the belligerents while limiting civilian casualties, but robust intelligence will be required. The threat has changed, and with it the capabilities to prevent that threat from materializing or to react to a crisis must also change. The threat today is not to the existence of one or all of the EU states, but to the stability of the wider European continent and the world as a whole and to the interests and values of the EU states. The capabilities required are not large standing armies made of massed ranks of tanks, but better intelligence, especially as the United States is reluctant to share its own, and smaller, highly responsive, and flexible forces capable of deploying into the periphery of Europe and beyond.

Finally, full autonomy, if taken literally, would also require a defense industrial base capable of producing the necessary equipment, spare parts, and upgrades for the whole range of potential operations envisaged by the Petersberg tasks. In addition, this would have to be done on a Europewide level to ensure the multinational nature of the supply, though on a more competitive basis than is currently used (allocating a share of work to each state). Perhaps one state could be the "prime contractor" for a particular equipment program, while others contribute their specialized skills.

Alternatively, one or two states could focus on one form of defense industry while another pair or group of states specialize in another, thereby ensuring that, within the EU, all necessary capabilities are covered. These are difficult, long-term political and economic decisions that have to be made, but without making them ESDP is likely to drift aimlessly for the foreseeable future.

Five years after St. Malo, the EU needs to move from institution building to capability building and institutional rationalization to ensure that ESDP becomes a successful policy. It needs to do this as soon as possible because it will take at least five to ten years to bring some of the capabilities the EU needs up to an operational level and it will take up to fifteen to twenty years for the EU to develop a fully autonomous military capability. The capability improvements will also require a refocusing of defense spending coupled with some short-term spending increases to develop and procure all the necessary equipment, though, as stated earlier, this is unlikely in the near future.

The EU did not achieve its goal of fulfilling the Helsinki Headline Goal by 2003, but it has put in place the institutional apparatus necessary for managing such a force, if and when it is developed and required. To have a fully autonomous force ready by 2010 at the earliest, by 2015 more realistically, difficult but crucial decisions have to be made now. Finally, these decisions should be coupled with the development of some form of strategic framework to give a basis from which to work when developing the capabilities and acquiring the equipment. Without knowing more precisely where, how, why, and when this force may be used, it will be extremely difficult to buy the appropriate equipment and provide the right force structures and training. Such a framework would also clarify how autonomous the EU states want ESDP to be, or more realistically, what level of autonomy can be agreed.

ESDP is now part of the EU's policy remit and significant progress has been made, especially in the first two years after St. Malo. It is now time to revive that momentum and tackle the hard issues, which still need to be resolved before ESDP can be declared fully operational.

Notes

1. Kofi Annan, press release, SG/SM/6598, June 15, 1998, www.un.org/news/press/docs/1998/19980615.sgsm6598.html.

2. Nicolas Burns, "U.S.-European Capabilities Gap Must Be Narrowed," press conference, Ljubljana, Slovenia, February 28, 2002, www.useu.be/categories/defense/feb2802burnsuseucapabilities.html.

3. Jack Straw, "EU-U.S. Relations: The Myths and the Reality," speech to the Brookings Institution, May 8, 2002, www.fco.gov.uk.

4. Richard N. Haas, *The Reluctant Sheriff: The United States After the Cold War* (New York: Council on Foreign Relations Press, 1997), p. 138.

5. Council of the European Union, *Presidency Conclusions: Copenhagen European Council* (Copenhagen, 2002), SN 400/02.

6. Council of the European Union, *Presidency Conclusions: Helsinki European Council,* annex 4, *Presidency Report on Strengthening the Common European Policy on Security and Defence* (Helsinki, December 1999), SN 300/99.

7. Council of the European Union, General Affairs, "Military Capabilities Commitment Declaration" (Brussels, November 20, 2000), press release, 13427/2/00. http://ue.eu.int/newsroom/oaddoc.cfm?ma...doc=!!!&bid=75&did=63995&grp=2957&lang=1.

8. Council of the European Union, General Affairs, *Statement on Improving European Military Capabilities* (Brussels, November 2001).

9. Ministry of Defense (UK), *The Role of the Reserves in Home Defence and Security: A Discussion Document* (London, June 2002), p. 5.

10. Fred Barnes, "Why the President Loses Little Sleep over Europe," *The Times,* May 21, 2002, p. 13.

11. Ibid.

2

Fifty Years of Failure

In May 1945, after six years of war, Europe was weak and defenseless:

> In the cities, the skyline was jagged with destruction: amid the ruins and craters, rubble and wreckage blocked the streets . . . machinery rusted in the bombed-out factories. . . . Roads were pitted with shell-holes. . . . Much of the countryside was charred and blackened. . . . Sheds on weekend vegetable plots became houses; cellars and caves were turned into houses. . . . The survivors . . . for them, this wasteland of rubble, rags and hunger was a prison without privacy or dignity; and like all prisons it smelled . . . of sweat and vomit, dirty socks and excrement; of decay and burning and the unburied dead.[1]

In addition, very soon the great wartime alliance would collapse. In 1945 the Allies had met at Yalta (February 1945) and Potsdam (July–August 1945). Between these meetings the atmosphere had begun to change. In May, Winston Churchill had already addressed the new U.S. president, Harry Truman, with his doubts about the future, and had referred to the "iron curtain" that was being drawn up. At Potsdam the final communiqué was vaguely worded and many of its commitments were broken almost immediately.

The year 1945 also saw the abandonment of the Morgenthau Plan, which had been adopted in 1944. It saw Germany as pervasively evil and consequently held that Germany should be permanently divided. The practical measures taken instead saw the military occupation of Germany into four zones and four years later the division of Germany into the Federal Republic and Democratic Republic.

Those four years had also witnessed the evolution of the Cold War.

15

Even during World War II, the Soviet Union had begun to exercise territorial expansion with the annexation of Estonia, Latvia, and Lithuania, and parts of Finland, Romania, Poland, northeastern Germany, and eastern Czechoslovakia, a total area of 180,000 square miles and 32 million people. The presence of the victorious Soviet armies and Communist infiltration effectively compelled Albania, Bulgaria, Romania, East Germany (Democratic Republic), Poland, Hungary, and Czechoslovakia to become Communist. There were problems too in Turkey and Greece, and in 1947 there were virulent campaigns of opposition in Western Europe to the established regimes, particularly in France and Italy. This evolving conflict was even more worrisome because of the dawning of the nuclear age, after atomic bombs were dropped on Hiroshima on August 6 and Nagasaki on August 9, 1945. Altogether, some 100,000 people were killed and another 100,000 wounded. In September 1949 the USSR exploded its first atomic bomb, ending the U.S. nuclear monopoly. Not only were these weapons awesome in their destructive power, but they had penetration, speed, relative ease of delivery, and increasing accuracy. The world looked frightening: it was atomic and bipolar.

In the West there was a clear determination to respond. In Missouri on March 5, 1946, Churchill again referred to the "iron curtain" and noted that for the Soviets, "There is nothing they admire so much as strength, and there is nothing for which they have less respect than for military weakness."[2] He went on to argue for an English-speaking "fraternal association" to counter Soviet expansion. In July 1947 the "X" article, written by George Kennan, the chargé d'affaires of the Moscow embassy, appeared in *Foreign Affairs*. The article argued:

> [T]he main element of any United States policy toward the Soviet Union must be that of a long-term vigilant containment of Russian expansive tendencies. . . . The Soviet pressure against the free institutions of the Western world is something that can be contained by the adroit and vigilant application of counter-force at a series of constantly shifting geographical and political points, corresponding to the shifts and manoeuvres of Soviet policy.[3]

Although he later disavowed the implementation of "containment," the notions implicit within it did strike a chord, and some were displayed in the formation of the North Atlantic Treaty (NAT) and other regional pacts.

The great states of Europe had once been the cauldron of international relations, but now they had to adjust to the loss of empire and the movement of truly global power to two extra-European superpowers. In addition, they had to look to the United States for help. Here began one of the continuing themes of European security and defense: Western Europeans needed to do something to help themselves, but they also had to rely upon the United States.

The United States had demobilized in Europe, from 3.1 million troops in 1945 to a dramatic drop to 391,000 in 1946, which was less than the total of British forces. It looked as if this number would fall further. Given the events in Europe, particularly after the British alerted the United States that it would be unable to continue to provide the economic and military aid necessary to assist Greece and Turkey, the United States stepped into the breach. In March and June 1947 two important policy developments took place. In the first, on March 12, 1947, President Truman told Congress that "it must be the policy of the United States to support free peoples who are resisting attempted subjugation by armed minorities or by outside pressures. I believe that we must assist free peoples to work out their own destinies in their own way. . . . Collapse of free institutions and loss of independence would be disastrous not only for them but for the world."[4] This was to be followed up by money ($400 million) and the dispatch of U.S. civilian and military missions to Athens and Ankara. The United States would supply military aid to those countries trying to support themselves, alone or in alliance.

In terms of the second factor, on June 5, 1947, Secretary of State George Marshall, speaking at Harvard, launched the economic equivalent of the Truman Doctrine, the European Recovery Program (the Marshall Plan). Marshall spoke of the "visible destruction" that was Europe, and of Europe's need to import food and other essential products. He went on:

> Any assistance that this Government may render in the future should provide a cure rather than a mere palliative. . . . [B]efore the United States Government can proceed much further in its efforts to alleviate the situation and help start the European world on its way to recovery, there must be some agreement among the countries of Europe as to the requirements of the situation and the part those countries themselves will take in order to give proper effect to whatever action might be undertaken by this Government. It would be neither fitting nor efficacious for this Government to undertake to draw up unilaterally a programme designed to place Europe on its feet economically. . . . The initiative . . . must come from Europe. . . . The programme should be a joint one, agreed to by a number, if not all, European nations.[5]

Between 1947 and 1952 some $17 billion was given to Western Europe, providing the latter with a considerable financial and psychological boost. In practice the European response to the Marshall Plan paved the way for subsequent economic integration.

A Military Worm?

On March 4, 1947, Britain and France signed the Dunkirk Treaty of Alliance and Mutual Assistance, which was to last for fifty years. In the treaty, Britain and France agreed to unite in the event of any renewed aggression by Germany. They also agreed to consult on problems affecting their economic relations, prosperity, and stability. Interestingly, in 1947 Germany was still seen as an aggressor. On January 22, 1948, Ernest Bevin, British foreign secretary, suggested a similar scheme for Western Europe. The coup in Prague in February 1948 gave these talks added edge, and on March 4, 1948, Britain, France, Belgium, the Netherlands, and Luxembourg met in Brussels to consider the terms of a mutual assistance pact. On March 17, 1948, they agreed the Treaty of Economic, Social, and Cultural Collaboration and Collective Self-Defense (the Brussels Treaty). Importantly, Article 4 (1948 version) said: "If any of the High Contracting Parties should be the object of an armed attack in Europe, the Other High Contracting Parties will, in accordance with the provision of Article 51 of the Charter of United Nations, afford the Party so attacked all the military and other aid and assistance in their power."[6] Unlike the North Atlantic Treaty of 1949, the parties also agreed "to consult with regard to *any* situation which may constitute a threat to peace, in whatever area this threat should arise." (Article 7, italics added).

In 1948 the Brussels Treaty also affirmed the danger of "a renewal by Germany of an aggressive policy." In view of later misrepresentation, it is important to note that the Brussels Treaty was to last for fifty years, after which time the High Contracting Parties could "cease to be a party" after having given notice. The Brussels Treaty provided for the creation of the Consultative Council, composed of the five foreign ministers, and under it, the Western Defense Committee, composed of the five defense ministers. In addition to the articles on defense, the 1948 treaty also had articles on promoting "the economic recovery of Europe . . . [member states will] so organise and coordinate their economic activities as to produce the best possible results, by elimination of conflict in their economic policies, the coordination of production and the development of commercial exchanges . . . social and other related services."

On June 24, 1948, the Berlin blockade began. It saw the Soviet Union closing all the West Berlin land borders so that it was accessible only by air. The blockade lasted until the May 9, 1949. It hastened the formation, in September 1948, of a military body under the Brussels Treaty, the Western Union Defense Organization (WUDO) with Field Marshall Bernard Montgomery in charge. The immediate effect of the Brussels Treaty was to provide the U.S. president with the evidence he needed to convince Congress of Western Europe's determination and ability to organize itself for defense.

In April 1948 the U.S. administration held talks about the European security situation with Senators Arthur Vandenberg and Tom Connally. On May 19, Vandenberg introduced the Vandenberg Resolution into the Senate.

Crucially, it recommended "the association of the United States, by constitutional process, with such regional and other collective arrangements as are based on continuous and effective self-help and mutual aid." It passed by a vote of sixty-four to four on June 11, 1948.[7]

Before the WUDO could become operational, it was overtaken by the signature of the North Atlantic Treaty on April 4, 1949. One result of the Berlin blockade was to accelerate talks about developing a concrete proposal to join the Brussels Treaty with North America. One of the key arguments about the NAT was the nature of the U.S. guarantee: Could the new treaty lead to an automatic guarantee to wage war if Western Europe was attacked? The United States did not want to be automatically committed to war. The NAT came into force on August 24, 1949, having been ratified by all twelve original signatories.[8]

In September of that year, the creation of the new structure began, including the Defense Committee and the Military Committee, which until 1966 also had an Executive Committee composed of the United States, the United Kingdom, and France. In December 1949 the Defense Committee agreed a strategic concept for the integrated defense of the area and in spring 1950 agreed a first draft of a four-year defense plan. However, it was only in 1952 that the NAT became an organization and the North Atlantic Treaty Organization (NATO) became a permanent organization.

On June 25, 1950, North Korean troops invaded South Korea. Three months later the North Atlantic Council (the supreme decisionmaking body created by the NAT) agreed that a forward strategy should be adopted for the defense of continental Europe so that aggression could be resisted as far east as possible. However, the plans for defense demanded extra troops; one solution was the creation of the integrated force under centralized command. At the end of the year, it was agreed that an American, Dwight D. Eisenhower, should be appointed Supreme Allied Commander for Europe (SACEUR). He took up the post in 1951, with the responsibility to organize, equip, train, and, if necessary, implement agreed plans. It was Korea that really put the "O" in NATO, and really copper-bottomed the U.S. commitment.

Europe Awakes?

It was also Korea that led to the most far-reaching European defense proposal—the European Defense Community (EDC). Previously, several Europeans had dreamed of an army of Europe. At the turn of the seventeenth century, the Duke of Sully (1559–1641) had argued for a European army of 100,000 infantrymen, 25,000 cavalry, and 120 cannon, with the support costs being shared among the nations. This army was to enforce the decisions of the Conseil Très Chrétien. Others later floated different versions of the same idea. In May 1944, six years before Korea, some European resistance leaders had argued for an "army at the disposal of this government [federal], no national armies being permitted."[9]

Now, in 1950, the Korean attack was perceived in the West as a possible precursor or diversion to a Soviet attack on West Berlin or Western Europe. In this situation, the United States began to think about the reservoir of manpower in West Germany. In July 1950, John McCloy, the U.S. High Commissioner in Western Germany, admitted that it would be "very difficult to deny the Germans the right and the means to defend their soil."[10]

In 1950, however, few Europeans were willing to envisage a rearmed West Germany. Robert Schuman, French foreign minister, had made clear during the French parliamentary debate on the North Atlantic Treaty that West Germany should and would remain unarmed. Even the new West German government was not willing to contemplate a reconstituted Wehrmacht, although in December 1949 its new chancellor, Konrad Adenauer, had said that he might be able to envisage a "German contingent in the army of a European federation, under European command."[11] The question was, however, how to mobilize and utilize this German reserve, just five years after the defeat of Germany in May 1945 and just six years after the end of the German occupation of France.

Against this background, Churchill—then Leader of the Opposition in Britain—made a celebrated speech in the Consultative Assembly of the newly founded Council of Europe, although the Council was not supposed to consider defense. His resolution was passed by a vote of eighty-nine to five, and he has been often seen as the "father" of the modern idea of a European army. Having said that the Assembly had no power apart from counsel, Churchill went on:

> There must be created, and in the shortest possible time, a real defensive front in Europe. Great Britain and the United States must send large forces to the Continent. I have already made my appeal to Germany. France must again revive her famous army. . . . All . . . must bear their share and do their best . . . we should make a gesture of practical and constructive guidance by declaring ourselves in favour of the immediate creation of a European army under a unified command, and in which we should all bear a worthy and honourable part. Therefore . . . I beg to move that: The Assembly . . . calls for the immediate creation of a unified European army subject to proper European democratic control and acting in full cooperation with the United States and Canada.[12]

Jean Monnet, and the same team that worked on the Schuman Plan to create the embryonic European Coal and Steel Community (ECSC), were equally concerned about the turn of events. They began to develop a proposal in the military area. Monnet was worried that, rather than taking up Churchill's idea, the United States might plan to arm up to ten West German divisions by putting them in NATO under the unified command of a U.S. general, Eisenhower. Monnet had planned that a political Europe would be the "culminating point of a gradual process," but now decided that "the federation of Europe would have to become an immediate objective. The army, its weapons, and basic production would all have to be placed simultaneously under joint sovereignty."[13] It would be a European solution to the problem of defense.

The French were concerned about the reestablishment of the West German army and wanted therefore to propose the same methods as for coal and steel: "a European Army with a single High Commissioner, a single organization, unified equipment and financing, and under the control of a single supranational authority (German units would gradually be integrated into this initial structure)."[14] He believed that Adenauer would agree. On October 24, 1950, René Pléven announced the French plan to the French National Assembly. He signaled that West Germany had a right to make its contribution to European security but also argued that there was now a need for a European army. In such a case,

> the creation, for our common defence, of a European Army tied to political institutions of a united Europe . . . only common institutions will do. The army of a united Europe, composed of men coming from different European countries, must, as far as is possible, achieve a complete fusion of the human and material elements which make it up under a single European political and military authority. A Minister of Defence would be appointed by the participating governments and would be responsible, under conditions to be determined, to those appointing him and to a European Assembly. . . . His powers . . . would be those of a national Minister of Defence. . . . The contingents furnished by the participating States would be incorporated in the European Army at the level of the smallest possible unit. The money for the European Army would be provided by a common budget. . . . The participating States which currently have national forces at their disposal would retain their own authority so far as concerned that part of their existing forces which was not integrated by them into the European Army. . . . The European force placed at the disposal of the unified Atlantic Command would operate in accordance with the obligations assumed in the Atlantic Treaty . . . to invite Great Britain and the free countries of continental Europe . . . to work together.[15]

Coming so soon after the Schuman speech of May 9, the tide of events seemed to favor the Pléven proposal.

The United States, at this stage, had not given up on the controlled rearmament of Germany, but found opposition in Germany to their plans. In Germany there were deep divisions over Pléven, but the government reacted favorably, as long as the Federal Republic was given full equality in the new scheme. Nonetheless, for a while there were two schemes: "an 'Atlantic' Germany Army, or a European Army."[16] The immediate response in the French National Assembly, despite a vote in favor of the Pléven proposal in principle, hinted at the problems ahead. Concern was voiced about the lack of British involvement, the creation of a camouflaged German general staff, and, indeed, the very idea of integration in this area.

The European Defense Community

The conference to discuss the proposal opened in February 1951 with five full participants: Belgium, the Federal Republic of Germany, France, Italy, and Luxembourg. The Netherlands initially was represented by an observer, but became a full participant in October 1951. Britain, Denmark, and Portugal were represented by observers.

Although the political debate became torrid, the European Defense Treaty was signed on May 27, 1952, by the six European Coal and Steel Community states.[17] It consisted of 132 articles and 12 associated protocols, and in addition there were a number of declarations and conventions, principally concerning reciprocal security guarantees and cooperation arrangement between (1) the European Defense Community and NATO, (2) the United Kingdom and the EDC, and (3) the United States, the United Kingdom, and the EDC.

The treaty defined the EDC as a "supranational European organization . . . supranational in character, comprising common institutions, common armed forces, and a common budget." It was supranational because its decisions would be binding, some could be taken by a majority vote, and it envisaged the "fusion" of the armed forces (under certain conditions), not just coordination or cooperation.

The EDC had an exclusively defensive remit, was to be within the NATO framework, and asserted that an attack on one member state would be regarded as an attack on all. It would ensure the security of its members "by taking part in Western defence within the framework of the North Atlantic Treaty." NATO's SACEUR would supervise the organization, equipping, and instruction of the force, and "shall exercise over them such authority and responsibilities as devolve on him by virtue of his mandate. . . . In time of war [he] shall exercise over the Forces . . . full powers and responsibility." Member states would be able to retain national forces for overseas defense and international missions.

The institutional system consisted of a Council, composed of a representative from each participating state's government, which was to harmonize the actions of the Board of Commissioners and the member states. Voting in the Council was to be weighted to reflect the military contributions made by each state. The Board of Commissioners, consisting of nine members serving six-year terms, was to be supranational, in that it would receive instructions from the Council but not from individual member states. It was to be the EDC executive organ. Initially the Assembly was to be shared with that of the European Coal and Steel Community, except that France, West Germany, and Italy would each have three additional members. Like the ECSC, the Assembly was to receive an annual report from the Board of Commissioners and it could force its resignation by a two-thirds majority. According to Article 38 of the treaty, the Assembly was also to "examine problems arising from the co-existence of different agencies for European cooperation . . . with a view to ensuring coordination within the framework of the federal or confederal structure." The EDC was to be part of a wider European political authority.

The basic military units would be composed of troops of the same national origin, but these would be dependent on supranational echelons, which would fulfill logistical and maintenance functions. The army units would form an Army Group (there were broadly similarly arrangements for the other services), composed of different nationalities, and the general staff would be integrated. Eventually the Board of Commissioners was to take over recruiting, the formulation of a common doctrine, plans for mobilization, and the territorial distribution of forces, all within a NATO framework. A military protocol laid down peace- and wartime establishments. All of this was to be supported by a common budget, financed by revenue from national contributions, the EDC's own income, and foreign aid. The Board of Commissioners was to prepare common equipment, arms, supply, and infrastructure programs, as well as authorize the import and export of war matériel. In addition, the Federal Republic had to accept continuing restrictions on the production of atomic, biological, and chemical weapons, missiles, large naval vessels, and military aircraft. The treaty was to last for fifty years and cover the European territory of the member states only, although its forces might be used to defend the European territory of non-EDC but NATO members. It is necessary to emphasize, then, that there was to be both a European army and a European defense identity and indeed community, but that the EDC was firmly within the NATO ambit.

In spring 1952 the treaty was approved in principle by the French National Assembly, German Bundestag, and Dutch States-General, but it was already clear that it faced a rough ride if ratification was to take place. This despite the fact that the European Coal and Steel Community came into existence on July 25, 1952. Moreover, the Ad Hoc Assembly, composed of the ECSC Assembly plus nine members co-opted from the

Council of Europe's Consultative Assembly and thirteen observers, began to examine the establishment of a European Political Committee (EPC), regarded by many as a sine qua non of the EDC's success.

French unease continued to grow with fears about West German rearmament, the apparent abandonment of France's own national forces, and the ability of the new European Defense Force to deter or stop a Soviet attack. There was also concern that, despite a gradual firming up of British and U.S. commitments, these assurances did not go beyond existing obligations and did not answer the fears about German revanchism. Moreover, the followers of de Gaulle objected to France accepting ties and constraints on its freedom that Britain had not. In addition, the French were increasingly preoccupied with events in Indochina, suffering a decisive defeat at Dien Bien Phu in May 1954. The question of the ability to fight for and defend their overseas territories was therefore of critical importance to them, and a majority believed that the EDC would further dilute that ability. The French government's attempts to meet these criticisms by proposing an additional protocol to the treaty that, in effect, would have allowed France to retain a national army were not accepted by the other five member states as part of the treaty, although they did accept the protocol as an interpretative text.

The Dutch parliament was the first to ratify the treaty. Although the Netherlands would have preferred a NATO solution, it accepted that France would only accept the rearmament of Germany on the basis of an integrated European army. Constitutional issues arose in both Belgium and the Federal Republic of Germany. In the former, the issue was whether the supranational character of the EDC clashed with Belgian constitutional provisions on sovereignty and the ability to make war and peace, but both Belgian chambers voted overwhelmingly to approve the ratification bill.

In West Germany, the opposition Social Democrat Party opposed the EDC. It complained that West Germany was not being treated as a genuinely equal partner, worried about its impact on German unification, questioned whether it had sufficient military power, and was anxious about the implications of rearmament in Germany itself. There were also questions about the compatibility of the EDC with the German Basic Law. Chancellor Adenauer only gained a sufficient majority after elections in September 1953 to change the Basic Law and secure ratification. He saw German membership in the EDC as a way of avoiding neutralization, or German incorporation into the Soviet bloc, as well as offering the positive advantages of easing historic Franco-German tensions and achieving full equality for Germany. In July 1954, as tensions and doubts mounted in France, Adenauer made it clear that the Federal Republic of Germany expected full sovereignty shortly, and in the absence of an EDC it would have a national army (although he preferred the EDC solution).

In Luxembourg ratification was overwhelmingly agreed, but in Italy there were a number of difficulties. Although a bill to allow ratification was finally presented to parliament in April 1954, and subsequently approved by the relevant parliamentary committees, it did not go before the full chamber before the summer recess. The French decision in August 1954 rendered the Italian debate irrelevant.

The crucial French vote was ultimately on a procedural motion that the occasion was not appropriate for a debate and the issue be rejected without further consideration. The EDC mustered only 264 supporters, while 319 opposed, 12 abstained, and a further 31 deputies (including 23 members of the government) took no part in the vote. All the Communists voted against the EDC, as did all but two of the Gaullists (one also abstained). Only the Movement Républicain Populaire (MRP) voted solidly for the EDC (though two voted against it and four abstained). Other parties were about equally divided.[18]

Although some of the urgency had now gone out of the European rearmament question, following the armistice in Korea in 1953, there was still the question of the position of the Federal Republic of Germany and German forces. It was the British, who had opposed the federal nature of the EDC, who were now responsible for salvaging the situation, convening a conference that led to the Paris Agreements of October 1954. By these agreements Italy and the Federal Republic of Germany were to join a remodeled Brussels Treaty Organization (BTO), the Western European Union (WEU), which was to be integrated militarily into the NATO framework, and a sovereign Federal Republic was to join NATO. With the collapse of the EDC, the EPC ambitions collapsed too, and the aspiration to build a federal or confederal structure had to be put in abeyance.

The Paris Agreements and the reformulated Brussels Treaty allowed the rearmament of the Federal Republic, but with certain guarantees regarding the development and deployment of atomic, biological, and chemical weapons. Machinery was set up to limit the size of German armed forces—which were to be the same as finally agreed in the EDC (twelve divisions and a thousand aircraft)—and the quantities of armaments. The WEU was to monitor the situation. The rearmament of West Germany was made palatable by Britain agreeing that it would

> continue to maintain on the mainland of Europe, including Germany, the effective strength of the United Kingdom forces which are now assigned to the Supreme Allied Commander Europe, that is to say four divisions and the Second Tactical Air force, or such other forces as Supreme Allied Commander Europe regards as having equivalent fighting capacity. She undertakes not to withdraw these forces against the wishes of the majority of the High Contracting Parties. . . . This undertaking shall not, however, bind her in the event of an acute overseas emergency [or] too great a strain on the external finances of the United Kingdom.

The United States undertook to maintain its forces too.

The new agreement involved nothing beyond intergovernmentalism and was therefore acceptable to the British. It made clear that the WEU would work in close cooperation with NATO; "recognising the undesirability of duplicating the Military Staffs of NATO, the Council and its agency will rely on the appropriate Military Authorities of NATO for information and advice on military matters."[19]

These arrangements seemed to resolve the outstanding issues, but before long the WEU became NATO's junior sibling and was soon engulfed by it. Nonetheless, many provisions of the 1948 Brussels Treaty remained, including the old Article 4 provision (now in Article 5) on automatic help to those attacked in Europe. That provision is still in force.

A New Direction

For the Six, the founders in 1952 of the European Coal and Steel Community and later the European Economic Community in 1958, the European Defense Community was a response to the Korean War, the problem of German rearmament, a development of the ECSC proposal of Monnet and Schuman, and partly a fulfillment of the dreams of Monnet and Pléven.

Policy actors were mindful that European integration had a political vocation. Indeed, one important mainspring of the European momentum had been the realization that in a "world dominated by political and economic units of continental dimensions, the European nations cannot hope to survive on a basis of political or economic independence."[20] Europe was becoming an object of the game of international politics rather than a participant in it. Many came to believe that only a united Europe would recover the continent's old greatness, significance, and influence. By the time of the Messina Conference of 1955, the path of unity was regarded as "indispensable if Europe is to maintain her position in the world, regain her influence and prestige."[21] The new Europe was to become an actor on the world stage in its own right, acting as a single unit. This basic aspiration surfaced on several subsequent occasions. In the Treaties of Rome of March 1957 they agreed to build the "foundation of an ever closer union among the peoples of Europe,"[22] but the Six acknowledged that the first step now should be taken in the "economic field."[23] The difficulty was that "supranationalism," for the time being, was a dirty word, and it was clear that the ECSC and drafts of the EDC and EPC were no longer to be models.

Defense continued to be a problem. In the negotiations for the Treaty Establishing the European Atomic Energy Community (Euratom), there were difficulties because of arguments about the manufacture of atomic bombs, with France not wanting to forgo its manufacture on military grounds. France also thought that such a treaty, with such a commitment, would be unacceptable to the National Assembly. The emphasis now was to be on low politics and so, in the Treaties of Rome, defense was scarcely mentioned.

Defense is mentioned in a negative way in Articles 223–225. Article 223 stated: "No Member State shall be obliged to supply information the disclosure of which it considers contrary to the essential interests of its security" and it "may take such measures as it considers necessary for the protection of the essential interests of its security which are connected with the production of or trade in arms, munitions and war material; such measures shall not adversely affect the conditions of competition in the common market regarding products which are not intended for specifically military purposes."

Article 224 allowed the member states to consult together "with a view to taking together the steps needed to prevent the functioning of the common market being affected by measures which a Member State may be called upon to take in the event of serious internal disturbances affecting the maintenance of law or order, in the event of war or serious international tension constituting a threat of war, or in order to carry out obligations it has accepted for the purposes of maintaining peace and security."

Article 225 enabled the Commission, and the European Court of Justice (ECJ), to become involved if "the conditions of competition in the common market" were distorted. These articles are still valid, in Articles 296–298 of the Consolidated Version. As Trevor Taylor has said:

> Thus there was no formal exclusion of defence from the Community agenda in the Treaty of Rome. Instead it was largely ignored and no commissioner was appointed with responsibility for this area. Unless the narrow view is taken that anything not specifically allowed is illegal, it would seem that the EC could expand into defence without actually violating the Treaty of Rome if its members so chose. Evidence favouring a wide interpretation of the treaty can be found in the Preamble, which noted members' determination to "strengthen the safeguards of peace and liberty," and in Article 235, [now Article 308 of the Consolidated Version] which provides for Community activity in areas not anticipated when the treaty was signed.[24]

This did not happen under the auspices of the Rome treaties. Nonetheless, the political vision (foreign policy, security, and defense) did not disappear. It was de Gaulle, coming to power in France in 1958, who lost no time in proposing that the Six, the members of the EEC, should engage in foreign policy discussions and cooperation. After some skirmishing, they agreed in November 1959 to meet quarterly outside the framework of the treaties and without the presence of the Commission: "The consultation will concern both the political extension of the activities of the Communities and other international problems."25

At a summit meeting in Bonn in 1961, the six members of the European Economic Community (EEC/EC) agreed to hold

> at regular intervals, meetings whose aim will be to compare their views, to concert their policies and to reach common positions in order to further the political union of Europe thereby strengthening the Atlantic Alliance. The necessary practical measures will be taken to prepare these meetings. In addition, the continuation of active cooperation among the Foreign Ministers will contribute to the continuity of the action undertaken in common.26

The Bonn summit also agreed to set up a committee to study a statute for a political union, with Christian M. Fouchet as its chairman.

The Fouchet talks of 1961–1962 on a treaty of political union faltered over the perennially disputed issues in European cooperation: whether to move away from supranationality, to circumvent the role of the EC Commission, and whether to deal with defense outside the NATO context, with the divergence of view being between the French and the Six minus France (or the Federal Republic of Germany, Italy, and Benelux). The first plan was put forward in November 1961, bearing the full imprint of de Gaulle's views. This union was to be of "states" not of "peoples." Fouchet proposed a "common foreign policy . . . to strengthen, in cooperation with other free nations, the security of the Member States against any aggression by adopting a common defence policy." Decisions were to be taken unanimously and there was to be a European Political Commission to direct its work. It was very much a Gaullist attempt to create an intergovernmental alternative to the Community method, the role of the Commission, and integration. The Political Commission was also charged with working toward a "unified foreign policy and the gradual establishment of an organization centralising, within the Union, the European Communities."27

A second draft was put forward in January 1962, but this was turned down as a basis for discussion since it seemed to disregard the suggestions of the others. The breakdown of these talks in April 1962, however, did not mean the end of these and related issues, which were back on the agenda at the end of the decade.

After the resignation of de Gaulle in April 1969, another attempt to put the integration movement back on course was made at The Hague. It became famous for its triptych: completion, deepening, and widening. "Deepening" embraced the objectives of "progress in the matter of political unification" and paving "the way for a united Europe capable of assuming its responsibilities in the world of tomorrow and of making a contribution commensurate with its tradition and its mission." Under this procedure, "all major questions of foreign policy" could be discussed.[28] "All" originally included the "political aspects of security" but, increasingly, EPC ministers found the distinction between the "political" and other aspects of security hard to maintain. In essence, they tried to uphold the old fiction of the Council of Europe: they would discuss questions that, within a national parliament, would be dealt with by a minister of foreign affairs but not those that would be handled by a minister of defense.

The system was to operate separately from the Community system per se, in that it was outside any treaty framework. The Commission was merely to be "consulted" and the European Parliament "associated." There was no role for the ECJ. There was to be no question of voting—every decision was to be made through consensus. In addition, the work of the EPC was to be chaired by the state occupying the Council presidency, with that state also hosting meetings and being responsible for providing "secretarial service and . . . practical organization of the meetings."[29]

This EPC or Davignon system was avowedly intergovernmental and was to run in parallel with the EC treaty system. Some, like Ralf Dahrendorf, initially saw this as a great strength, recognizing the reality of interaction between sovereign states.[30] The Commission saw the avoidance of existing institutions as a retreat from Community to intergovernmental action. However, a common policy, as distinct from cooperation in foreign policy, remained only a long-term objective.

Strengthening Europe's Voice in NATO

In 1961 and 1967 Britain had applied to join the EC. On both occasions de Gaulle said no. As part of the British attempt to become more overtly European, in 1968 Denis Healey, the British secretary of defense, played a pivotal role in creating Eurogroup. For a while Healey had been organizing informal dinners of the European defense ministers in the evenings before the NATO Council meetings, and with the help of Helmut Schmidt, German defense minister, managed to change this gathering into Eurogroup in November 1968. Eurogroup was started without agreement on its constitution, powers, and organization. Given that the Mansfield amendment, which argued that unless the Europeans contributed more to the common NATO defense the numbers of Americans present in Europe should be reduced, was being debated in the U.S. Senate, Healey had U.S. support, from both Lyndon Johnson and Richard Nixon, for a European caucus in NATO.

The idea that Western Europe could show what it was collectively doing was a publicity mechanism by which the European contribution could be better appreciated in Washington. Another motivation may have been a growing uncertainty about U.S. commitments:

> [T]o put it more bluntly—the thought may have been occasionally thought, even though hardly expressed, that it might not necessarily be possible to count indefinitely on the American presence being maintained. . . . [I]f there was any risk of diminution or loss of the American presence, it would be a valuable precaution that the Europeans should have some means already established, even if in a shadowy form, by which they could consult on defence matters.[31]

Some worried that doing anything might turn the diminution of the U.S. presence into a self-fulfilling prophecy. This was one reason for keeping the group informal. It was not going to be another EDC. As Denis Healey himself said, "Differences on strategic policy have prevented it from providing that European pillar inside NATO for which I originally hoped; but it has been of some value in developing common European projects for arms and equipment."[32]

Eurogroup's official aim was

> to help strengthen the whole Alliance by seeking to ensure that the European contribution to common defence is as strong and cohesive as possible . . . in two ways. It: enables its members to improve the effectiveness of their contribution to the Alliance by co-ordinating their defence effort more closely, thereby making the best use of resources available for defence: provides an informal forum for an exchange of views by Defence Ministers on major political/strategic questions affecting the common defence.[33]

It was hoped that a more European voice could be articulated. Given the events in France of May 1968, de Gaulle was not the force he had been. Europe was back on the agenda. However, France did not become a member of Eurogroup. To further European defense at this time seemed inopportune and, in the French view, Eurogroup was too closely tied to NATO—meeting on the eve of the NATO's Defense Policy Committee, of which France was no longer a member.

It also must be remembered that in 1965–1966 de Gaulle had engineered the biggest crisis that the European Community suffered, the "empty chair" crisis. This came about, at least partly, from de Gaulle's view that "nothing of any importance either in the initial planning or the later operation of the Common Market" should be decided upon except by national governments. Otherwise member states would "be ruled by some sort of technocratic body of elders, stateless and responsible to no one."[34] In 1959 de Gaulle had launched a similar attack on NATO, when he refused the NATO tenet of "integration" and emphasized: "It is necessary that the defence of France be French . . . the concept of war or even of a battle in which France would no longer be herself and would not act on her own accord, following her own goals, such a concept could not be accepted." Integration could not be accepted: "each country must play its own part."[35] Portugal also did not take part until after the revolution of 1974, claiming that the focus of its activity was Africa, given its colonial commitments.

Eurogroup also suffered because there was a plethora of other fora for consultation of wider defense and foreign policy interests; indeed, the acronyms of organizations resembled "alphabet soup." Eurogroup did, however, contribute to increasing defense coordination, and in 1970 it agreed the European Defense Improvement Program, supplementary to existing national plans, with a total outlay of $1 billion between 1970 and 1975.

There was perhaps another reason for the formation of Eurogroup in 1968, namely the invasion of Czechoslovakia on August 20–21, 1968. The period 1945 to the late 1960s had seen a number of crises: Berlin in 1948, Korea in 1950–1953, Hungary in 1956, the Berlin Wall crisis of 1961, and the Cuban missile crisis of 1962, among others. For the West, the invasion of Czechoslovakia with 40,000 troops following the Czech government's liberalization program, the "Prague Spring," seemed to sum up the attitude of the Soviet Union. Little seemed to have changed since the invasion of Hungary in 1956. Making matters worse at the end of the 1960s was the Brezhnev Doctrine, or the doctrine of limited sovereignty. In November 1968 the general secretary of the Communist Party of the Soviet Union (CPSU), Leonid Brezhnev, announced:

> When internal and external forces hostile to Socialism attempt to turn the development of any Socialist country in the direction of the capitalism system, when a threat arises to the cause of Socialism in that country, a threat to the security of the Socialist commonwealth as a whole, it already becomes not only a problem for the people of that country but also a general problem, the concern of all Socialist countries.[36]

While the doctrine did little more than reiterate the central tenets of Soviet policy, it alarmed the West because it implied a greater Soviet willingness to intervene. After 1968 it looked as if even greater control was to be exercised over Soviet states.

Czechoslovakia also killed off one of de Gaulle's pet ambitions, of a European entente "from the Atlantic to the Urals," so that Europe could be the center of civilization once more.[37] Part of this involved a deal with West Germany (the 1963 Franco-German Treaty) and the reunification of Germany. It was also about taking on the Anglo-Saxon hegemony in NATO. If France could lever some room to maneuver in NATO, perhaps others could follow suit in the Warsaw Pact. France, for de Gaulle, was the only European power capable of taking the lead to achieve the reunification of the two halves of Europe, so that Europe could play a significant role in the world independent of the two superpowers. De Gaulle hoped that the 1963 treaty with West Germany could lead to a Franco-German bloc at the heart of European politics to act as a check on U.S. power. However, the West Germans, (un)fortunately at the time, also valued the U.S.-NATO connection—coming just two years after the erection of the Berlin Wall.

De Gaulle had a view of restoring French grandeur and a global and European role for France. This was seen in his proposals for a directoire between France, the UK, and the United States that would be able to make decisions on global questions affecting their security, with France resuming its historic role. It was also seen in the priority de Gaulle gave to the force de frappe—the independent nuclear force of France. As Lawrence Freedman says: "French nuclear strategy became linked to the challenge to the very concept of an Alliance. . . . French enjoyed the frank disclosure of the unreliability of America's nuclear guarantee."[38] For de Gaulle the force de frappe was the major factor in allowing French influence in international power. Without it, France would always be dependent on the United States. The force de frappe put France on an equal status with Britain, and crucially in a different league from the Federal Republic of Germany. For de Gaulle, as for Monnet in 1950, the long-term relationship between France and West Germany was key.

Britain had a different perspective. It too wished to be "great," but for much of this period it simply assumed this to be true, even if economic resource issues occasionally became a problem. In 1952 Sir Anthony Eden, British foreign secretary, had explained, partly in the context of the EDC:

> Frequent suggestions have been made that the United Kingdom should join a federation on the continent of Europe. This is something which we know, in our bones, we cannot do. We know that if we were to attempt it, we should relax the springs of our action in the Western democratic cause and in the Atlantic association which is the expression of that cause. For Britain's story and her interests lie far beyond the Continent of Europe. Our thoughts move across the seas to the many communities in which our people play their part, in every corner of the world. These are our family ties. That is our life: without it we should be no more than some millions of people living on an island off the coast of Europe, in which nobody wants to take any particular interest.[39]

The traditional attitude was to be one of "cordial caution."[40] The plans for a federal Europe concerned the continent much more than Britain, and fundamentally Britain was not solely a European power. As Churchill had said in Zurich in 1946, Britain saw itself as the "friends and sponsors of the new Europe" but not, it would seem, an integral part of it.[41] In 1953 he had

said that Britain's relationship with Europe "can be expressed by preposi-
tions, but the preposition 'with' but not 'of'—we are with them, but not of
them."[42]

These traits had been made manifest in Britain's attitude toward the
Schuman Plan of 1950 and subsequent negotiations on the EDC. Britain
liked intergovernmental organizations such as NATO, the Council of
Europe, and even the Brussels Treaty and the WEU. Gradually some elements of this changed with the British application to join the European
Economic Community in 1961 and 1967. Britain came to appreciate that
there were problems in secular trends in economic power; that the "special
relationship" was not as special after Suez and the Cuban missile crisis; and
that its leadership of the Commonwealth was troubled. However, at its root,
British thinking remained the same.

For the "independent" deterrent, Britain had at first relied on the "V-
bombers," but increasingly found that there needed to be a missile replacement. Given the trauma of trying to develop a missile system in 1962, the
UK accepted the offer by the United States at Nassau for Britain to buy
U.S. Polaris missiles but supply the submarines and warheads themselves.
There were many questions about how "independent" the British bombs
were, although it was maintained that the decision to use them was to lie
with the British. The agreement at Nassau said that the Polaris missiles
were "for the purpose of international defence of the Western Alliance in all
circumstances . . . except where [Her Majesty's Government] may decide
that supreme national interests are at stake."[43]

The British deterrent was a contribution to the NATO deterrent and
made the risk calculations of the USSR much more difficult. In 1967 the
leader of the opposition, Edward Heath, gave a tantalizing clue as to his
thoughts, when he argued that there may be a "nuclear force based on the
existing British and French forces which could be held in trusteeship for
Europe as a whole," although he did not expand on that argument.[44] A
major problem for the British was accepting that Britain alone could only
do so much—it needed allies, but were they to be U.S. or European? In this
period the unequivocal answer of the British was the United States and
NATO.

The answer for West Germany on defense was also the United States
and NATO, but it was more complicated. Throughout the 1945–1970 period
the problem of Germany was at the heart of the European enterprise. It was
this problem that led Monnet, in 1950, to take his initiative, since he feared
an "increasing acceptance of a war that is thought to be inevitable," not
because Germany "might initiate something but because other countries
were treating her as the stake in their power games."[45] The decisive
German influence on policy was Chancellor Konrad Adenauer, who was
elected in 1949 and held the office for fifteen years. Adenauer placed his

trust in Western values and had a profound distrust of the Soviet Union and communists and their various unification offers, which invariably had conditions attached such as the neutralization of a united Germany. Adenauer also favored European integration over the discredited nationalism that had besmirched Germany. There was also the belief that identification with Western European developments offered a path to moral, political, and economic rehabilitation, as well as to strengthening national security, given the perceived threat from the communist East, especially the USSR. There was a real debate over the relative priorities to be given to a Western orientation as against a hope of reunification, but the distrust of the Soviets and the desire to be under the security umbrella provided by the West led to the opting for European integration and ultimately the Atlantic Alliance. The Federal Republic of Germany was thus a founder member of the ECSC and of the abortive EDC, and in 1955 joined NATO. It had already been under the NATO strategy of forward defense, which was agreed in New York in September 1950. This remained the position until the end of the Cold War.

Being at the heart of the Cold War, Germany could not afford the luxury of the French position—France knew that the United States was in West Germany and would protect it anyway. Germany needed to be a solid and loyal member of the Alliance. It also knew that it needed France's help in rebuilding its position, and at times, such as in the relationship between Adenauer and de Gaulle and the 1963 Franco-German Treaty, some feared that Adenauer was too much under the sway of de Gaulle (although on key issues like the Fouchet Plans, Germany was adamant that any such proposals had to be seen within the context of the Alliance and as strengthening it). By the end of the 1960s, Germany had become preoccupied by Ostpolitik under the guidance of Willy Brandt—foreign minister from 1966 to 1969 and then chancellor from 1969 to 1974. He chose to endorse a new approach, namely that the Federal Republic needed to recognize realities in order to change them and thus to establish closer relations with the East. Ostpolitik began in earnest in October 1969 with the ultimate aim of increasing cooperation with East Germany. In 1970 the Federal Republic, the USSR, and Poland signed treaties accepting the postwar frontiers as inviolable (though not immutable).

A New Beginning

On January 1, 1973, the six EC members became nine with the accession of Denmark, Ireland, and the United Kingdom. After the departure of de Gaulle, the agreement of The Hague, and the successful agenda-setting summit in Paris in October 1972, there was an air of excitement about the new start for European integration. However, early in its existence, the nine-member Community came under a strain that was to prove almost too great. The activity and interest was belied by the absence of the political will to move forward in a fundamental way. That absence was both caused by, and symptomatic of, the uncertain environment generated by the Yom Kippur War of October 1973, as a result of which Arab oil states embargoed exports to the Netherlands and, partly as a result of the war, began to force up oil prices, generating the energy crisis.

Contrary to expectations that external crises might stimulate centripetal behavior, it instead produced centrifugal pressures for each state to seek to arrange its own deal to its own best advantage. The UK and France were quick to make oil deals with Arab states, and the Community was seen to show little backbone when Arab ministers showed up in Copenhagen at a summit meeting in December 1973. In this climate it is perhaps not surprising that the members only produced a thin document (twenty-three paragraphs) on "European identity" in Copenhagen. It reiterated much of what had been said in the past, and ironically claimed that they now had the "political will to succeed." They said they were looking for "common attitudes and, where possible and desirable, common action" so that they could transform "the whole complex of their relations into a European Union." They acknowledged that individual states could not play a "major role on the international scene . . . alone," so that "Europe must unite and speak increasingly with a single voice if it wants to make itself heard and play its proper role in the world."

On security, those of them who were NATO members acknowledged the role of U.S. nuclear weapons and forces and agreed that member states should "hold to their commitments and make constant efforts to ensure that they have adequate means of defence at their disposal." However, they did not say how. They were adamant that "European unification is not directed against anyone, nor is it inspired by a desire for power," although they did say that nothing should "conflict with the determination of the Nine to establish themselves as a distinct and original entity."[46] The obsequiousness of the rhetoric camouflaged their inability to agree on more substance.

Indeed, the lukewarm response to the wave of reports on a "European Union," which reached their climax with a report on the subject by the Belgian prime minister, Leo Tindemans, in December 1975, showed that conditions were not right for decisive progress on the major questions of the political and economic future of Europe, or indeed for a significant development of the EPC.

Tindemans had tried to alert his colleagues to the fact that "the security of one member necessarily affects the security of others. No foreign policy can disregard threats, whether actual or potential, and the ability to meet them. Security cannot therefore be left outside the scope of the European Union. . . . European Union will not be complete until it has drawn up a common defence policy." Noting that this was not likely to happen at the moment, Tindemans nevertheless proposed to hold regular exchanges of views on defense matters, so that "one day" member states would be able to "reach a common analysis of defence problems." He also proposed that they should cooperate in the manufacture of armaments, "with a view to reducing defence costs, and increasing European independence and the competitiveness of its industry." The new European Union should therefore have a "common industrial policy."[47] At the time, these ideas came to nothing, but like other ideas in his report, twenty years later they came into vogue.

The second half of the 1970s saw a period of disenchantment, and the report of the "three wise men" (Barend Biesheuvel, Edmund Dell, and Robert Marjolin) made at the request of the European Council in 1979 agreed that the "present time seems to us ill-suited to futuristic visions which presuppose a profound and rapid transformation of attitudes within the Community. The chance of such transformation in the next few years seems to be exceedingly slight."[48]

New Activity

Despite this inauspicious background, the new decade of the 1980s brought a bout of renewed activity. The renewal arose from a variety of factors, including an increasing disillusionment with the United States as the leader of the Western world and a consequent acceptance of the need for greater European consultation and greater autonomy from U.S. leadership. In addition, there was the pervasive concern to reinforce Europe's capacity to act as a single entity in world affairs, particularly the perceived need to allow the ten EC members (the Nine plus Greece, which had acceded in 1981) to be more positive and to take a longer-term view, instead of merely reacting to world events as had tended to be the case. There was, perhaps, also something of a sense that the battering that the European idea had received in the 1970s had demonstrated the dangers of simply living on a plateau. Moreover, the inept and delayed response to the Soviet invasion of Afghanistan in December 1979 had revealed that all was not well with the machinery, while the calls for action over the U.S. hostage crisis in Tehran and the Afghan and Polish crises reemphasized the artificial nature of the distinctions being drawn between economic, political, and security issues, especially when consideration began to be given to the imposition of sanctions against the Soviet Union and Iran.

In winter 1980–1981 a series of initiatives began to appear, partly to breathe new life into the EPC and to enable it to respond to crises, but also partly to relaunch the movement toward a European Union. The British foreign secretary, Lord Carrington, was associated with the first; the German and Italian ministers, Genscher and Colombo, with the second. The Carrington initiative resulted in the London Report on EPC of October 1981, while the Genscher-Colombo initiative resulted in the Solemn Declaration on European Union of June 1983. Both had a degree of significance for the Single European Act (SEA). In any event the initiatives overlapped.

It was at Venlo in May 1981 that the EPC dimension of the question was discussed, and it became controversial because of the desire of the West Germans to include defense questions in the ambit of the EPC. While this was ruled out, it was agreed that broad aspects of security could be discussed, as indeed they had been for several years.

Given the role of nonalliance member Ireland, and with help from other states, the narrow formal interpretation of security was maintained in the formal London Report—that is, the EPC was identified with the political aspects of security, although it was quite clear that the distinctions between the political, economic, and military aspects of security were difficult, if not impossible, to maintain. The London Report reaffirmed the agreement that "having regard to the different situations of the Member States" (which Dublin interpreted as a nod in the direction of their apparent neutrality), the ministers agreed "to maintain the flexible and pragmatic approach which has made it possible to discuss in political cooperation certain important foreign policy questions bearing on the political aspects of security."[49]

Wider questions of institutional reform remained on the agenda given the Genscher-Colombo initiative of November 1981, and some of these proposed reforms touched upon the EPC. Noting what had gone before, Germany and Italy now proposed that "the security of Europe must also be guaranteed by joint action in the field of security policy which at the same time helps to maintain the common security of the partners in the Atlantic Alliance." Member states needed to have a "common foreign policy" and "the coordination of security policy and the adoption of common European positions in this sphere in order to safeguard Europe's independence, protect its vital interests and strengthen its security." In order to bring this about, they suggested that "the Council may convene in a different composition if there is a need to deal with matters of common interest in more details," that is, defense ministers.[50] It took until 1998 before defense ministers met informally in Austria. In 1983 the agreed Solemn Declaration on European Union made in Stuttgart only expanded the scope of EPC discussion to "the political and economic aspects of security."[51] Moreover, the declaration could hardly resolve the dilemma, because although "solemn," it was not law.

These debates appeared to culminate in the arrangements laid out in

Title III of the Single European Act of 1986, which contained the basic organizational structure and operational parameters of the EPC up to the Gulf and Yugoslav crises of 1990–1993, and the Maastricht decisions of December 1991. The SEA reasserted the distinct juridical base of the EC and EPC systems. The SEA confirmed the existing practices and ensured that the commitments remained political rather than legal, if only in the sense that there was no way of enforcing them (although the EPC was at last provided with a legal basis by the SEA).

There was consternation in Ireland about the wording of Article 30.6(a) of the SEA, which now legally reiterated the political position that the member states were "ready to coordinate their positions more closely on the political and economic aspects of security."[52] Some in Ireland claimed that this wording was ambiguous and that it was a misrepresentation to claim that the SEA specifically or categorically excluded the military aspect of security, since all it did was not specifically include it. After heated debate, the Irish finally deposited their instrument of ratification in June 1987, but they also deposited with it a declaration. Its second clause read:

> The Government of Ireland note that the provisions of Title III do not affect Ireland's long-established policy of military neutrality and that coordination of positions on the political and economic aspects of security does not include the military aspects of security or procurement for military purposes and does not affect Ireland's right to act or refrain from acting in any way which affect Ireland's international status of military neutrality.[53]

The Fianna Fáil government believed that this removed any possible ambiguity or misunderstanding of Ireland's position and would prevent any possible erosion of it. In a referendum the Irish people accepted the SEA by 69.9 percent, but in a harbinger of the future only 44 percent voted.

Second, there was the question of the WEU and NATO. The Italians favored the creation of a mechanism for consultation between the EPC and the Western European Union. At that time the United Kingdom, and to some extent West Germany and the Netherlands, favored primarily using NATO and the WEU. This subject caused difficulties for the Danes and Greeks, who were not members of the WEU, but most particularly for the Irish, given their rhetorical neutrality and nonadhesion to NATO and the WEU. In a further harbinger of things to come, the SEA acknowledged that those who wished to were to be free to pursue "closer co-operation in the field of security . . . within the framework of the Western European Union or the Atlantic Alliance." The SEA again acknowledged the need to promote "a European identity in external policy matters," as well as the need to "maintain the technological and industrial conditions necessary for . . . security," albeit within the framework of existing competent institutions.[54]

The debate about security raised other questions of definition. It is clear that the EPC system worked well, for example, during the Conference on Security and Cooperation in Europe (CSCE) meetings, which dealt with, among other things, military confidence-building measures. The history of the EPC and the EC, however, showed quite clearly that it was not possible to draw rigid demarcation lines between the political, economic, and military aspects of security, or indeed between the EC and EPC systems and policies. An example from the early 1980s was the EPC decision to condemn the Soviet invasion of Afghanistan and the EC decision to ensure that Community products did not replace the grain sales cut off by the United States as part of the coordinated Western response. However, it was not all plain sailing. There was nit-picking in April–June 1982 over the question of sanctions against Argentina after the invasion of the Falklands, although the initial Community decision to embargo imports from Argentina for the first time referred in its preamble to the agreement reached in the EPC on the taking of economic measures.

The SEA, therefore, did not end the debate. The Italians, for example, felt that the SEA did not go far enough toward political cooperation, while the Danes suffered the embarrassment of their parliament, the Folketing, narrowly rejecting the reforms and demanding a renegotiation, a possibility ruled out by the other member states. It went to a referendum, which saw a 56.2 percent "yes" majority. The SEA position on the EPC was of course overtaken by the 1991 intergovernmental conference (IGC) on political union, but the arrangements outlined in Title III provided the basic framework of the EPC in the crises of 1990–1992.

That divisions occur on such issues is not surprising. Roger Morgan noted perspicaciously many years ago that the development of a common foreign policy was likely to be hampered by the legacies the member states brought with them into the EPC, especially their centuries of distinctive experience. He identified four problems:

- The states in the Community were far from agreement on many aspects of their internal arrangements, and some of those disputes had external repercussions (for example, was Europe progressing toward a federal system or retaining intergovernmentalism?).
- The inevitably divisive factor of straightforward commercial competition.
- The differing geographical perspectives from which they viewed the outside world, a factor specifically relating to the varying but long-standing historical traditions of each state's view of its place in the world.
- The different substantive interests of the EC members in the international system as a whole, and in both economics and strategy.[55]

In addition, mention must be made of the sovereignty issue, especially in the sensitive areas of defense and security. The history of the EPC seemed to embody Margaret Thatcher's "Bruges credo" of "willing and active cooperation between independent sovereign states is the best way to build a successful European Community."[56] Member states seemed ready to forgo economic sovereignty, but not sovereign decisionmaking over foreign policy, security, or defense. Whatever the view about contract theory as the foundation of states, policymakers clearly believe that the ability to make foreign policy and defense decisions is crucial to what makes a state a state.

On many issues the other divergences were submerged to some extent, given the highly declaratory nature of the EPC—the fact that it consisted largely of statements and had few other instruments. This was coupled with a tendency for the participants to unite "behind a common position sufficiently loosely defined to allow each to add his own interpretation, so producing some forward movement without confronting the major obstacles ahead."[57]

The 1990–1991 Intergovernmental Conference

The foregoing provided the environment within which individual states, societies, policymakers, and institutions had to determine their responses to the debate about the nature and scope of the EPC in the context of the ICG on political union. It had already been agreed (in Strasbourg, 1989) that there should be an ICG on economic and monetary union in 1991. The preliminary decision to call a parallel IGC on political union was taken at the special April 1990 Dublin European Council, and was a response not only to the sweeping events unfolding in Eastern Europe, including the approaching unification of Germany, but also to the renewal of the stumbling debate within the twelve EC members (including Portugal and Spain, who joined in 1986) in the 1980s over their political future. The crises in the Gulf and Yugoslavia added a compelling, urgent, and complicating factor to the debate about the unity, coherence, and motivation of the EC's international action, and called for a reexamination and revitalization of the EPC.

Initially it seemed as if the debate would focus on improving the organization of the EPC and, perhaps, extending its scope. However, it became clear that a number of member states wished to evaluate the importance of the issue in response to the Gulf and Yugoslav crises, with the Gulf crisis changing the parameters of the debate on the EPC in a very profound sense. The appearance of an "out-of-area" threat and the possibility of war lent urgency to the discussion of EPC reform and foreign and security policy. There were two main themes in the debate on EPC reform. The first was the call for a common foreign and security policy (CFSP), which would represent a "quantum leap forward." With varying degrees of priority, Italy, Germany, Belgium, the Netherlands, and Greece declared their interest in this first approach.

The second approach was a concern to improve the internal workings of the EPC, a gradualist approach. Britain, Ireland, and to some extent Denmark and Portugal voiced reservations about departing too far from the current arrangements for coordinating policy by consensus and avoiding defense matters usually left to NATO and the WEU. The Irish had problems with their rhetorical attachment to neutrality, and reiterated that the SEA did not cover the military aspects of security. The Danish parliament had long been loath to endorse political union and the development of a strong security profile by the EC.

The United Kingdom did not support developments that undermined NATO or the WEU and showed little enthusiasm for majority voting in this area, being clear that decisions should be consensual. It accepted that some lessons might have to be learned from the Gulf, but felt it was wrong to catapult the EC into a defense role for which it was not prepared. In the UK view, the defects in the Community's common response to the Gulf War were not caused by the absence of machinery, but by differences in view on substance. What was needed, therefore, was a greater unity of analysis and an event-by-event approach, gradually working toward a more effective common policy.

Apart from the problems of the EPC already discussed, one of the difficulties facing European states was the problem of which institution should do what, and how to rationalize the activities of a number of defense-related institutions in Europe with overlapping functions and heterogeneous memberships. For example, France had remained in NATO, but outside the integrated military commands. It had also refrained from direct involvement with Eurogroup, although it was in the Independent European Program Group (IEPG). All twelve members of the EC, except Ireland, were in NATO, but France was not the only one to have had a form of "special status." Spain had joined the Alliance in 1982 but for fifteen years took no part in the integrated military structure. Denmark had national legislation that did not allow nuclear weapons or foreign troops to be stationed on its territory in peacetime. In addition, as noted earlier, there were the differing commitments under the arrangements of NATO and the Brussels Treaty Organization, the latter of which is the foundation of the WEU and obliges states to provide military assistance, while the former requires that they provide the help they deem necessary.

The Gulf and Yugoslav crises focused attention on the Western European Union. With the accession of Spain and Portugal in 1988, the

WEU had nine of the twelve EC states as members, but not Ireland, Denmark, or Greece. Moribund for many years, it was revived in 1984 precisely because of the perceived need to agree and articulate a European view on security. The WEU was almost thrust into a role in the Gulf crisis by default, given the EC's reluctance to become involved too directly in military affairs and the refusal of NATO to take on out-of-area responsibilities. The WEU had some success because its treaty permitted out-of-area action, which was particularly important to the NATO members, who wanted a mechanism for coordinating such issues. The WEU played a role in attempting to work out an agreed European response, in providing an umbrella under which states could contribute, and in coordinating the activities of NATO's European members. The WEU also sought to show that the Europeans were interested in intervening in matters that affected both their own and international security more generally.

France was especially keen to see a WEU role and sought to underline the close links between the WEU's security interests and the broader process of European integration. It did this, for example, by inviting all twelve members of the EC to attend a WEU meeting in August 1990, even though only nine of the twelve were members. Denmark and Greece agreed to send observers, while Ireland declined the invitation.

Also in the minds of those discussing a CFSP were the deliberations of NATO, which led to the NATO summit in Rome on November 7–8, 1991, just a few days before the Maastricht meeting. Rome produced the "Declaration on Peace and Security" and the Alliance's "New Strategic Concept."[58] The Rome Declaration on Peace and Cooperation confirmed the Alliance's belief that it would continue to play a key role in European security, but was clear that, in the new security environment, NATO, the CSCE, the EC, the WEU, and the Council of Europe all complemented one another, and all had a role to play if instability was to be prevented. It stressed that appropriate links would have to be established between NATO, the WEU, and the twelve EC members to ensure that all were adequately informed about decisions that might affect their security. The NATO states said that they welcomed the prospect of the reinforcement of the role of the WEU, "both as a defence component of the process of European unification and as a means of strengthening the European pillar of the Alliance." These two processes were regarded as mutually reinforcing, with the Alliance seen as the buttress of strategic unity and indivisibility of security.

Equally important was the issue of whether it should be an "Atlantic European" defense (i.e., predominantly NATO) or a "European European" defense (i.e., predominantly WEU in the short term, but EC in the longer term). Reflecting on the Gulf experience and the approaching IGC, in March 1991 Jacques Delors, while acknowledging that a European common defense policy had to be built on what existed, namely the WEU, also noted the divisions that existed regarding its role. He summarized these as follows: "should it be a forum for increased co-operation between the countries of Europe, a bridge to the Atlantic Alliance, or should it be a melting-pot for a European defence embedded in the Community, the second pillar of the Alliance?" For Delors, only the second option was acceptable, it being the goal that separated the approaches.[59] Still, others believed that, in the changed situation post-1989, any defense or security arrangements should be focused on the pan-European level, namely the post-Paris November 1990 revived CSCE.

Another fundamental division underlay the discussions. For the French it was prudent for Europe to make preparations independently of the United States; from a British standpoint, this was the kind of attitude that would make the United States leave. This divide took on a particular edge in 1991–1992 with the Franco-German proposal to develop their joint brigade (at that time, 4,200 soldiers of two French regiments and two German battalions) into a joint corps of 35,000–40,000 by 1995, which they hoped could be the nucleus of, or model for, a future European army. Belgium, Italy, Luxembourg, and Spain were all reported as expressing interest in being involved.

In some minds the pervasive uncertainty surrounding the new European environment counseled the cautious view that institutions and arrangements that had served them well should not be tampered with.

The Gulf and Yugoslavia

The major factor in the environment that provided the backdrop to Maastricht was the mixed performance, at best, of the twelve EC members during the Gulf and Yugoslav crises. Initially the analysis from EC officials on the response to the Gulf crisis was upbeat. Its reaction had been "light years ahead of any of its previous actions to major international crises both in speech and in content."[60] Supporters of this view pointed to the aid effort to the frontline states, the trade embargo, the concord at the UN, and the series of declaratory statements. Skeptics, rather than looking at the rhetoric, however, saw the resurfacing of old national positions and divergences of interests and views. They pointed to the limitations in the Community's response and particularly the clear divergence between those who were reluctant to back any policy and the more resolute British attitude.

There were twelve different contributions to the international coalition effort in the Gulf from EC members, with no two states contributing in the same way. As a result, it exposed the fragility of European cooperation (see Table 2.1). Indeed, Delors observed during the Gulf crisis that "the

Table 2.1 Contributions to the Coalition Effort in the Gulf, 1991

	Belgium	Denmark	France	Germany	Greece	Italy	Luxembourg	Netherlands	Portugal	Spain	United Kingdom	Ireland[a]
Took part in offensive air operations in Iraq and Kuwait			■			■					■	
Took part in offensive land operations in Iraq and Kuwait			■								■	
Took part in offensive naval operations in the Gulf			■			■		■			■	
Took part in naval embargo operations	■	■	■		■	■		■			■	
Took part in mine-clearing operations	■		■	■		■		■			■	
Defended key areas in Saudi Arabia			■								■	
Deployed medical units	■		■			■		■			■	
Provided practical or financial assistance to the coalition	■	■	■	■	■	■	■	■	■	■	■	
Took part in defensive operations in the NATO area	■	■		■	■	■		■	■	■	■	

Source: Statement on the Defence Estimates: Britain's Defence for the 90s, vol. 1, Cm. 1559-1 (London: HMSO, 1991), p. 9.
Note: a. Ireland agreed to allow refueling of U.S. planes at Shannon Airport.

Community had neither the institutional machinery nor the military force which would have allowed it to act as a Community."[61] He later observed during the Yugoslavia crisis that EPC had only three weapons at its disposal: public opinion, the threat of withholding diplomatic recognition, and economic sanctions.[62] This is one reason why he and others called for new treaty provisions to allow for common defense issues to be discussed by the Community, instead of just intergovernmentally, as had happened.

These events were happening simultaneously to serious negotiations in the context of the IGC on political union discussing the nature and shape of a common foreign and security policy, even a defense role for the Community, and its relationship with the WEU and NATO. Problems raised included the questions as to whether there was a dearth of instruments for the EPC; whether the EPC was more than rhetoric and declaration; and the especially difficult questions on a security or defense input. Most important, they raised the question of whether "Europe is an economic giant, a political dwarf and, even worse, a worm until it concerns itself with elaborating a defence capability."[63]

At first there did seem to be a degree of consensus over Yugoslavia. The EC certainly felt some responsibility for Yugoslavia, on the grounds of geographical propinquity; the existing trade, aid, and cooperation agreements; and the dangers that events in Yugoslavia posed to European peace, stability, and security. It may also have been relevant that, after the Gulf crisis, this was seen as a European problem with which the new power broker in Europe, that is, the EC, could and should deal.

The Community sought to bring financial and economic levers to bear. It also turned to the other instruments that Delors had identified. It did consider the military options. However, each instrument was to pose problems for policy coherence and arouse friction between the member states. It tried to arrange a peaceful settlement, sending fifty European observers to monitor a cease-fire. On the practicalities of a cease-fire observer force, divergences arose among the twelve EC members over questions relating to the nature of the force, who should authorize its functioning, at what stage it should become involved and under what circumstances, and ultimately the question of whether it should be armed or supported by a force with arms. Observers were sent but failed to bring peace.

The failure of all these efforts, and the problems encountered by the monitors, led to a key disagreement among the twelve EC members over the issue of military intervention. It also led to questions about the relationship between the member states and the WEU. On September 19, 1991, the EC foreign ministers met in The Hague, in conjunction with a special meeting of the WEU, and examined ways of strengthening the EC's cease-fire monitoring operation. This meeting broke new ground in the relationship between the EC and the WEU, and it became clear over the next few weeks that the WEU was, on this matter at least, becoming the military arm of the EC. Of a number of options considered, the UK was alone in opposing all of them, partly influenced by its experience in Northern Ireland. In general, Belgium, the Netherlands, Luxembourg, France, Germany, and Italy backed some sort of intervention. The Greeks were cautious, as were the Spanish.

Fortunately for the member states, the continuing fighting in Yugoslavia made the question of military intervention largely hypothetical, since few were really willing to go in to separate the warring parties. There was a world of difference between maintaining an already established cease-fire and fighting one's way in. Nonetheless, it was the sort of issue that demonstrated that if the member states wished to move to a common foreign and security policy, a change of attitude would be required. The cumulative impact of the Gulf and Yugoslavia crises gave pause for thought about the future and did influence decisions at Maastricht.

Maastricht

Debate about the inadequacies in the EPC process led to the European Council at Maastricht agreeing to establish a CFSP, although Title V in the treaty and Article J both promised rather more than was actually produced.[64] CFSP was to be one of three pillars of the European Union: Pillar I—the European Community; Pillar II—CFSP; and Pillar III—cooperation in the area of justice and home affairs. Each had its own decisionmaking system. Pillars II and III remained essentially intergovernmental. CFSP was not part of the European Community system per se, not subject to the same decisionmaking procedures, or subject to judicial review by the ECJ. The Commission was to be "fully associated" with CFSP (in reality, this meant merely that it attended all CFSP meetings and was part of the presidential troika). While the Commission could speak and represent the European Union on Pillar I matters, it was the EU Presidency that spoke on Pillar II matters. This often led to confusion among nonmembers. The Commission was given a joint right of initiative, together with member states, on CFSP. Decisions, however, remained the prerogative of the member states.

The European Parliament was to be kept regularly informed of CFSP developments, and consulted on the principal issues, but it could not enforce its views on the Council. It could hold an annual debate on the progress in implementing CFSP, though, again, in practice this had very little impact on policy. The one strong potential instrument the Parliament had was in the realm of funding. It was decided that the administrative costs of CFSP and, if agreed by the member states, the operational costs would be paid for by the Community budget, over which the Parliament had the power of approval and discharge. Therefore, in theory the Parliament could threaten to block the entire EU budget over a CFSP matter to make its opinion heard and to influence policy. However, this would have been an extremely crude way of influencing policy and was not tried. The most supranational elements of Pillar I were eschewed, as most states would not allow such issues of "high politics" to be heavily influenced by the Commission, the Parliament, or the European Court of Justice.

In addition, Article J.8.2 made it clear that "the Council shall act unanimously, except for procedural questions," and where it had unanimously agreed "matters on which decisions are to be taken by a qualified vote" (Article J.3.2), that is, joint actions. The principal decisionmaking body for CFSP was the Council, with ministers of foreign affairs meeting as the General Affairs Council. However, it was the Political Committee and to a lesser extent the Committee of Permanent Representatives (Coreper) that carried out the majority of the groundwork. The EU Presidency was also heavily involved in the day-to-day management of CFSP, while the European Council set the overall policy guidelines and direction of CFSP.

The Treaty on European Union (TEU) introduced two new instruments that the EU could use to implement CFSP decisions: common positions and joint actions. These two instruments were to enable the EU to move beyond just talking about foreign and security policy to actually playing a role in international affairs. Common positions, broadly speaking, were interpreted as being about intentions, objectives, and priorities, while joint actions were about the specific implementation of decisions to achieve the desired objectives. Both of these instruments commit the member states to the actions and positions the EU adopts. However, there was some confusion as to when to use these instruments, and which instrument suited what problem. The dominance of unanimity and intergovernmentalism within Pillar II slowed decisionmaking, but safeguarded the capacity of the member states to block decisions they did not agree with.

A crucial statement was contained in Article J.4, in which it was agreed that a CFSP "shall include *all* questions related to the security of the Union, including the eventual framing of a common defence policy, which might in time lead to a common defence" (emphasis added). This implicitly drew a distinction between a joint, collaborative defense policy and the more expansive idea of common defense per se, as mooted by Jacques Delors and recognized as the ultimate goal.

However, the twelve EC members had effectively subcontracted "decisions and actions of the Union which have defence implications" to the WEU by requesting it "to elaborate and implement" decisions of the Union that had such implications. This could be interpreted as a separation of CFSP among the twelve members from defense in the WEU and the Alliance, but the WEU was described as an "integral part" of the European Union, so the question remained about how separate these activities would be. There was also the curious wording that the WEU was "to elaborate and implement" defense-oriented actions, which seemed to avoid a direct statement of who would take such decisions, the implicit actor being the Council of the European Union. Given this, it was perhaps not surprising that the Council of the Union and the WEU were to agree suitable practical arrangements to govern their relationship.

Concomitantly, the nine members of the WEU (all of which were members of the EC) agreed a "Declaration on the Role of the Western European Union and Its Relations with the European Union and with the Atlantic Alliance."[65] In this the nine WEU members agreed to develop "a genuine European security and defence identity and a greater European responsibility on defence matters." They noted that the WEU was integral to the development of the European Union, but immediately linked this to the Union's contribution to enhancing solidarity within the Atlantic Alliance. WEU states agreed with Article J.4 of the TEU, adding that such common defense was to be compatible with the Atlantic Alliance. Most important, the nine WEU members said that the WEU was "prepared, at the request of the European Union, to elaborate and implement decisions and actions of the Union which have defence implications."

The WEU states proposed synchronization of WEU/European Union meetings, closer cooperation between staffs, and harmonization of the presidencies. However, to balance this, working links between the WEU and NATO were also to be strengthened, as were the contribution, role, and responsibility of the nine WEU members within NATO. It is worth noting that, having agreed to be the defense arm of the European Union and to implement its decisions, they also agreed that the "WEU will act in conformity with the positions adopted in the Atlantic alliance."

In a new development the nine WEU members agreed to try to coordinate their policies on Atlantic issues, such as to seek to introduce the "joint positions agreed in the WEU into the process for consultation in the Alliance," reiterating that the alliance was *the* vehicle for security and defense matters under the North Atlantic Treaty. To increase the WEU's operational role they agreed to establish "a planning cell; meetings of WEU Chiefs of Staff; a study of military units answerable to WEU and closer cooperation with the Alliance in logistics, transport, training and strategic surveillance."

The nine WEU members also agreed to consider enhanced cooperation in the field of armaments with a view to creating a European armaments agency and making sure that the WEU's stronger operational role was compatible with NATO. All of this endeavor was to be fully compatible with the military dispositions necessary to ensure the collective defense of all the Allies. In addition, the WEU Council and secretariat would move to Brussels, and Alliance and European Union representatives would be "double-hatted." In a further declaration the nine WEU members invited the three European Union nonmembers of the WEU (Ireland, Greece, and Denmark) either to join it or to assume observer status. Norway, Turkey, and Iceland, as European members of NATO, but members of neither the European Union nor the WEU, were invited to become associate members of the WEU.

Given that these arrangements did not really resolve the issue of "Atlantic European" defense versus "European European" defense, it was not surprising that, in Article J.4.6 of the Treaty on European Union, the twelve EC members agreed to review the European Union/WEU and CFSP components of the treaty in 1996.

The Maastricht text leaves a central ambiguity in interpretations of the goal of a "common defense," namely: Was the long-term objective of the Union to change the basis of defense from membership of the Alliance to membership of the Union itself? Is it true, as Genscher said in April 1991, that the "development of a common European foreign, security and defence policy is not intended to create an ersatz NATO, but to reinforce the European pillar. . . . A growing sense of identity in Europe does not make the Atlantic wider?"[66]

Having made this linkage with the WEU, a linkage reciprocated by the nine WEU members in their declarations, the twelve EC states, in Article J.4 of the TEU, went on to say that their policy should "not prejudice the specific character of the security and defence policy of certain Member States," or the obligations of signatories of the North Atlantic Treaty. Presumably the former was a rather indirect sop to Ireland, with its traditional policy of nonalliance involvement, and perhaps also an acknowledgment of both the nuclear and Security Council roles of Britain and France. It was also agreed that bilateral cooperation was permissible between states, as long as it was compatible with the above.

There still remained some residue of the debate as to whether the EU states should follow, on the one hand, an institutional approach, which sought to strengthen the institutions of the twelve EC members and of the Community as a whole, and to arrive at "binding" procedures that would necessarily advance the common interest; or, on the other hand, the "problem-oriented" approach, which attempted to sort out the problems most amenable to solution or influence by the Community, and tried to bring the collective weight of the Community to bear on them.

At Maastricht it was not possible to resolve the underlying debates about a European security identity or CFSP, though a CFSP was established. There was no resolution of the alphabet soup of institutions, of the definitive role of the European Union, the WEU, and NATO, of "Atlantic Europe" or "European Europe," of whether the future was to be intergovernmental or federal, a common defense policy or a common defense, incremental drift or real change. Maastricht left as an open question what the role of the European Union was to be. A further complication was the impending membership of Sweden, Finland, and Austria, the former European neutrals, in the Union and CFSP.

Common Interests

The real issue, perhaps, was not institutional, whether to have joint integrated commands or corps, the lead played by NATO, the WEU, or the EU, but whether there was an emergent identification of common political and security interests that guaranteed unity. Effective institutions, alliances, and policies in the CFSP area require military capability, a working consensus on the conditions under which the capabilities should be used, and a credible willingness to act when agreed conditions exist. These did not exist at the time and some would say that they still do not.

The post-Maastricht period had caused problems for CFSP, which only came into existence in November 1993. Indeed, in the 1991–1992 IGC, it had been acknowledged that there was a degree of studied ambiguity about the decisions and that the member states would need to return to the issues, particularly defense.

Notes

1. Richard Mayne, *The Recovery of Europe* (London: Weidenfeld and Nicolson, 1970), pp. 29–30.

2. Winston Churchill, *Vital Speeches of the Day,* Vol. 12 (New York: City News Publishing, 1946), p. 332.

3. "X," "The Sources of Soviet Conduct," *Foreign Affairs* 25 (July 1947): 556–582.

4. Harry S. Truman, "The Truman Doctrine: Special Message to the Congress on Greece and Turkey, 12 March 1947," *Public Papers of the Presidents of the United States, 1947,* pp. 177–179.

5. U.S. Department of State bulletin, Washington, D.C., June 15, 1947.

6. Command Paper 7599 (London: HMSO, 1949).

7. *NATO: Facts and Figures 1989* (Brussels: NATO Information Services, 1989), p. 11.

8. Belgium, Canada, Denmark, France, Iceland, Italy, Luxembourg, the Netherlands, Norway, Portugal, the United Kingdom, and the United States.

9. W. Eichler, ed., *Europe Speaks* (London: Militant Socialist International, 1944), p. 45.

10. *New York Times,* July 23, 1950.

11. Jean Monnet, *Memoirs*, trans. Richard Mayne (London: Collins, 1978), p. 338.

12. Consultative Assembly, Council of Europe, *Proceedings,* August 11, 1950.

13. Monnet, *Memoirs,* p. 343.

14. Ibid., p. 346.

15. Richard Vaughan, *Post-War Integration in Europe* (London: Edward Arnold, 1976), pp. 57–58.

16. Monnet, *Memoirs,* p. 350.

17. For text of the European Defense Treaty, see *The European Defence Community,* Command Paper 9127 (London: HMSO, 1954).

18. See Edward Fursdon, *The European Defence Community* (New York: St. Martin's Press, 1980).

19. *Protocol Modifying and Completing the Brussels Treaty* (October 1954), Command Paper 9304 (London: HMSO, 1954).

20. International Council of the European Movement, *Declaration of Political Principles of European Union* (February 28, 1949), reproduced in Vaughan, *Post-War Integration in Europe,* pp. 37–39.

21. The Messina Resolution is reproduced in Miriam Camps, *Britain and the European Community* (London: Oxford University Press, 1964), pp. 520–522.

22. *Treaty of Rome Establishing the European Economic Community* (March 1957), Command Paper 4864 (London: HMSO, 1972).

23. See Camps, *Britain and the European Community,* pp. 520–522.

24. Trevor Taylor, *European Defence Cooperation* (London: Routledge and Kegan Paul, 1984), p. 18.

25. Quoted in P. Gerbet, *La construction de l'Europe* (Paris: Imprimerie Nationale, 1983), p. 275.

26. Reproduced in European Parliament, Committee of Institutional Affairs, *Selection of Texts Concerning Institutional Matters of the Community from 1950 to 1982* (Luxembourg, n.d.), pp. 107–108.

27. A. Silj, *Europe's Political Puzzle: A Study of the Fouchet Negotiations and the 1963 Veto,* Occasional Papers in International Affairs no. 17 (Harvard: Harvard Center for International Affairs, 1967), p. 12.

28. *Communiqué of the Conference of the Heads of State and Government of the European Community's Member States* (The Hague, December 2, 1969), Bulletin of the European Communities 1-1970 (Luxembourg: Office for Official Publications of the European Union, 1970), pp. 11–18; and *Report by the Foreign Ministers of the Member States on the Problems of Political Unification,* Bulletin of the European Communities 11-1970, pp. 9–14.

29. *Report by the Foreign Ministers,* pp. 9–14.

30. See Ralf Dahrendorf, "A New Goal for Europe," in M. Hodges, ed., *European Integration* (Harmondsworth: Penguin, 1972), pp. 74–87.

31. Bernard Burrows and Geoffrey Edwards, *The Defence of Western Europe* (London: Butterworths European Studies, 1982), pp. 44–45.

32. Denis Healey, *The Time of My Life* (London: Michael Joseph, 1989), p. 316.

33. *Eurogroup* (Brussels: NATO Information Services, n.d.), pp. 9–10.

34. Aidan Cawley, *De Gaulle* (London: Collins, 1969), p. 443.

35. John Bayliss, "French Defence Policy," in John Bayliss, Ken Booth, John Garnett, and Phil Williams, *Contemporary Strategy: Theories and Policies* (London: Croon Helm, 1975), p. 294.

36. Michael Sheehan and James Wyllie, *Pocket Guide to Defence* (Oxford: Blackwell and Economist, 1986), p. 37.

37. *L'Année politique 1960,* Paris, pp. 647–649.

38. Lawrence Freedman, *The Evolution of Nuclear Strategy,* 2nd ed. (London: Macmillan, 1989), p. 313.

39. Sir Anthony Eden, British foreign secretary, University of Columbia,

January 11, 1952, cited in Nicholas Mansergh, *Documents and Speeches on British Government Affairs, 1931–1952,* vol. 1 (London: Oxford University Press, 1953), pp. 1156–1157.

40. *Internal British Foreign Office Minutes on the Briand Plan* (1930), quoted in Trevor Salmon and William Nicoll, eds., *Building European Union: A Documentary History and Analysis* (Manchester: Manchester University Press, 1997), pp. 14–15.

41. Winston Churchill, quoted in Randolph Churchill, ed., *The Sinews of Peace* (London: Cassell, 1948), p. 202.

42. Winston Churchill, May 11, 1953, *House of Commons Debates,* 5th ser., vol. 450, cols. 1314–1319.

43. Lawrence Freedman, *Britain and Nuclear Weapons* (London: Macmillan, 1980), pp. 17–18.

44. Edward Heath, *Old World, New Horizons: Britain, the Common Market, and Atlantic Alliance* (London: Oxford University Press, 1970), p. 73.

45. Monnet, *Memoirs,* pp. 288–292.

46. *The European Identity* (December 14, 1973), Bulletin of the European Communities 12-1973, pp. 118–122.

47. Leo Tindemans, *Report on European Union* (December 1975), Bulletin of the European Communities Supplement 1/76.

48. *Report on European Institutions Presented by the Committee of Three to the European Council* (Luxembourg, 1980), published by the Council of the European Union under catalog no. BX-30-80-011-EN-C.

49. *Report on European Political Cooperation* (London, October 13, 1981), Bulletin of the European Communities Supplement 3/81, pp. 14–17.

50. *Draft European Act Submitted by the Governments of the Federal Republic of Germany and the Italian Republic* (November 6, 1981), reproduced in European Parliament, Committee of Institutional Affairs, *Selection of Texts Concerning Institutional Matters,* pp. 490–499.

51. Bulletin of the European Communities 6-1983.

52. *Single European Act,* Bulletin of the European Communities Supplement 2/86.

53. *Ireland Today* (Dublin, Department of Foreign Affairs) nos. 1037, 1039 (1987).

54. *Single European Act.*

55. Roger Morgan, *High Politics, Low Politics: Towards a Foreign Policy for Western Europe,* Washington Papers no. 11 (London: Sage, 1973), pp. 21–25.

56. Rt. Hon. Mrs. Thatcher, *39th Academic Year of the College of Europe* (Bruges, September 20, 1988), reproduced in Salmon and Nicoll, *Building European Union,* pp. 208–214.

57. William Wallace, "Cooperation and Convergence in European Foreign Policy," in C. Hill, ed., *National Foreign Policies and European Political Cooperation* (London: Allen and Unwin, 1983), p. 10.

58. *NATO Review* no. 6 (December 1991): 19–22, 25–32.

59. Jacques Delors, "Address to the International Institute for Strategic Studies," March 7, 1991, reproduced in *Survival* 33, no. 2 (March–April): 107–108.

60. *Financial Times,* September 6, 1990.

61. Delors, "Address to the International Institute for Strategic Studies," p. 102.

62. European Parliament, *The Week* (Strasbourg), September 9–13, 1991, PE 152.616/rev., pp. 17–18.

63. Mark Eyskens of Belgium, 1991, www.wsws.org/articles/1999/sep1999/belg-s13.shtml.

64. *Treaty on European Union* (Luxembourg: Office for Official Publications of the European Communities, 1992).

65. *Declaration on Western Union,* attached to ibid.

66. Genscher, foreign minister of Germany, *International Herald Tribune,* April 11, 1991.

3

A Successful Relaunch?

Despite the much heralded introduction of the Common Foreign and Security Policy (CFSP), and with it the implicit objective to create a common defense policy, the Treaty on European Union (TEU) was always an unfinished project with regard to CFSP and its defense component. Consequently, a review of the operation of CFSP, in the form of another intergovernmental conference (IGC), was scheduled (in Title V, Article N of the TEU) for 1996.

In fact, defense was one of the key motives that there needed to be another IGC. The treaty stated: "With a view to furthering the objective of this Treaty, and having in view the date of 1998 in the context of Article 12 of the Brussels Treaty, the provisions of this Article may be revised . . . on the basis of a report to be presented in 1996 . . . which shall include an evaluation of the progress made and the experience gained."[1] The report would reopen many vexed questions, but no one expected that, by 1996–1997, the EU would have had so little experience in a CFSP. To complicate matters, the one major European security crisis in this period, the disintegration of Yugoslavia, saw the European Community/European Union (EC/EU) perform disastrously in its attempts to control events.

The 1996–1997 Intergovernmental Conference

The 1996–1997 IGC faced a number of issues and problems to be resolved in the area of foreign, security, and defense policy. Most fundamentally there were divergences about the role of the EU in European security and about the very nature of security. Other issues to be tackled included the scope of CFSP, whether defense should be left to the North Atlantic Treaty

Organization (NATO), and what role the Western European Union (WEU) should have—specifically, whether it should be absorbed into the EU.

These divergences were not petty issues over structure but rather represented fundamentally different views as to the nature and direction of the EU and its role in the new European security order. The maximalist approach wanted the EU to be able to make decisions on security and defense, to integrate the WEU, and to have a real capability in the defense field, at least in the long term. In contrast, the minimalist approach looked to intergovernmentalism and the tradition of the alliances with a veto for all. For this faction NATO should be central. Due to these very different perspectives, the IGC continued well into 1997 as the member states continued to argue for their preferred solutions and to protect what they saw as their vital interests in foreign and security policy. These differences could be seen in the statements and memoranda that the EU states produced in the run-up to the IGC, elaborating their positions on the wide variety of issues up for discussion. Each had a section on CFSP and on the prospects of the EU developing a security and defense role.

During this IGC, the Benelux states of Belgium, Luxembourg, and the Netherlands all supported a greater role for the EU in security and defense. They announced their support for the development of an EU defense policy and the phased integration of the WEU into the CFSP pillar, which should also incorporate the Petersberg tasks and collective defense.[2] The Dutch did, however, continue to emphasize the importance of NATO, stating that the practical implementation of collective defense should remain a matter for NATO and that the EU should establish specific links in the defense field with NATO's.[3]

In the 1996–1997 IGC the French took a weaker stance in advocating the "European Europe" than they had previously. By this time France's external environment had changed significantly. In particular the French had observed that they had been rather marginalized in the Gulf War by their semidetached relationship with NATO. Second, they realized that the EC and EU respectively had been ineffective with regard to the disintegration of Yugoslavia and the subsequent train of events. Third, they saw that NATO and the United States had largely won the arguments over the European security architecture and, indeed, had moved toward rejoining parts of NATO's integrated military structure and created an expectation that it would completely rejoin.[4] Therefore, this issue did not have the same salience for the French as it once had. On defense, therefore, the French advocated developing the WEU's operational capabilities, the inclusion of the WEU Petersberg tasks into the remit of CFSP, and eventually the integration of the WEU into the EU.[5] In the meantime, they advocated developing the WEU both as an element of EU defense policy and as a means of strengthening the European pillar of NATO, reforming NATO from within.

On defense, while reaffirming that NATO was the indispensable basis of European security, the Germans continued to advocate that Europeans should shoulder more responsibility. To this end, and to make CFSP more effective, Germany supported proposals to increase the WEU's operational capability and to strengthen organizational links with the EU, pending the medium-term objective of merging the WEU into the EU. It also argued for greater interoperability of armed forces and the joint provision of equipment.[6] Specifically on WEU capability the Germans argued that the WEU should develop into a common defense structure capable of carrying out the Petersberg tasks, and that the concept of combined joint forces enabling the WEU or coalitions of EU/WEU members to act should be developed.[7] Together with the French the Germans proposed the inclusion of a "political solidarity clause" applying to all member states and the incorporation of the Petersberg tasks into CFSP competence.

At the beginning of the decade Italy made CFSP a priority. For them the Gulf War showed that the competencies of the Union needed to be extended "to all aspects of security without limitations" and they called for the "transfer to the Union [of] the competencies presently being exercised by the WEU."[8] By 1996 the Italians had moved slightly in the direction of accepting that securing a consensus on the principles and substance of foreign policy was a prerequisite for action. On defense, the Italians continued to argue that the WEU should be an instrument of the EU, and indeed absorbed into the EU.[9] Not surprisingly, therefore, during the IGC it was one of those who supported the incorporation of the Petersberg tasks into CFSP who argued that, pending absorption, the WEU structures should be brought under the aegis of the EU. In line with this approach, Italy suggested that the WEU and EU membership should be harmonized, that WEU operational capacity be strengthened, and that cooperation in the field of armaments be tightened.[10] However, rather like their final position in 1991, the Italians were anxious that these developments fully respect the transatlantic agreements.[11]

For Ireland, neutrality and CFSP continued to be a very sensitive issue. Officially Ireland has always opposed membership in existing alliance systems, but in line with its long-standing policy it did accept that it would participate, if the EC/EU developed its own security system. By 1996 the government argued in a White Paper that the majority of Irish people cherished Ireland's military neutrality and that it would not be changed unless agreed to in a referendum. Ireland would not seek membership in NATO or the WEU, or assume mutual defense guarantees.[12] Ireland did, however, take up the 1992 WEU offer to become an "observer," which allowed it to attend and speak at WEU Ministerial Council meetings and participate in WEU working groups and committees. Observer status, however, did not involve any mutual defense commitment or military obligation, and Ireland could not be part of the final decisionmaking process. The question did arise, however, of whether, given its long-term tradition of contributing to UN peacekeeping forces, Ireland should participate, on a voluntary basis, in operations encompassed by the Petersberg tasks. This would not be a massive shift in policy, as Ireland had also contributed fifty people, in the role of military police, to the Implementation Force (IFOR) and Stabilization Force (SFOR) operations, despite the fact that IFOR was, and SFOR still is, a NATO-led operation. Ireland also joined NATO's Partnership for Peace program, further complicating its position within European security structures. On a common defense policy Ireland argued it should "take account of the level of political and economic integration achieved by the European Union, be responsive to broader developments in European security, and reflect the varying experiences and capacities of the Member States."[13]

The Danes have also been cautious about foreign policy, security, and defense cooperation. Most Danish parties agreed that they did not want to include defense in CFSP. They decided to maintain their opt-out from defense matters, attained at the Edinburgh European Council, and made it clear that this position was not up for negotiation: "Nothing in the Treaty on European Union commits Denmark to become a member of the WEU. Accordingly, Denmark does not participate in the elaboration and implementation of decisions and actions of the Union which have defence implications, but will not prevent the development of closer co-operation between Member States in this area."[14]

Denmark remained opposed to an EU-WEU merger, although it came to favor somewhat closer links between the two. Like Ireland, it too declined the invitation to join the WEU, accepting observer status instead. Denmark remained, however, a member and strong advocate of NATO. It also took a broad view of security, believing that EU cooperation in security should be broadened to include the so called soft-security issues of trade, aid, and the environment, so that minor problems could be prevented from escalating.[15] In this vein it supported the emergence of the Petersberg tasks, as long as individual states could decide for themselves whether to participate or not. The Danes are not opposed to participating in these sorts of operations, as can be seen by their involvement, through the UN and NATO, in the United Nations Protection Force (UNPROFOR), IFOR, and SFOR, but they do not wish to be involved through the EU. They do, however, believe that other EU states should have the opportunity to participate in such EU-led operations.[16]

The UK was another state with skeptical views on the role of the EU in defense matters. The basis for its position in the 1996–1997 IGC was a March 1995 memorandum on its approach to the treatment of European defense issues at the 1996 IGC:

The nation state remains in particular the fundamental entity for co-operation in the field of defence. The defence of its citizens is the most fundamental duty of any Government . . . it is the national Government's duty
to answer to national Parliament when troops are sent into action.
European action in the defence and security field should be inter-governmental, based on co-operation between national states.[17]

Continuing traditional British policy, NATO's "overriding" importance
was stressed, especially the Article 5 commitment to mutual aid, as was the
crucial commitment of the United States to European security. The UK
argued that, given this U.S. commitment, it was wrong to develop separate,
wholly European military structures, although the Europeans should shoulder more of the burden for European security.[18] Thus there was support for
the WEU remaining as the European pillar of NATO and as the defense
component of the EU. The WEU should leave collective defense to NATO,
but should develop its operational capabilities with regard to the Petersberg
roles.[19] This was all the more important since the Europeans could no
longer expect the North Americans to participate in each and every aspect
of European security. All these developments should be judged on a "hard-
headed assessment of what European states can realistically expect to do
together" and there should be a "task-based approach" to defense.[20] Thus,
future structures should take account of "the circumstances in which our
armed forces are likely to be operating" and states should be left to choose
for themselves the operations in which they wished to participate: "variable
geometry" was the way forward.[21]

Greece, during the 1990–1991 IGC, favored abandoning previous
restrictions on the types of security issues that could be discussed within
the EU, and the inclusion of defense. It enthusiastically joined the WEU
after changes at Maastrict allowed EU members to join the WEU as members or observers, a change the Greeks had lobbied strongly for. In the
1996–1997 IGC the Greeks continued their support for strengthening the
EU's role in security and defense. They wanted to strengthen CFSP and
wanted it to "include a clear guarantee concerning protection of the external frontiers of the Union and the Member States and a mutual assistance
clause."[22] This obviously reflected their preoccupations with the perceived
security threat from Turkey, the disputes over Cyprus, and the problems in
the Balkans, including their continuing unhappiness over the newly independent Former Yugoslav Republic of Macedonia (FYROM). The Greeks
felt somewhat let down by their partners, who wished Greece to express
solidarity on matters affecting them but did not return the compliment on
issues close to Greek hearts. Not surprisingly, the Greeks favored the evolution of a common defense policy, supported the integration of the WEU
into the EU as a long-term objective, and endorsed the incorporation of the

Petersberg tasks.[23] In the meantime they accepted a division of labor between the WEU and NATO, with the WEU being responsible for security and NATO maintaining its primary defense position.[24]

Portugal was another state that approached negotiations on CFSP and defense in a cautious manner, wary of damaging NATO and the transatlantic link. It wanted CFSP to remain intergovernmental and remained attached to NATO's primacy, with its fundamental responsibility for the collective territorial defense of its member states.[25] It also hoped that NATO would continue to have prime responsibility for major military action, although the WEU should be developed to allow it to deal with smaller-scale peacekeeping, crisis management, and other Petersberg tasks. Any change to the WEU should respect NATO and, although somewhat closer ties between the WEU and the EU should be developed, there was to be no defense "fourth pillar."[26]

Spain, too, believed that defense was so linked to national sovereignty that it had to remain an intergovernmental issue, although some flexibility would be beneficial.[27] While willing to see the WEU developed, especially in relation to the Petersberg tasks, it regarded NATO and the United States as vital to European security. Spain believed that in the medium term, and "when the time was ripe," the incorporation of crisis management tasks and even the Brussels Treaty's Article 5 guarantee of collective defense could be incorporated into the EU.[28] In the meantime there should be the gradual institutional convergence of the EU and the WEU, with the EU able to give instructions to the WEU for EU actions (similar to the Petersberg tasks), but with the WEU remaining autonomous for its own operations. Accordingly the WEU operational capacity should be enhanced.[29] However, Spain stressed that the development of the EU and WEU capability in security and defense should aim at reinforcing the Atlantic Alliance.

The discussions in 1996–1997 were complicated by the accession to the EU, in 1995, of Austria, Finland, and Sweden, all neutral states. There had been some debate within Austria over the possibility of joining NATO, but it has sought to maintain its neutral position. It did, however, become an observer at the WEU. Its general orientation toward security and defense is illustrated by its emphasis on the existing TEU objectives for CFSP as being appropriate and on the EU's contribution to European stability and conflict prevention. It did support CFSP developing an operational capability in the sphere of the Petersberg tasks, although Austria wanted to have "civil protection" added to the list.[30] It rejected notions of some member states being able to undertake action on behalf of the EU unless the entire EU had endorsed that action. It was adamant that any military-related decision would require unanimity, although a cautious approval was given to the gradual transition to majority voting in nonmilitary areas of CFSP.[31]

Although Finland and Sweden also only became members of the EU in

1995 and observers at the WEU shortly after that, they were significant players in the 1996–1997 IGC. In particular, they were keen to follow up on the WEU's 1992 Petersberg declaration "on strengthening the WEU's operational role" and incorporate some of these ideas into CFSP. On April 25, 1996, Finland and Sweden issued a memorandum to their colleagues on the IGC and the security and defense dimension—toward an enhanced EU role in crisis management. The memorandum accepted the "need for the European Union to enhance its role and capabilities in conflict management" and referred specifically to the Petersberg tasks and those aspects of "conflict management where military organisations are used."[32] It argued for a linkage between the WEU and the EU, but clarified that, "at the same time, it is not necessary for the Union itself to perform military tasks."[33] Finland and Sweden were, however, acutely aware of the need for the EU to be able to act in peacekeeping and crisis management, although it would be the WEU that actually conducted the operations.[34] All EU member states would have the option of being involved, even if they were not full WEU members. To facilitate this, EU states were to provide the WEU with details of the forces they had available for such tasks.

Despite this support for a strong institutional link between the EU and the WEU to enable the WEU to carry out operations on the instructions of the EU, the memorandum emphasized its origin from these neutral states:

> An enhanced competence in the security and defence dimensions of the Union will respect the specific character of the defence solutions of the members and will not affect their status as states pursuing independent or common defence. It is understood that co-operation in military crisis management is separable from collective defence commitments.[35]

The Finns drew a distinction between the political leadership provided by the EU and the implementation of crisis management by the WEU. They preferred the strictly intergovernmental approach on military matters, but conceded that the use of qualified majority voting concerning the implementation of some CFSP measures should be examined.[36] Sweden, reflecting its record in UN peacekeeping, wanted to see the EU move into the Petersberg area, giving the EU a peacekeeping capability, but not into collective defense. It wished to be fully in control of its own decisions on defense, to maintain its neutrality, and made it clear that it had no intention of joining the WEU or any other alliance.[37]

Given the nature and extent of the divisions, it is not surprising that the 1996 IGC staggered on until Amsterdam in June 1997, the delay in completion being symptomatic of the difficulties encountered in resolving CFSP matters, as well as other issues. Toward the end of the negotiations informed sources suggested that opinion on defense matters was divided as follows: (1) on the issue of including defense in the EU, Austria, Belgium,

France, Germany, Greece, Italy, Luxembourg, the Netherlands, Portugal, and Spain were broadly in favor, while Denmark, Finland, Ireland, Sweden, and the UK were not; and (2) on the issue of merging the WEU into the EU, Belgium, France, Germany, Greece, Italy, the Netherlands, and Spain were supportive, whereas Austria, Denmark, Finland, Ireland, Luxembourg, Portugal, Sweden, and the UK were opposed.

All except Germany wished to retain the intergovernmental character of CFSP and no state formally pushed for the abandonment of unanimity in CFSP. Eventually, compromises were found and agreements reached, which were formalized in the 1997 Amsterdam Treaty.[38]

The Amsterdam Treaty

The security and defense discussions during the 1996–1997 IGC, based on the positions outlined above, led the Amsterdam Treaty to make a number of revisions to CFSP in an attempt to improve its operational development. Of particular note, at least in rhetorical terms, is the replacement of the phrase "*eventual* framing of a common defence policy" with "the *progressive* framing of a common defence policy."[39] This single-word change implied that the development of a common defense policy was already under way and would be a continuous process. The Amsterdam Treaty also outlined what sort of military operations the EU would participate in. For this the EU incorporated the so-called Petersberg tasks adopted by the WEU in 1992. These were "humanitarian and rescue tasks, peacekeeping tasks and tasks of combat forces in crisis management, including peacemaking."[40] This was a significant step, defining the possible military actions to be undertaken by the EU.

However, exactly what sort of action remained undefined, and the phrase "use of combat forces in crisis management" is itself ambiguous, with a wide range of interpretations regarding the type and scale of forces involved. François Heisbourg argues that even an operation as large and demanding as the Korean War could be deemed to be covered by the peacemaking segment of the statement, given that it was a UN-mandated military intervention to restore peace.[41] Although such an operation by the EU is highly unlikely, it illustrates the ambiguous nature of the Petersberg tasks, which has so far facilitated agreement but will, in the medium to long term, create problems in defining exactly where and how the EU will act. The one point made clearly, by its absence, is that the Petersberg tasks firmly steer clear of the notion of a security guarantee for the EU member states. This issue was a very sensitive point during the negotiations and, in the Irish Draft Treaty, there was a discussion on the exact wording.[42] The first draft suggested the wording "territorial defence," but this was argued by some to imply a defense guarantee (still the prerogative of NATO) and also to infringe on the neutrality of some EU member states. Eventually the wording was changed to the rather ambiguous phrase of "safeguarding . . . the integrity of the Union."[43]

To answer Henry Kissinger's age-old question of whom to call in Europe in a time of crisis and in an attempt to reduce the confusion over whom to contact with regard to CFSP, the Secretary-General of the Council was to be given the title of High Representative for CFSP. The High Representative was to contribute to the "formulation, preparation and implementation of policy decisions, and, when appropriate and acting on behalf of the Council at the request of the Presidency, through conducting political dialogue with third parties."[44] In short, he/she was to improve the coordination and effectiveness of CFSP.

The High Representative would also be responsible for a new institutional development agreed in the Treaty of Amsterdam, the Policy Planning and Early Warning Unit (PPEWU). This unit is staffed by personnel on secondment from the member states, in addition to personnel from the Council's general secretariat, the Commission, and the WEU.[45] The PPEWU's core tasks were to monitor, analyze, and provide assessments, including policy option papers, and early warning on all areas of interest to CFSP.[46]

The Amsterdam Treaty also expanded the number of instruments and mechanisms available in the CFSP arena. In addition to joint actions and common positions, common strategies were introduced to cover areas where the member states all had common interests, to be decided by the European Council on the recommendation of the Council. A common strategy, which was agreed by unanimity, sets out the objectives of an EU policy, its duration, and the means to achieve that objective within the period.[47] Its implementation can then be decided by qualified majority voting, if all agree to do so. This was only the second time qualified majority voting had been introduced in the context of CFSP, the other being the implementation of joint actions, again, if all parties agreed to this method first. There was also an attempt to clarify the roles of joint actions and common positions. The former was to address "specific situations where operational action by the Union is deemed to be required," while the latter shall "define the approach of the Union to a particular matter of a geographical or thematic nature."[48]

The dominance of unanimity and intergovernmentalism within Pillar II (the CFSP) slowed decisionmaking. In an attempt to speed the process, without imposing a decision on a member state, the Amsterdam Treaty introduced the concept of constructive abstention. This allowed a member state to abstain from a decision and release itself from obligation to apply that decision, though the membership accepted that the decision committed the EU to that policy.[49] This mechanism was designed to allow the EU to make better progress in CFSP matters. However, if a state objected for "important and stated reasons of national policy," a vote would not be taken and the matter would be referred to the European Council. Hence the dominance of intergovernmentalism remained within the decisionmaking process of CFSP. This dominance of intergovernmentalism was even stronger for all matters related to the European Security and Defense Policy (ESDP). The limited use of qualified majority voting and constructive abstention would not apply to any matter with military or defense implications.[50]

Even the inclusion of the European Parliament in CFSP did not diminish the dominance of the member states. It obtained a role in CFSP through its budgetary powers. It was decided that all expenditure, except from operations having military or defense implications incurred while applying CFSP, was to be paid for by the EU budget, which the Parliament must approve. However, it still had no say on operational decisions, and any expenditure relating to military or defense issues remained the responsibility of the member states (except those who excluded themselves from that particular operation).[51] At the Seville European Council this changed slightly when it was agreed that so-called common costs, even relating to operations such as transport, communications, and barracks, could be covered by the EU.[52]

Finally, on the issue of military operations, the Treaty of Amsterdam retained the WEU as the body with operational capability in CFSP but went one step further than the Maastricht Treaty by suggesting that, if the European Council so decided, the WEU could be integrated into the EU.[53] However, the Treaty of Amsterdam further complicated the situation between the WEU and the EU. It stated that the European Council was able to instruct the WEU in areas where the EU has made use of the WEU's capabilities, thereby allowing the fifteen EU states to instruct the ten WEU states as to what their policy and operational decisions shall be.[54] This appeared, in 1997, to further exacerbate the institutional complexity of the European security landscape and gives former neutral states a voice in what a military organization, of which they were not full members, does.

Though far from perfect, the formal inclusion of CFSP, and with it the possible inclusion of defense matters, into the structure of the European Union at Maastricht, and the refinements made at Amsterdam, have given the EU a foothold in a critical area of international relations. It can also be seen as the first step toward resolving the perennial criticism of the EU being an economic giant but a political dwarf. However, this first step was not initially followed up.

Despite the much heralded introduction of CFSP in the 1992 Treaty on European Union, and the amendments made in the 1997 Treaty of

Amsterdam, the EU saw little progress in developing a clearly defined and effective CFSP during the 1990s. As a result there was no progress in developing a common defense policy, a stated objective of CFSP in both of these treaties. Throughout most of the decade there was a distinct lack of enthusiasm among the major European states to genuinely develop such a common defense policy, and even less enthusiasm for developing the military capabilities that would be required to operate it.

Only the last eighteen months of the decade saw a marked shift in attitude, process, and progress in the field of European security policy. This shift was so swift that, even before the Amsterdam Treaty came into effect (May 1999), it appeared that the changes that had been agreed for CFSP in Amsterdam were to be superseded. The period from mid-1998 to early 2000 saw a definitive shift toward the establishment of a European security and defense policy and, more tangibly, the military capabilities to support such a policy, which in turn was to support CFSP.

1998–1999: Portschach to Helsinki

A series of bilateral and multilateral European summits and continuous behind-the-scenes discussion and negotiation during October 1998 through December 1999 set the EU on course for potentially one of the most significant additions to its competencies during its history. The primary reason for this definitive shift was the change in attitude of just one state, the UK. Its new approach to European security under the recently elected Labour government started to emerge during 1998, under the Austrian Presidency of the EU. The UK had been traditionally opposed to the development of an EU security capability on the grounds that it might weaken, or even lead to the disintegration of, NATO. By autumn 1998 it became apparent that the UK was beginning to favor an EU initiative on security and defense policy on the basis that, if it improved capabilities, it could strengthen NATO and rebalance the Atlantic Alliance.

At the October 1998 informal European summit in Portschach, Austria, the first signs emerged that a CFSP and even an ESDP were taking a higher profile than had been the case during much of the 1990s. In a press conference at the end of the summit, UK prime minister Tony Blair said that "there was a strong willingness . . . for Europe to take a stronger foreign policy and security role."[55] During questioning he went into more detail, stating that "as Kosovo has brought home to us, it is right that Britain and other European countries, as part of Europe, play a key and leading role and we enhance our capability to make a difference in those situations."[56] These comments indicated a significant shift in UK policy and encouraged other European states, notably France, to reopen discussions on what is a very sensitive issue for many governments. It was also possibly one of the first occasions since the end of the Cold War that a European leader had alluded to improving, rather than reducing, defense capabilities. Tony Blair's comments were intensely analyzed by the press and other politicians. He had generated genuine interest in the subject and, although many questions were still to be answered, the issue of a CFSP and even a common defense policy had been well and truly established high on the European political agenda.

The heightened profile of security within the EU was made further apparent by the first ever meeting of the EU member states' defense ministers at an informal council in Vienna on November 3–4, 1998. This was a significant event in the evolution of a security role for the EU, despite the meeting not being made public and no official records of the meeting being produced.[57] Meanwhile, the British prime minister's reference to enhancing European military capabilities was reinforced a month later by then–UK secretary of defense George Robertson in a speech given to the Assembly of the WEU on December 1, 1998. His speech covered a wide range of fundamental issues relating to the debate on European defense, including a specific section on military capabilities. He opened the section by saying, "If Europe is to have a stronger voice in the world, then European armed forces need to be capable of supporting that position."[58] This seemed to be an attempt to address the long-standing criticism of CFSP, that it was increasing expectations of what the EU could do while failing to improve its actual capabilities in the field of foreign and security policy. Or, as Christopher Hill argued, creating a "capability-expectations gap."[59]

The statements made in Portschach and Paris regarding enhancing European military capabilities were quickly consolidated by the "Joint Declaration on European Defence," issued at the British-French summit in St. Malo on December 4, 1998. This document was arguably the most important development in fifty years of debate on European security and defense cooperation. The declaration raises the issues of European autonomous action, credible military forces, and a "European" defense industry. Previously, these issues were side-stepped whenever they arose. Paragraph 2 of the declaration states that "the Union must have the capacity for autonomous action, backed up by credible military forces, the means to decide to use them, and a readiness to do so, in order to respond to international crisis."[60] This statement was supported by Paragraph 4, which argues that "Europe needs strengthened armed forces that can react rapidly to the new risks, and which are supported by a strong and competitive European defence industry and technology."[61] This declaration is probably the most significant development for EU security policy because the two strongest military powers in Europe (Britain and France) agreed a framework for the future development of EU security cooperation. This was in stark contrast to some of the opposing positions these two states have taken on several other EU issues.

A week later (December 11–12) at the Vienna European Council, the other EU member states indicated their support for the ideas raised in St. Malo and the renewed impetus this gave to ESDP, stating in the Presidency Conclusions that the European Council "welcomes the Franco-British Declaration." It went on to say that "in order for the European Union to be in a position to play its full role on the international stage, CFSP must be backed by credible operational capabilities."[62] The Presidency Conclusions also advocated the swift appointment of the High Representative for CFSP and argued that he/she be a personality with a "strong political profile," presumably in the hope that this would lead to a more coherent and effective CFSP. In just two months it was becoming apparent that the UK and France were making a concerted effort to improve the operational effectiveness of CFSP by moving toward an ESDP combined with the institutional arrangements required to give the EU a greater role in European security. Importantly, the focus of these statements was on military capabilities rather than institutional arrangements. The military capabilities were the real problem for the EU states, while the institutional aspects were important, to manage both developments and future operations. However, the EU has rarely had difficulties in developing new bodies and institutions to manage new competencies.

It is clear from Tony Blair's statements at Portschach, George Robertson's address to the WEU Assembly, and the wording of the St. Malo Declaration that a significant and fundamental shift was under way in the UK's position toward an effective CFSP for the EU. This shift in UK policy raised the debate in the rest of Europe and signs emerged that other states were moving in the same direction, with France emerging as the UK's strategic partner in this field. At the time of the St. Malo Declaration, and since, some journalists, politicians, and analysts have argued that the UK was merely posturing to gain a voice and a role in the EU after the launch of the single currency on January 1, 1999 (which the UK has not yet joined). However, subsequent events have shown that there existed a concerted effort by the UK and a number of other EU states to develop a common defense and security policy and, even more important, to develop the military capabilities to support the policy.

The importance of this issue was also recognized outside of purely European institutions. For example, its importance was evident at the NATO Washington summit on April 23–24, 1999. Both the New Strategic Concept and the Washington Declaration mention enhancing military capabilities, but the true importance of this issue was highlighted at the launch of the Defense Capabilities Initiative (DCI). This initiative aims to "improve defence capabilities to ensure the effectiveness of future multinational operations across the full spectrum of Alliance missions . . . with a special focus on improving interoperability among Alliance forces, and where applicable also between Alliance and Partner forces."[63] The other significant announcement at the Washington summit was that NATO would make its assets and capabilities available to the EU for "operations in which the Alliance as a whole is not engaged militarily as an Alliance."[64] This was a potentially very significant move in the shakeup of the European security structure, especially if, as was rumored at the time, the WEU were to be in some way absorbed into the EU. It indicated a stream-lining of the complex European institutional framework. It also improved the possibility of the EU successfully undertaking autonomous military operations by providing the EU with NATO's planning capabilities as well as some other assets. This would allow NATO expertise to filter into the embryonic EU military apparatus and allow the EU to focus on acquiring crucial military equipment without having to duplicate expensive planning facilities.

It was therefore becoming clear that one of the priorities among many EU governments in the late 1990s was to develop some form of security and defense cooperation within the EU. It was also clear that within this broad aim was a specific focus on improving the military capabilities of national and multinational forces to enable them to carry out a set of specif-ic missions. The missions the Europeans agreed to act on were established in June 1992 during a meeting of WEU foreign and defense ministers in Petersberg, Germany, to consider the implementation of the TEU (the Petersberg tasks). This meant that the EU was not trying to replace NATO's central role as the guarantor of Europe's collective defense; rather it would focus on crisis management operations of the type that EU states had failed to address in the Balkans throughout the 1990s.

From the signing of the TEU in 1992, the WEU became more and more closely linked to the EU. First, the TEU allowed the EU to request the WEU "to elaborate and implement decisions and actions of the Union that have defence implications."[65] Then, in 1997, the Amsterdam Treaty offi-cially incorporated the Petersberg tasks into the EU and confirmed the importance of the WEU's role. Article J.7.1 (new Article 17.1) states: "The Western European Union is an integral part of the development of the Union providing the Union with access to an operational capability notably in context of paragraph 2 [Petersberg tasks]."[66]

Meanwhile, even as the Amsterdam Treaty was entering into force on May 1, 1999, the German Presidency of the European Union was already preparing a report on strengthening the common European security and defense policy. The final version of the report was approved and adopted by the EU member states at the Cologne European Council in June 1999. The report brought a major change to the evolution of CFSP and ESDP, making far-reaching proposals on institutional, policy, and capability enhancements. The report stressed that "the CFSP must be backed by credible operational capabilities."[67] Paragraph 2 of the report confirmed the objectives and scope of a common European security and defense policy as the Petersberg tasks. It stated, "The focus of our efforts therefore would be to assure that the European Union has, at its disposal, the necessary capabilities (including military capabilities) and appropriate structures for effective EU decision making in crisis management within the scope of the Petersberg tasks."[68]

It also suggested the formation of what were to become the Political and Security Committee (PSC), the EU Military Committee (EUMC), and the EU Military Staff (EUMS), as well as suggesting the need for a satellite center and security studies institute. The new bodies were to provide the decisionmaking capability in the field of security and defense policy as well as the political control and strategic direction of operations. These additions would give the EU militarily oriented bodies within its institutional structure for the first time in its history.

The implementation of such a policy and conduct of such an operation were also touched upon, raising the two alternatives available to the EU. The first was an EU-led operation using NATO assets and capabilities. This would require the development of the agreements reached at the NATO summits in Berlin in 1996 and Washington in 1999, which would provide the EU with assured access to planning capabilities and the presumed access to other assets. The second option was for an EU-led operation without recourse to NATO assets. This type of operation would rely on the national and multinational command structures already available within the EU member states.[69]

Aside from confirming and formalizing the discussions and statements made during the previous six months, the report's other real significance was its adoption by all fifteen EU member states, including the neutral states of Austria, Finland, Ireland, and Sweden. These states have traditionally avoided becoming part of organizations and institutions with defense and military attributes, but they were now taking part in the transformation of the EU from economic giant into a more balanced and powerful player on the international stage. Finally, at the Cologne meeting, Javier Solana was appointed as the High Representative for CFSP.[70] As the Secretary-General of NATO, he was the high-profile political figure that many member states felt was needed to give CFSP and ESDP the direction and coherence they needed. His experience as NATO Secretary-General, particularly his difficult role gaining political consensus during the Kosovo crisis and air campaign, would stand him in good stead. That experience would hopefully provide the EU with the credibility it needed in establishing its ESDP, good relations with NATO, someone with experience in developing a plan for improving capabilities (the DCI), and the leadership required to drive through these improvements.

Just prior to the meeting in Cologne, the Franco-German summit in Toulouse also produced a declaration on defense and security. In it the two states reaffirmed "their determination to put their full weight behind the effort to secure for the European Union the necessary autonomous assets it needs to be able to decide and act in the face of crises."[71] The declaration went on to announce that they had "decided on a concerted development of the capabilities needed to achieve that autonomy, including the pooling of certain assets."[72] It was becoming apparent that the lead taken by the UK to push for progress on the practical level of European security cooperation (i.e., the military capabilities) was being taken up by several of its most influential EU partners. With the Germans in agreement on the need to improve military capabilities within the EU member states, the three largest states hoped they could make a success of this policy.

In July 1999 it became clear that Italy, also an important military power in the EU, was in support of these efforts. The "Anglo-Italian Joint Declaration Launching the European Defence Capabilities Initiative" suggested a new practical and tangible approach to improving military capabilities. The approach suggests a "timetable to achieve: European wide goals for enhanced military capabilities to undertake crisis management including peacemaking [and]; national capability objectives to achieve the European aim."[73] This appeared to be an attempt to set definitive targets and objectives aimed at improving the armed forces of the EU member states, both to create the option of autonomous EU action and to better contribute to NATO capabilities.

In November 1999 the areas of military capability that needed to be improved within the WEU states became clear. These were announced in the WEU "Audit of Assets and Capabilities for European Crisis Management Operations." The audit states that collective capabilities need to be improved in the field of strategic intelligence and strategic planning. In addition, the main areas of operational capabilities in need of improvement are "availability, deployability, strategic mobility, sustainability, survivability and interoperability and operational effectiveness."[74] It went on to argue that the second focus for operational capabilities should be on "multinational, joint Operation and Forces HQs, with particular reference to C^3 (command, control and communications) capabilities and deployability of Force HQs."[75] The EU states now had a clear idea, if they did not before, of the collective deficiencies in their armed forces for crisis management operations.

The WEU audit was swiftly followed by the Helsinki European Council meeting in December 1999, which produced the most significant steps yet taken by the EU in deciding on the necessary military assets for an

EU security and defense policy. The Presidency Conclusions outlined the military forces that should be available to the EU for crisis management operations. They stated that "cooperating voluntarily in EU-led operations, Member States must be able, by 2003, to deploy within 60 days and sustain for at least 1 year military forces up to 50,000–60,000 persons capable of the full range of Petersberg tasks."[76]

This objective was elaborated upon in the accompanying "Presidency Progress Report on Strengthening the Common European Policy on Security and Defence." This report was split into three main parts, dealing with the decisionmaking aspects, relations with non-EU European states and with NATO, as well as the military headline goal. The report was the most detailed and focused step yet taken in the development of an EU security and defense policy.

The report elaborated on the headline goal, arguing that the 50,000–60,000-strong force should be "militarily self-sustaining with the necessary command, control and intelligence capabilities, logistics, other combat support services and additionally, as appropriate, air and naval elements."[77] It also gave further details on time scale of the deployments. The sixty-day limit was for the deployment of the full-size force, whereas the smaller, rapid response elements were to be available at "very high readiness."[78]

The decisionmaking aspect of the report further elaborated the details of the new political and military bodies proposed at the Cologne European Council, announcing that interim bodies along these lines would be established as of March 2000. The PSC would be composed of national representatives at the senior/ambassadorial level dealing with all aspects of CFSP and ESDP and exercising political control and strategic direction of an EU operation. The EUMC would be composed of military representatives of the Chiefs of Defense, who themselves would meet when necessary and would advise the PSC and direct the EUMS. The EUMS would provide military expertise and support, including early warning, situation assessment, and strategic planning.[79] Finally, an ad hoc Committee of Contributors would be established for the duration of any operation and composed of the member states (and partners) contributing to the mission. The states on this committee would be the states directing and shaping the operation.

The presence of an ad hoc Committee of Contributors, which included partner states, indicated that there had been further discussion on the issue of relations with non-EU European states and NATO. In this respect the report stated that mechanisms for dialogue, consultation, and cooperation with NATO and its non-EU European states, EU applicant states, and other potential partners would be developed. If an operation was to use NATO assets, non-EU European NATO states could participate if they so wished;

other states might be invited to join once the Council had decided to launch an operation.[80] At this point they would be able to take part in decisionmaking within the ad hoc Committee of Contributors.

Finally, the role of the Secretary-General/High Representative was also made clearer at Helsinki. Overall, it would appear that the High Representative's primary role is to coordinate the actions of the various EU institutions and the member states to produce a coherent EU CFSP and thereby contribute to a coherent ESDP. The High Representative's relationship with the Commission was less clear, particularly concerning the division of responsibilities between the Secretary-General/High Representative and the Commissioner for External Relations.

The period from autumn 1998 through the end of 1999 was the most significant in the history of the EC/EU's attempts to develop a defense and security policy. This period saw the most progress yet achieved in the realm of defense and was coupled with a focus on military capabilities that raised hopes that, this time, the initiative would produce more than simple institution building.

By the end of 1999 the framework for how the EU was to develop its ESDP was in place; it was time to start building on the words to create the institutional and, more important, the military dimensions of ESDP. In addition there were still some issues to be further refined in the realm of military capabilities. These were to further clarify and prioritize what capabilities were needed, how they were to be procured, and what they would cost. Tackling these issues and making a reality of the framework were to be the focus of discussions throughout 2000 and beyond.

After the Helsinki European Council in December 1999, the frameworks for both the institutional and military aspects of ESDP were in place. In the period from early 2000 through to mid-2002 the EU focused on developing ESDP so that it could be declared operational at the end of 2001 and be capable of undertaking some missions, if necessary, in 2002–2003. There was good progress through 2000 on implementing the concepts agreed at Helsinki, but the pace of developments slowed considerably in 2001 and 2002.

2000: Helsinki to Nice

There were a number of significant events in 2000 that moved the development of ESDP forward considerably: the establishment of interim committees to oversee ESDP, discussions on how to implement the headline goal, the Feira European Council, the WEU Marseilles Declaration, the Capabilities Commitment Conference, and the Nice European Council.

As authorized at the Helsinki European Council, the General Affairs

Council (meeting on February 14–15, 2000) established the interim military structures to manage ESDP. This allowed establishment of the PSC and the Military Body (to become the EUMC) and authorized the secondment of national military experts to the Council's general secretariat as of the beginning of March.[81] These national military experts would form the nucleus of the future Military Staff. The first meetings followed quickly. On March 1, 2000, the interim Political and Security Committee held its first meeting. A week later, on March 7, the first meeting of a committee of uniformed military officers was held, and the next day, March 8, the Head of Military Experts (Brigadier Graham Messervy-Whiting) was appointed.[82] The third interim body, the interim Military Body in Chiefs of Defense session (the future Military Committee), met on May 11, 2000. The first meetings of these bodies were a very significant step forward for the EU. It signaled their intent to turn rhetoric into reality in the field of security and defense policy. Never before had military officers met within the framework of the EC/EU, and never before had security and defense been officially discussed within the EU. The primary discussions at these meetings were twofold. First, especially for the Military Body, was how to get everything and everyone in place and get the bodies running as effectively as possible, as quickly as possible. Second, the bodies had to get to work quickly on the development of the "Force Catalog" as part of the process of fulfilling the Helsinki Headline Goal.

Two weeks after the General Affairs Council meeting that agreed the establishment of the new bodies, at an informal meeting of defense ministers in Sintra, in-depth discussions were held on how to implement the headline goal. The defense ministers proposed the establishment of a Headline Task Force (HTF) to identify the capabilities the EU required to respond to the full range of Petersberg tasks. This meeting also put forward proposals on how the military bodies in the EU could plan and conduct an EU operation. This meeting proposed several significant ideas that would become central to how the EU's military capability developed (these are covered in later chapters). These proposals were worked on through the spring and then officially endorsed at the Feira European Council.

In June 2000, the Feira European Council saw the next set of institutional decisions and structural developments. The summit established the HTF mechanism, endorsed the idea of a Capabilities Commitment Conference for the end of 2000, and outlined the modalities for the consultation and participation of the non-EU NATO members and the EU applicant states in EU crisis management operations. A framework was laid out for both the interim and permanent phases of the EU military structures and, within the permanent phase, for both routine and crisis scenarios.[83]

The meeting also established four EU-NATO working groups, on security, defining capability goals, EU access to NATO assets and capabilities, and permanent arrangements for EU-NATO relations. These four groups would, by the time the EU military structures became permanent, elaborate ways for establishing permanent EU-NATO arrangements in the field of security and defense.[84]

Outside of the EU, two significant events occurred in the next few months that would impact on the EU's development of ESDP. The first was the signing of a framework agreement on restructuring the defense industry on July 27, 2000, by six EU states. The other was the Western European Union's Marseilles Declaration of November 13.

The "Framework Agreement Concerning Measures to Facilitate the Restructuring and Operation of the European Defence Industry" was signed by France, Germany, Italy, Spain, Sweden, and the UK. This agreement followed from a 1998 Letter of Intent (LOI) that these six states had signed (as a result they have become known as the "LOI states"). Some observers believe that these six states are the ones that possess the greatest capability for transforming their military capabilities and, hence, for giving the EU a credible security and defense policy. This is because these six states have the largest and most developed defense industries in the EU. The most interesting element of this agreement is that it includes a "postneutral" state, Sweden, primarily because of its long history of arms production and its solid foundation in the defense industry. However, it must also be remembered that Sweden, together with Finland, came up with the idea to introduce the Petersberg tasks into the EU's remit. As such they may well have some additional contributions to make to the direction in which ESDP develops, though probably at the humanitarian assistance and peacekeeping end of the Petersberg tasks.

As a result of the EU's drive toward an ESDP, assuming the crisis management and conflict prevention roles of the WEU along the way, it appeared that the WEU was verging on becoming redundant. In November 2000 the WEU Council met in Marseilles to agree a new role for itself. The resulting declaration stated that the WEU would continue as a collective defense organization for its members and would continue to host the Western European Armaments Group (WEAG). The WEU Council also expressed its satisfaction that the EU would, in principle, take over the WEU's security studies institute and satellite center.[85] The EU would also assume responsibility for the Multinational Advisory Police Element (MAPE) agreement with Albania.

Throughout 2000, discussions continued in the national ministries of defense, and in the interim EU committees, on how best to achieve the Helsinki Headline Goal, focusing on which states would contribute what military capabilities. These discussions came to their initial conclusion at the Capabilities Commitment Conference, held in Brussels on November 20, 2000. This conference of defense ministers established the Force

Catalog—forces committed and available to the EU for crisis management operations where "NATO as a whole is not engaged."[86] Table 3.1 shows the estimated commitments made by the states contributing to the European Rapid Reaction Force (ERRF).

As the table below shows, fourteen of the fifteen EU member states, including the neutrals (Denmark having obtained an opt-out on defense policy matters at the Edinburgh European Council in 1992),[87] made a com-

Table 3.1 Estimated Commitments Made for the ERRF

EU Country	Ground Forces	Naval Vessels	Air Forces
Austria	2 battalions[a]	N/A	N/A
Belgium	1,000	9 (2 frigates, 6 antimine, 1 support vessel)	27 (14 F-16s, 11 C-130s, 2 Airbus)
Denmark (opted out)	0	0	0
Finland[a]	1,430	1 mine sweeper	N/A
France	12,000	15	75 and 2 AWACs
Germany	13,500	20	93
Greece[a]	4,000	7 (6 surface vessels, 1 submarine)	40
Ireland	850[a]	N/A	N/A
Italy	12,000	19	47
Luxembourg	100	N/A	N/A
Netherlands	2 battalions, 1 brigade	1 frigate, 1 task force	1–2 squadrons, 1 Patriot missile battery[a]
Portugal	1,000	4 (3 surface vessels, 1 submarine)	13 (8 F-16s, 3 C-130s, 2 P-3 Orions)
Spain	6,000	Surface and amphibious vessels, 1 naval air group	40 (2 squadrons ground attack, 1 transport squadron)
Sweden	1 battalion, 1 MP company	9 (8 surface vessels, 1 submarine)	8 (4 transport, 4 reconnaissance)
United Kingdom[a]	12,500	18	72

Sources: Based on table in Thomas Skold, "States Pledge Resources for Crisis Management," *European Security Review* no. 3 (December 2000): 3. Additional information also taken from Centre for Defence Studies, *Achieving the Helsinki Headline Goals* (London, November 2001), annex A; "Les Progres de la defense europeenne," *Lettre d'Information* no. 31 (Ministre de la Defense Groupe de Liaison, February 2001); and various national press reports.

Note: a. Confirmed.

mitment to provide forces toward establishing the ERRF. In total they committed over 100,000 troops and approximately 400 aircraft and 100 naval vessels.[88] This was another significant step toward giving the EU the capabilities necessary for intervening effectively in a security crisis in the regions surrounding the EU's borders, and possibly beyond, by 2003.

In December 2000, less than a month after the Capabilities Commitment Conference, the French Presidency hosted the Nice European Council. The main focus of this summit was to agree on reforms that would prepare the EU for its next round of enlargement, but a number of ESDP issues were also decided upon. The EU states confirmed they would incorporate the majority of the functions of the WEU and assume the crisis management functions of the WEU and a number of its institutions, but they refrained from incorporating the Article 5 collective defense element. The most significant structural components formally incorporated were the Torrejon Satellite Center and the Institute for Security Studies, while the operational component taken over by the EU was the management of the police technical cooperation mission in Albania, replacing the WEU's MAPE.[89] In a declaration attached to the Nice Treaty, it was stated that a decision on the operational status of the EU in ESDP was to be made as soon as possible, by the Laeken European Council in December 2001 at the latest. It was clear that the EU wanted some level of operational capability by the end of 2001, though it was equally clear that it would not be able to declare itself fully operational within that time frame. It was partly due to this declaration that the Irish rejected the Nice Treaty in a referendum in 2001, fearing that it impinged upon their declared neutrality.

The Nice European Council also announced the decision to confer permanent status on the interim committees set up at Helsinki. Principally, these three committees were to organize, manage, and direct the forces pledged at the Capabilities Commitment Conference in Brussels. The EUMS was to advise and report to the EUMC, which in turn was to report to the PSC, which was to retain privileged links to the Secretary-General/High Representative for CFSP.

Finally, the Nice European Council further elaborated the Feira proposals on relations with NATO, non-EU European NATO states, and the accession candidate states. It set out detailed proposals on the ideas developed at the 1999 NATO Washington summit whereby the EU would have guaranteed access to NATO planning capabilities and presumed access to other preidentified assets and capabilities, the so-called Berlin Plus.[90]

Just five days after the Nice summit, NATO's North Atlantic Council (NAC) held its meeting and discussed the Nice suggestions on EU-NATO relations. No agreement could be reached regarding the EU proposals because of Turkey's veto. It wanted to be able to veto the deployment of EU forces anywhere in its region, fearing adverse effects on its own security.

2001: Nice to Laeken

From the beginning of 2001 the pace of developments slowed as the project reached the more difficult stages of actually trying to implement the military dimension of the objectives expressed during the previous two years. This was exacerbated by reduced political interest in ESDP, leading to a loss of leadership and fading momentum. In 2001 the most significant events were the conferral of permanent status on the committees overseeing ESDP, the Gothenburg European Council in June, the Capabilities Improvement Conference in Brussels, and the Laeken European Council at the end of the year.

The Nice decision to make permanent the three new committees was approved by the General Affairs Council meeting of January 22–23, 2001. The PSC became permanent on January 22, 2001; the EUMC became permanent, with the appointment of its first permanent chairman (Gustav Hagglund of Finland), on April 9, 2001; and the EUMS officially became a permanent body of the EU on June 11, 2001.[91]

The bodies swiftly began consolidating arrangements to ensure their efficient functioning and their interaction with the existing EU structures and with each other. The intensity of the work schedule is apparent in the number of meetings held during the first few months of the committees' permanent status. Between its first formal meeting on March 23, 2001, and the end of October, the PSC held 105 meetings, while the EUMC held 27 meetings between its inaugural meeting on May 2, 2001, and the end of October 2001.[92]

The Gothenburg European Council, held in June 2001, achieved further developments in the EU's security and defense apparatus, although they were less significant than progress achieved at previous European Council meetings. The summit announced that the final decisions on the establishment of the EU Satellite Center and the EU Institute for Security Studies should be able to take place in the "near future."[93] The EU Satellite Center is crucial to the development of an autonomous military capability, while the Institute for Security Studies is a useful tool for further developing the debate regarding the concepts, direction, and utility of ESDP. The Swedish Presidency also announced it had initiated work on "identifying principles applying to the financing of operations having military or defence implications."[94]

However, the central aspect of the work carried out under the Swedish Presidency focused on relations with the non-EU European NATO states and the EU applicant states. The Presidency Report confirmed that permanent arrangements had been established with NATO for consultation and cooperation.[95] The first formal EU-NATO ministerial meeting took place on May 30; in addition, a number of PSC-NAC and EUMC-NATO military committee meetings had taken place during the Swedish Presidency. These were important steps in establishing a working relationship between the EU and NATO, allowing the EU to learn from NATO's experiences while making sure NATO was kept informed of developments. The ad hoc working groups also continued to meet and made good progress in further defining EU-NATO relations and in developing EU capability objectives.[96] These formal and working group meetings began to allow a useful working relationship in crisis management to develop between the two institutions. This was most apparent in the extent of cooperation in FYROM, an issue on which a large number of meetings and actions took place in an attempt to stabilize the rising tensions in that part of the Balkans. In this particular instance a division of labor emerged, which was roughly that NATO provided the military instruments, while the EU provided the diplomatic, financial, and political tools. The important point was that neither institution, at that time, possessed all the instruments necessary to reduce tensions. This cooperation has been a success. The issue for the EU states is that if NATO had not wanted to become involved in FYROM, from where would the military instruments have come, and how would they have been organized? This is one of the primary rationales behind the arguments for ESDP.

However, the Swedish Presidency failed to reach an agreement on one of its central objectives, finalizing arrangements to permit guaranteed EU access to NATO assets and capabilities, as outlined at the Nice summit. Turkey continued to be the primary stumbling block in the negotiations, maintaining its desire to participate in ESDP decisionmaking in return for access to NATO planning capabilities. From the EU's point of view, a Turkish veto over EU operations in regions with a security interest to Turkey (not an EU member) would impinge upon the autonomy of the EU.

The Swedish Presidency also implemented the cooperation with non-EU European NATO members and EU applicant states, as described at the Nice European Council. The first meetings of EU foreign and defense ministers with their counterparts from the non-EU European NATO states and applicant states in the EU+15 format and just the non-EU European NATO states in the EU+6 format took place on May 15, 2001.[97] Cooperation with other international organizations, in particular EU-UN cooperation, was also further developed during the first half of 2001. The Swedish Presidency identified themes and areas for EU-UN cooperation, which included conflict prevention and the civilian and military aspects of crisis management.[98] In particular, the need for cooperation in the western Balkans, the Middle East, and Africa were highlighted. Coordination with the Organization for Security and Cooperation in Europe (OSCE) and the Council of Europe was also raised as an area of importance with the potential for mutual reinforcement. Aside from these institutional issues, large parts of the Swedish Presidency focused on the civilian crisis management issues and, in particular, the further development of police contributions and arrangements.

In July 2001, as predicted at the Gothenburg European Council, the Council of the EU finally established the EU Institute for Security Studies and the EU Satellite Center.[99] The two joint actions establishing these facilities will, in the long term, enhance ESDP and the EU Satellite Center, an important addition to the development of the EU's military capabilities. In November 2001, following up the Capabilities Commitment Conference of November 2000, EU defense ministers met again in Brussels at the Capabilities Improvement Conference. This meeting was held to discuss the progress achieved toward fulfilling the Helsinki Headline Goal and remedying the fifty remaining capability shortfall areas listed at the Capabilities Commitment Conference. The defense ministers announced that new offers had been received and that these remedied the shortfalls in a further ten capability areas. The remaining forty shortfalls were divided into areas where the situation had improved (ten) and areas where no improvement was yet discernible (thirty). The important point of the Capabilities Improvement Conference is that many of these remaining forty capability shortfalls are critical to the military effectiveness of ESDP. The shortfalls included strategic transport, C^3I (command, control, communications, and intelligence), aerial refueling, precision-guided munitions, and deployable communications. The conference also agreed on a European Capability Action Plan (ECAP) to help remedy some of the capability shortfalls by rationalizing national defense efforts and increasing synergy between national and multinational projects.[100]

At the Laeken European Council summit in December 2001, the ERRF was declared partially operational. The EU declared itself able to "conduct some crisis management operations" and to be "in a position to take on progressively more demanding operations, as the assets and capabilities at its disposal continue to develop."[101] Declaring an initial operational capability was no great surprise, as it covered the easier potential operations, which several member states could organize from a national headquarters. Nevertheless, it was still another step toward an effective ESDP. However, despite an agreement being brokered with Turkey for guaranteed access to planning capabilities, no final agreement could be announced at Laeken as the Greeks objected to the deal arranged with Turkey.

2002: Laeken to Copenhagen

Through the first half of 2002 the Spanish Presidency worked on further developing ESDP and trying to establish its operational credentials. In particular it worked on attempting to strengthen EU instruments and to take greater account of the capabilities required to combat terrorism, and the European Council adopted a declaration on this matter at the Seville European Council.[102]

The Seville meeting also gave a more detailed account of the financing of EU-led crisis management operations with military or defense implications. It outlined that there can be common costs for operations with military implications and defined what common costs would encompass. This was another issue that had been a difficult sticking point until then, and the clearer delineation of what would be common costs and what would be considered individual costs is another step toward making ESDP operational. The report on ESDP also announced that ECAP was fully under way and work had started in trying to rectify the military capability shortfalls that had already been identified.

The Seville European Council also announced that the EU was in position to undertake its first crisis management operation in January 2003, when it would take over the UN police mission in Bosnia, becoming the EU Police Mission (EUPM). It also reaffirmed its willingness to take over the NATO operation in Macedonia when NATO's mandate ends, as first suggested at the Barcelona European Council in March 2002. However, this would only occur on the basis that the Berlin Plus arrangements had been agreed (the guaranteed access to NATO planning capabilities and presumed access to other assets). However, these arrangements were still not agreed and it looked increasingly unlikely that the EU would be ready to assume responsibility for the operation in Macedonia.

Finally, at the Seville summit, the European Council adopted a declaration by Ireland on its neutrality and reciprocated with its own declaration on ESDP and its effects on member states. The declaration stated that Ireland's participation in CFSP "does not prejudice its traditional policy of military neutrality."[103] It went on to stress that "Ireland is not bound by any mutual defence commitment . . . nor party to any plans to develop a European army."[104] Ireland hoped that by having this declaration inserted into the Presidency Conclusions it might convince the Irish public to vote for the Nice Treaty in the autumn referendum, having rejected it once already, allegedly on the grounds that it would undermine Ireland's neutral status. The Declaration of the European Council reinforced this effort by acknowledging Ireland's policy of military neutrality and confirming that "the policy of the Union shall not prejudice the specific character of the security and defence policy of certain member states."[105] In the second referendum, in October 2002, the Irish population approved the Treaty of Nice, removing the major obstacle to the adoption and implementation of the treaty and perhaps indicating that the declaration had eased their fears of the treaty impinging on Irish military neutrality.

The second half of 2002 saw discussions on ESDP being chaired by Greece as Denmark, the holder of the EU Presidency from July to December 2002, had opted out of participation in ESDP. Although there appeared to be little prospect of substantial advances in the development of ESDP, the Copenhagen European Council was highly significant. As is discussed in more detail in Chapter 6, the EU and NATO managed to overcome Greek and Turkish objections and conclude an agreement on the Berlin Plus arrangements. This meant that the EU was now guaranteed access to NATO planning structures and as such could contemplate undertaking crisis management operations. The European Council immediately confirmed "the Union's readiness to take over the military operation in FYROM [Macedonia] as soon as possible in consultation with NATO."[106] If and when the EU takes over this operation, it will be a highly significant moment for ESDP, and the success or otherwise of the operation will be crucial to the future of ESDP.

This is particularly pertinent because the Copenhagen Presidency Conclusions also "indicated the Union's willingness to lead a military operation in Bosnia following SFOR."[107] If the EU were to be able to undertake these operations, it will have taken a large step toward fulfilling its ambition of becoming an actor in European security with the full range of instruments necessary to operate on the international stage.

Conclusion

The period 1993–2002 saw massive change in the perspectives and positions of the EU member states toward developing a defense and security role for the EU. As is detailed in subsequent chapters, they have developed the institutional structures necessary for running a military operation, though they still need to be refined and rationalized, and have pledged military capabilities for ESDP and identified the continuing military shortfalls. Compared with the previous forty years, this appeared to be a definitive shift toward ESDP.

Notes

1. *Treaty on European Union* (Luxembourg: Office for Official Publications of the European Communities, 1992), art. J.4.6.
2. European Parliament, *White Paper on the 1996 Intergovernmental Conference,* vol. 2, *Summary of Positions of the Member States of the European Union with a View to the 1996 Intergovernmental Conference* (1996), p. 17, www.europa.eu.int/en/agenda/igc-home/eu-doc/parlment/peen2.htm.
3. Ibid.

4. William Nicoll and Trevor C. Salmon, *Understanding the European Union* (Harlow: Pearson Education, 2001), p. 365.

5. European Parliament, *White Paper on the 1996 Intergovernmental Conference,* vol. 2, p. 62.

6. Ibid., p. 31.

7. Ibid.

8. Finn Laursen and Sophie Vanhoonacker, *The Intergovernmental Conference on Political Union: Institutional Reforms, New Policies, and International Identity of the European Community* (Dordrecht: Martinus Nijhoff, 1992), p. 292.

9. European Parliament, *White Paper on the 1996 Intergovernmental Conference,* vol. 2, p. 71.

10. Ibid.

11. Ibid.

12. Department of Foreign Affairs (Ireland), *White Paper on Foreign Policy* (Dublin, 1996), par. 36.

13. Ibid., par. 4.113.

14. Council of the European Union, *Presidency Conclusions: Edinburgh European Council,* Bulletin of the European Communities 12-1992 (Luxembourg: Office for Official Publications of the European Communities, 1992), par. 1.37.

15. Ministry of Foreign Affairs (Denmark), *The Agenda for Europe: The Intergovernmental Conference 1996* (Copenhagen, June 9, 1996).

16. Ministry of Foreign Affairs (Denmark), *Basis for Negotiations Open Europe: The 1996 Intergovernmental Conference, Chief Task* (Copenhagen, 1995).

17. Foreign and Commonwealth Office (UK), *Memorandum on the United Kingdom's Approach to the Treatment of European Defence Issues at the 1996 Inter-Governmental Conference* (London, 1995) par. 21.

18. Ibid., par. 10.

19. Ibid., par. 11.

20. Ibid., par. 7.

21. Ibid., par. 24.

22. Government of Greece, *Memorandum of the Greek Government of 24 January 1996 on the IGC: Greece's Positions and Comments* (Athens, January 1996).

23. Greek minister of foreign affairs, *A Summary of Greek Positions at the IGC* (September 1996), par. 4.4.

24. European Parliament, *White Paper on the 1996 Intergovernmental Conference,* vol. 2, p. 38.

25. Ibid., p. 96.

26. Ibid.

27. Ibid., p. 57.

28. Ibid.

29. Ibid., p. 56.

30. Ibid., p. 88.

31. Ibid.

32. Memorandum from Finland and Sweden, *The IGC and the Security and Defence Dimension Towards an Enhanced EU Role in Crisis Management* (April 25, 1996).

33. Ibid.

34. Ibid., par. 9.

35. Ibid., par. 11.

36. European Commission, *Finland's Points of Departure and Objectives at the European Union's Intergovernmental Conference in 1996* (Brussels, February 1996).

37. European Parliament, *White Paper on the 1996 Intergovernmental Conference*, vol. 2, p. 108.

38. For further reading on the 1996 IGC and the Treaty of Amsterdam, see A. Duff, ed., *The Treaty of Amsterdam: Text and Commentary* (London: Federal Trust, 1997); G. Edwards, *Politics of European Treaty Reform* (London: Pinter, 1997); A. Moravcsik and K. Nicolaidis, "Explaining the Treaty of Amsterdam," *Journal of Common Market Studies* 37 (1999); and House of Commons Library Research Papers by Tom Dodd and V. Millar during 1996 and 1997.

39. *Consolidated Version of the Treaty on European Union* (Luxembourg: Office for Official Publications of the European Communities, 1997), art. 17.1.

40. Ibid., art. 17.2.

41. François Heisbourg, "Europe's Strategic Ambitions: The Limits of Ambiguity," *Survival* 42, no. 2 (Summer 2000): 6.

42. See the comment in Irish Presidency, *A General Outline for a Draft Revision of the Treaties* (Dublin European Council, December 1996).

43. *Consolidated Version of the Treaty on European Union*, art. 11.1.

44. Ibid., art. 26.

45. Ben Soetendorp, *Foreign Policy in the European Union* (London: Pearson Education, 1999), p. 73.

46. *Declaration on the Establishment of a Policy Planning and Early Warning Unit* (Luxembourg: Office for Official Publications of the European Communities, 1997).

47. Nicoll and Salmon, *Understanding the European Union*, p. 370.

48. *Consolidated Version of the Treaty on European Union*, arts. 14.1, 15.

49. Ibid., art. 23.1.

50. Ibid., art. 23.2.

51. Nicoll and Salmon, *Understanding the European Union*, p. 376.

52. Council of the European Union, General Affairs, *Presidency Report on European Security and Defence Policy*, annex 2 (Brussels, June 22, 2002), 10160/2/02 REV 2, p. 17.

53. *Consolidated Version of the Treaty on European Union*, art. 17.1.

54. Nicoll and Salmon, *Understanding the European Union*, p. 368.

55. Tony Blair, press conference at Portschach after the Austrian Presidency's informal summit, October 25, 1998, cited in Information Centre Releases, www.number-10.gov.uk/publi...eech_display.asp?random=0&index=1.

56. Ibid.

57. See Peter Truscott, *European Defence: Meeting the Strategic Challenge* (London: Institute for Public Policy Research, 2000), p. 19; and Nicoll and Salmon, *Understanding the European Union*, p. 379.

58. George Robertson, "Defence in Europe," presentation to the Assembly of the Western European Union, December 1, 1998, www.mod.uk/news/speeches/sofs/98–12–01.htm.

59. Christopher Hill, "The Capability-Expectations Gap, or Conceptualising Europe's International Role," *Journal of Common Market Studies* 31, no. 3 (September 1993): 305–328.

60. *Joint Declaration on European Defence Issued at the British-French Summit* (St. Malo, France, December 3–4, 1998), par. 2.

61. Ibid., par. 4.

62. Council of the European Union, *Presidency Conclusions: Vienna European Council,* Bulletin of the European Union 12-1998 (Luxembourg: Office for Official Publications of the European Communities, 1998), par. 76.

63. NATO, "Defence Capabilities Initiative," press release, NAC-S (99) 69, April 25, 1999, par. 1.

64. NATO, "Washington Summit Communiqué," press release, NAC-S (99) 64, April 24, 1999, par. 10.

65. *Treaty on European Union,* art. J.4.2.

66. *Consolidated Version of the Treaty on European Union,* art. 17.1.

67. Council of the European Union, *Presidency Report on the Strengthening of the Common European Policy on Security and Defence,* in European Council, *Presidency Conclusions: Cologne European Council,* Bulletin of the European Union 6-1999.

68. Ibid.

69. Ibid.

70. Council of the European Union, *Presidency Conclusions: Cologne European Council,* sec. 2, par. 4.

71. Franco-German Summit, Defense and Security Council, *Toulouse Declaration* (May 29, 1999), www.ambafrance.org.uk/db.phtml?id=2842.

72. Ibid.

73. *Anglo-Italian Joint Declaration Launching European Defence Capabilities Initiative* (Italy, July 19–20, 1999), par. 4.

74. Western European Union, Council of Ministers, *Audit of Assets and Capabilities for European Crisis Management Operations: Recommendations for Strengthening European Capabilities for Crisis Management Operations* (Luxembourg, November 23, 1999), www.weu.int/eng/mini/99luxembourg/recommendations.htm.

75. Ibid.

76. Council of the European Union, *Presidency Conclusions: Helsinki European Council,* Bulletin of the European Union 12-1999, sec. 2, par. 4.

77. Ibid.

78. Ibid.

79. Ibid.

80. Ibid.

81. Council of the European Union, General Affairs, *Strengthening of European Security and Defence* (Brussels, February 14–15, 2000), press release, 6108/00.

82. Taken from "Remarks by Dr. Javier Solana, High Representative of the EU for CFSP on the Occasion of the Official Launching of the Political and Security Committee" (March 1, 2000); "Remarks by Dr. Javier Solana, High Representative of the EU for CFSP at the Inaugural Meeting of the Interim Military Body" (March 7, 2000); and "Appointment of the Head of the Military Experts Seconded by Member States to the EU Council Secretariat" (March 8, 2000). See http://ue.eu.int/newsroom.

83. Council of the European Union, *Presidency Conclusions: Feira European Council,* Bulletin of the European Union 6-2000.

84. Ibid.

85. WEU Ministerial Council, *Marseilles Declaration* (November 13, 2000), par. 6.

86. Council of the European Union, General Affairs, "Military Capabilities Commitment Declaration" (Brussels, November 20, 2000), press release,

13427/2/00, par. 1, http://ue.eu.int/newsroom/oaddoc.cfm?ma...doc=!!!&bid= 75&did=63995&grp=2957&lang=1, 23/11/00.

87. Council of the European Union, *Presidency Conclusions: Edinburgh European Council.*

88. Council of the European Union, General Affairs, "Military Capabilities Commitment Declaration."

89. Council of the European Union, General Affairs, *Draft Presidency Report on the European Security and Defence Policy* (Brussels, December 13, 2000), 14056/3/00 REV 3, p. 10.

90. Ibid., p. 58.

91. Council of the European Union, General Affairs, *Presidency Report to the Gothenburg European Council on European Security and Defence Policy* (Brussels, June 11, 2001), 9526/1/01 REV 1, p. 7.

92. Data from Council of the European Union, General Secretariat, October 2001.

93. Council of the European Union, General Affairs, *Presidency Report to the Gothenburg European Council,* p. 8.

94. Ibid., p. 9.

95. Ibid., p. 10.

96. Ibid., p. 11.

97. Ibid., p. 13.

98. Ibid., p. 12.

99. Council of the European Union, General Affairs, *Council Joint Action of 20 July 2001 on the Establishment of a European Union Satellite Centre* (2001/555/CFSP) and *Council Joint Action of 20 July 2001 on the Establishment of a European Union Institute for Security Studies* (2001/554/CFSP).

100. Council of the European Union, General Affairs, *Statement on Improving European Military Capabilities* (Brussels, November 19, 2001).

101. Council of the European Union, *Declaration on the Operational Capability of the Common European Security and Defence Policy,* in Council of the European Union, *Annexes to Presidency Conclusions: Laeken European Council,* Bulletin of the European Union 12-2001, annex 2.

102. Council of the European Union, *Draft Declaration of the European Council on the Contribution of CFSP, Including ESDP, in the Fight Against Terrorism,* in Council of the European Union, *Presidency Conclusions: Seville European Council,* Bulletin of the European Union 6-2002, annex 5, p. 31.

103. Council of the European Union, *National Declaration by Ireland,* in Council of the European Union, *Presidency Conclusions: Seville European Council,* annex 3, p. 27.

104. Ibid.

105. Council of the European Union, *Declaration of the European Council,* in Council of the European Union, *Presidency Conclusions: Seville European Council,* annex 4, p. 29.

106. Council of the European Union, *Presidency Conclusions: Copenhagen European Council,* Bulletin of the European Union 12-2002.

107. Ibid.

4

ESDP's Institutions

This chapter looks in detail at the institutional aspects of the European Security and Defense Policy (ESDP) and sets out to describe and analyze the structures that have been and still are being put in place to manage and implement it. These institutional structures and developments are designed to allow an informed and effective decisionmaking process for the range of missions the EU is hoping to be capable of in the field of crisis management—namely the Petersberg tasks. The majority of the structures, such as the Political and Security Committee (PSC), the European Union Military Committee (EUMC), and the European Union Military Staff (EUMS), have been established since the Cologne European Council in June 1999. In addition there are institutional linkages and mechanisms that have been or are still being established to facilitate cooperation with the North Atlantic Treaty Organization (NATO), the non-EU European NATO states, the EU candidate states and other international organizations.

This leads into a discussion, later in the chapter, on the two most contentious issues within ESDP: first, the planning and conduct of military operations, and second, leadership (which states are likely to take the lead and how this affects intra-EU relationships). The first significant institutional structure to be developed specifically for the Common Foreign and Security Policy (CFSP), and therefore for ESDP, was the position of High Representative for CFSP, together with the Policy Planning and Early Warning Unit (PPEWU), which was to report to the High Representative on security issues.

The High Representative for CFSP and the PPEWU

The position of High Representative for CFSP was created to establish a single contact point for member states and others in times of international crises. The new post was allocated to the Secretary-General of the Council, who was given the additional title of High Representative for CFSP. The Secretary-General/High Representative was to improve the coordination, coherence, and effectiveness of CFSP and to try to ensure that the EU would be able to speak with one voice on international issues. The Treaty of Amsterdam outlined the High Representative's role as contributing to the "formulation, preparation and implementation of policy decisions, and, when appropriate and acting on behalf of the Council at the request of the Presidency, through conducting political dialogue with third parties."[1]

At the signing of the Amsterdam Treaty, which formally created this position, it was still unclear whether it was to be filled by a high-profile politician or a senior civil servant from within the Council. This issue was not resolved until the announcement at Cologne that the Secretary-General of NATO, Javier Solana, would become the first High Representative for CFSP.[2] This gave CFSP, and ESDP, the "heavyweight" player that several states, notably France, had argued for. Many member states felt that such a figure was necessary to give CFSP and ESDP the direction and coherence they needed. On the other hand, some argued that having a former Secretary-General of NATO as High Representative for CFSP merely confirmed the EU's status as secondary in security issues to NATO. However, this appointment was a strong indication that the EU really did want to make an impact on the international stage. Solana had recently guided NATO through its air campaign over Kosovo and Serbia, Operation Allied Force (OAF), the first offensive campaign undertaken in NATO's history, and was generally well respected in the international arena.

The High Representative's role in the EU and within CFSP, in particular, was made clearer at the Helsinki European Council in December 1999. The Secretary-General/High Representative was to accomplish the following:

- Assist the EU Presidency in coordinating work in the Council, to ensure coherence on the various aspects of the Union's external relations.
- Contribute to preparing policy decisions and formulating options for the Council on foreign and security policy matters, so that it constantly focuses on the major political issues requiring an operational decision or political guidance.
- Contribute to the implementation of foreign and security policy decisions in close coordination with the Commission, member states, and other authorities responsible for effective application on the ground.[3]

The High Representative was also given responsibility for another new institutional development agreed in the Treaty of Amsterdam, the PPEWU. The unit was established to strengthen the collective planning and analysis capabilities of the EU in foreign and security policy, creating independent CFSP options for the High Representative and the Council. The unit is staffed by personnel on secondment from the member states, in addition to personnel from the Council's general secretariat, the Commission, and the former Western European Union (WEU).[4] The PPEWU had a number of tasks assigned to it:

- Monitoring and analysing developments in areas relevant to CFSP.
- Providing assessments of the Union's foreign and security policy interests and identifying areas where CFSP could focus in the future.
- Providing timely assessments and early warning of events or situations which may have significant repercussions for the Union's foreign and security policy, including potential political crises.
- Producing, at the request of either the Council or the EU Presidency or on its own initiative, argued policy option papers to be presented, under the responsibility of the EU Presidency, as a contribution to policy formulation in the Council and which may contain analyses, recommendations, and strategies for CFSP.[5]

However, as Figure 4.1 illustrates, the High Representative's relationship with the Commission was less clear. The distinction between the High Representative and the Commissioner for External Relations in CFSP remained rather vague and ill defined and this was even more apparent with regard to the emerging ESDP. This lack of clarity, which the role of Secretary-General/High Representative was supposed to eliminate, raises significant leadership issues within the CFSP and ESDP area of the EU, and the question of coherence of the pillar structure.

The leadership issue within the EU goes much further than just who, or which states, lead which operation. There is also the need for a distinctive figurehead within the EU to represent its views to third parties. However, given the continuing confusion over the roles of various EU senior personnel, namely the High Representative and the Commissioner for External Relations, but also the Commission President and the rotating presidency, a single figurehead does not appear to be forthcoming in the near future. States from outside the EU often complain about the lack of leadership and being unsure of whom to contact. This problem is even greater in times of crisis, when quick, decisive actions are almost impossible to achieve in the EU. There have been suggestions for a division of labor between the Commissioner for External Relations and the High Representative, but there are no easy dividing lines in foreign and security policy. Indeed, one of the main claims the EU makes in support

Figure 4.1 CFSP/ESDP Structures Post-Amsterdam, 1999: Enhanced Clarity?

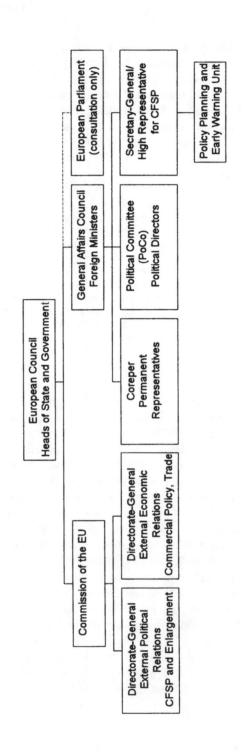

Notes: The Amsterdam Treaty added the position of High Representative to the EU's CFSP structures to enhance clarity and provide a point of contact. However, there was still a division of labor between the Council and Commission and even within the Council itself.

of its moves into the field of ESDP is that it can provide "comprehensive" security solutions ranging from economic assistance and conflict prevention to military intervention and postconflict reconstruction. If this is to be possible, a divided structure is likely to reduce effectiveness and efficiency.

This is an important issue, but given the lack of progress and the power struggle between the Commission and Council over control of EU external relations, it is unlikely to be effectively resolved in the near future. The recent suggestion by the Commission for one person to lead CFSP is a step in the right direction.[6] However, given the position and sensitivities of the member states, the idea that this should occur as a result of CFSP/ESDP being subsumed into Pillar I (the Community) is unrealistic. An alternative suggestion by some member states, notably France, for a form of EU President to be established to head the European Council and the Council of Ministers to provide the clear leadership requested by third parties, also seems to simply add to the confusion, creating another layer of bureaucracy. It would also continue the four-way struggle for leadership in international affairs between the High Representative, the Commissioner for External Relations, the Commission President, and the new EU President. However, such a position would presumably replace the six-month rotating presidency, which also creates a lot of confusion for states outside the EU as personnel and priorities change so regularly. The simplest and most effective solution is for one person to have overall responsibility for CFSP and ESDP. However, the EU's internal power struggles, member states' concerns over sovereignty, and the jostling for position of the member states mean that a great deal of time and effort will be required before this becomes a reality. At that point the EU would be more able to clearly and succinctly project its policies on the international stage.

Security and Military Structures

Through the first half 1999 the EU member states decided, in line with the St. Malo Declaration, to significantly enhance the EU's capabilities and decisionmaking structures to allow it to act more decisively in conflict and crisis situations. In support of this, at the Cologne European Council meeting in May, the German Presidency produced a report on strengthening the common ESDP. The most dramatic aspect of the report was the proposal to incorporate the functions of the WEU necessary to carry out the Petersberg tasks. This decision was to be taken by the end of 2000 and, at that point, the original WEU organization would come to an end.[7] The report suggested the EU would need:

- Regular (or ad hoc) meetings of the General Affairs Council, as appropriate, including Defence Ministers.
- A permanent body in Brussels (Political and Security Committee) consisting of representatives with political-military expertise.
- An EU Military Committee, consisting of Military Representatives making recommendations to the Political and Security Committee.
- An EU Military Staff, including a Situation Center.
- Other resources, such as an EU Satellite Center and Institute for Security Studies.[8]

In effect, most of these institutional arrangements provided very similar capabilities and functions to those previously provided by the WEU. In the case of the satellite center and security institute the EU simply took over the WEU's role. The one exception to this is the WEU's collective defense role, which the WEU has retained. These new institutions should allow the EU to carry out effective crisis management operations. The new political and military bodies proposed at Cologne were further developed and then confirmed at the Helsinki and Nice European Councils in December 1999 and December 2000 respectively.

The Political and Security Committee

The PSC, commonly referred to by its French acronym, COPS (Comité Politique et de Sécurité), is the pivotal security and defense element of ESDP, composed of senior national representatives at ambassadorial level. It deals with all aspects of CFSP, including ESDP, as defined in Article 25 of the Nice Treaty (now ratified), and without prejudice to Community competence as set out in Article 207 of Treaty of Rome Establishing the European Economic Community.[9] The PSC keeps track of international events that fall within the remit of ESDP and CFSP, helping to define policies for the Council and monitoring the implementation of policies. It also forwards guidelines to the Military Committee and receives recommendations and opinions from the EUMC. In the case of a military crisis management operation, the PSC will exercise, under the authority of the Council, the political control and strategic direction of the operation. It will evaluate the strategic military options and chain of command, as well as the operational concept and plan, before submitting it to the Council. It is the Council that decides to launch an operation within the framework of a joint action.[10] The High Representative may chair the PSC meetings, especially in times of crisis, and he/she will keep the Council informed. The chairman of the EUMC may also take part in PSC meetings when necessary.

The first meeting of the interim Political and Security Committee took place on March 1, 2000, and the PSC became permanent on January 22, 2001.[11] It holds two meetings a week and has been extremely active since its inception, as illustrated by the 105 meetings it held between its first formal meeting on March 23, 2001, and the end of October 2001. It has also established links with NATO, as will be described later in this chapter, and was very actively engaged with NATO during the tensions in Macedonia in 2001.

The institutional problem that remains for the PSC in 2002 is that it is still unclear how the work between it, the Political Committee (PoCo), and the Committee of Permanent Representatives (Coreper) is to be divided. Until these different bodies are either given clear and distinct remits or rationalized, there will always be some overlap in preparing CFSP and ESDP issues for the General Affairs Council (GAC). This may create confusing or conflicting opinions, advice, and tensions within the Council structures at the precise moment that the member states are trying to harmonize and strengthen ESDP. It appears from the statements and documents that emerged between 1999 and 2001 that the PSC has become the lead player in ESDP and it is this body that should be given sole responsibility for ESDP, thus reducing tensions and turf battles within the EU structures.

The EU Military Committee

The EUMC is composed of the fifteen EU chiefs of defense, represented by their military delegates, meeting at the level of Chiefs of Defense as and when necessary, but at least twice a year. The military delegates are normally double-hatted with each state's NATO representative. A four-star officer acting solely in an international capacity and responsible to the EUMC chairs the EUMC. The EUMC gives military advice and makes recommendations on military matters to the PSC and provides military direction to the Military Staff. The chairman of the EUMC will attend meetings of the Council when decisions with defense implications are to be taken.[12]

The EUMC is the principal forum for military consultation and cooperation between the EU member states in conflict prevention and crisis management. Day-to-day business is conducted at the level of national military representatives.[13] The chairman would participate in and contribute to, but not be a member of, the PSC and NATO Military Committee, as appropriate. He also attends Council meetings when decisions with defense implications are being discussed. The EUMC would also see the participation of the Deputy Supreme Allied Commander for Europe (DSACEUR) when appropriate, reflecting his responsibilities for NATO's European pillar and his potential role in EU-led operations.[14]

In crisis management situations the EUMC, under direction of the PSC, instructs the EUMS to develop strategic military options. The EUMC then evaluates these options and passes the options and its evaluation and advice to the PSC. During an operation the EUMC monitors the execution of the military operations.

The interim Military Body in Chiefs of Defense session (the body that preceded the EUMC) met for the first time on May 11, 2000. It gained its permanent status with the appointment of its first permanent chairman (Gustav Hagglund of Finland)[15] on April 9, 2001, holding twenty-seven meetings in its first six months.

The EUMC is the highest military body in the EU and its inception marked a major change in the nature of the EU, or at least in the issues the EU was to cover. Never before had such high-level military officers met regularly as part of the EU, and several states, notably the former neutrals, were wary of what they saw as the militarization of the EU. However, it must be stressed that these military bodies were under the authority of the PSC, a political body, which was in turn answerable to the GAC.

The EU Military Staff

The EUMS, under the direction of the EUMC, provides military expertise and support to EU bodies. Its three main tasks during peacetime are "early warning, situation assessment and strategic planning for Petersberg tasks including the identification of European national and multinational forces." In addition, it implements policies and decisions as instructed by the EUMC.[16] The Director-General of the EUMS (DGEUMS) is a three-star officer, General Rainer Schuwirth, who is responsible for a staff of 135 military and civilian personnel seconded from the member states. The DGEUMS is subordinate to the chairman of the EUMC.[17]

The EUMS is organized around a permanent core that handles the full range of Petersberg tasks and performs five main staff functions: intelligence assessment, situation monitoring, strategic planning, force preparedness (including training and logistics), and administration. During a crisis management situation the EUMS expands its duties to developing and prioritizing the military strategic options for the military advice of the EUMC to the PSC. It also identifies, in coordination with national planning staffs and, if appropriate, NATO, the forces that may be used in a potential EU-led operation. Finally, during such an operation the EUMS continuously monitors the situation, under the direction of the EUMC, and conducts strategic analysis, providing new options in response to operational developments.[18]

The EUMS held its first meeting on March 7, 2000, and Brigadier Graham Messervy-Whiting was named Head of Military Experts the following day.[19] The EUMS then became a permanent body on June 11, 2001, with General Schuwirth as DGEUMS and Brigadier Messervy-Whiting as his deputy. It spent much of its first year bringing in new staff and organizing itself, while its main task during that period was developing the Capabilities Commitment Declaration and assisting with the Force Catalog.

Again, as with the PSC, there still appears to be some overlap with another body within the Council secretariat, the PPEWU. Both bodies are tasked with the role for monitoring international events and providing early warning and situation assessment, ultimately, to the GAC. For an effective policymaking process it seems unnecessary to have both perform the same tasks and, again, it would be better to rationalize the number of bodies, or at the very least to give them clearly separate roles. The EUMS has put a huge amount of time and effort into the military capability side of ESDP and has been crucial in drawing up the Force Catalog and identifying the shortfalls alongside the Headline Task Force (HTF). Without this sort of military expertise the EU would be unable to develop a credible ESDP.

These three new structures, the PSC, EUMC, and EUMS, are now at the center of the development of ESDP, as can be seen in Figure 4.2. Their establishment hopefully indicates a serious effort to make ESDP work. However, as this organizational chart illustrates, it would be beneficial if some of the institutional overlap were removed to provide a more streamlined and effective ESDP structure. The other major issue for ESDP is that if it is to be welcomed by other states and organizations, and to help its own development, it has to establish links with these other states and organizations.

Institutional Arrangements with Non-EU European States

The numerous Presidency Reports have also stressed the need to accommodate those states that were NATO, but not EU, members and to develop "effective mutual consultation, co-operation and transparency between NATO and the EU."[20] Consideration was to be given to the possibility of EU candidate states being involved in EU-led operations and for all participants to have equal rights in respect to the conduct of operations. The EU was keen to receive military contributions from these states, but the principle of the EU's decisionmaking autonomy had to be respected.[21] These institutional decisions and structural developments were elaborated at the Santa Maria da Feira European Council in June 2000 and confirmed in Nice at the end of 2000. The permanent modalities for participation by non-EU European NATO members and EU candidate states are quite complex, as they need to take into account the different requirements for different situations. There are arrangements for both noncrisis and crisis periods.

Figure 4.2 CFSP/ESDP Structures, 2002: Whom to Call?

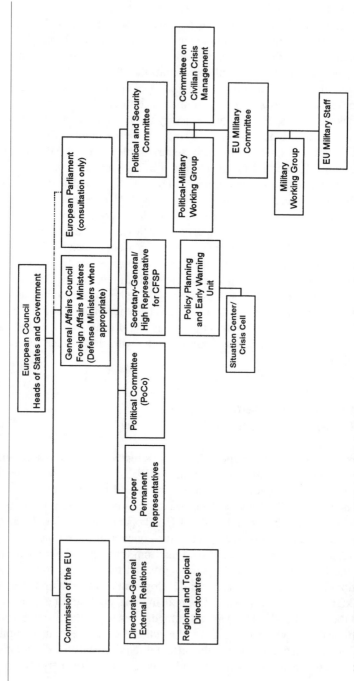

Notes: The EU now has a new capability to undertake crisis management operations. However, there is additional confusion and overlap in tasks and responsibility. For example, the PSC and Coreper are both advising the GAC on CFSP and ESDP, while the EUMS and Situation Center have similar roles and tasks and, now, a Joint Situation Center.

Noncrisis Periods

The noncrisis phase sees exchanges on various issues of security and defense policy and particularly on progress within the EU on the establishment of crisis management capabilities. During each EU Presidency there are at least two meetings of the EU+15 (candidate states and non-EU European NATO members) at the appropriate levels, at least two meetings of the EU+6 (the non-EU European NATO members), and additional meetings if the Council or PSC decides they are necessary.[22] The PSC plays a leading role in implementing these arrangements and they should include military-level exchanges. There will also be at least one meeting at ministerial level for both the EU+15 and EU+6 formats during each EU Presidency and two meetings at the EUMC level, as well as exchanges at the EUMS level.[23] The objective is to keep these states informed and, if they desire, involved in ESDP matters such as enhancing military capabilities and viewing strategic options in response to emerging situations. Third countries may also have a representative as a link to the PSC and an officer assigned to the EUMS to further enhance relations and information exchanges.

Crisis Periods

During crisis periods there will be two phases. The first, the preoperational phase, would see dialogue and consultations intensified and options for action considered. If an option included the use of NATO assets and capabilities, particular emphasis would be placed on consultations with the six non-EU European NATO states. The second, the operational phase, would start when the Council has chosen the strategic military option(s). At this point those non-EU European NATO states and EU applicant states that plan to take part in the operation are shown the options so that they can decide on their contribution. The Council of the EU then approves the operational concept. Once a plan is approved, other states may be invited to participate based on the arrangements agreed at Helsinki. The non-EU European NATO states will participate if NATO assets are used and they will be invited if NATO assets are not required. Applicant states may also be invited to take part.[24] Exchanges of information on operational planning and contributions continue until a Force Generation Conference is held, where contributions are confirmed. The Council of the EU then formally launches an operation and a Committee of Contributors is established.[25]

Committee of Contributors

During an EU-led operation there would be an ad hoc Committee of Contributors for the duration of any operation. It would play a central role in the day-to-day management of the operation by providing opinions to the PSC, which has political control over the operation. The Nice Presidency Report stated that "all EU member states are entitled to be present at the committee's discussions, irrespective of whether or not they are taking part in the operation, but only contributing states will take part in the day-to-day management of the operation. Non-EU European allies and candidate countries deploying significant military forces under an EU-led operation will have the same rights and obligations, in terms of day-to-day management of the operation, as EU member states taking part in the operation."[26] However, it is important to stress among these various new bodies that it is the Council of the EU that makes the critical decisions to launch an operation and to terminate an operation.

Hence, within the ad hoc Committee of Contributors, the non-EU European NATO states and applicant states that contribute *significant* military forces will have the same rights and obligations as the participating EU member states,[27] although once again this was not acceptable for Turkey. The ambiguity needed to reach agreement on the sensitive issues involved in the establishment of an ESDP is evident again here, with the use of the phrase "significant military forces." What "significant" means is not at all clear in the documents. It makes perfect sense that contributors to an operation have a say in how it is executed and that this allows the EU to involve other interested parties and possibly benefit from their capabilities, while giving those states some control over what the operation does and how it does it. This statement was presumably put in place partly to try to incorporate Turkey, reduce its concerns, and hopefully remove its objections to the EU's use of NATO assets. However, achieving a working definition of "significant" is a very difficult task, and until it is resolved some states may still see this as a means for the EU to dictate who can and cannot take part in the decisionmaking.

Despite this detail, the Committee of Contributors is clearly a critical element of the EU's institutional structure during an operation. It will be chaired by a representative of the Secretary-General/High Representative or the EU Presidency and supported by the chairman or deputy of the EUMC. It will usually comprise the representatives of the PSC or EUMC and may include the DGEUMS and the operation commander.[28] Finally, it was explicitly stated that an operation would end on the decision of the Council, after consultation between the members of the ad hoc Committee of Contributors.[29] However, the Committee of Contributors may be asked to provide an assessment of the operation and the lessons learned.

Finally, it should be noted that during the Swedish Presidency a lot of work was done on cooperation with other international organizations, in particular EU-UN cooperation, wherein themes and areas for cooperation were endorsed by the Council, but also with the Organization for Security and Cooperation in Europe (OSCE). Some have suggested that the European Rapid Reaction Force (ERRF) could act on behalf of the UN in some circumstances and that, for some of the former neutrals within the EU, a UN mandate would be crucial for participation in an EU-led operation.

Permanent NATO–EU Arrangements

As well as the arrangements outlined above for EU relations with non-EU European NATO members and EU candidate states, a specific set of arrangements was established for relations with NATO. This has been necessary to keep a number of EU members supportive of ESDP, for example the UK, to retain the support of the United States, and to ensure that the EU has access to the necessary capabilities to launch a military operation. The twin goals were to safeguard EU autonomy while trying to achieve "full and effective consultation, co-operation and transparency" between the EU and NATO.[30] The Feira European Council saw the establishment of the principles for consultations with NATO and the framing of the issues and modalities in which they would be discussed. The two key principles for the EU were:

- Development of consultation and cooperation between the EU and NATO must take place in full respect of the autonomy of EU decisionmaking.
- Arrangements and modalities for relations between the EU and NATO will reflect the fact that each organization will be dealing with the other on an equal basis.[31]

With these two principles the EU was attempting to establish itself as an equal to NATO in European crisis management, while recognizing the differences between the two organizations. It also asserted that the parallel processes within each organization, concerning their transformation and further development, should be mutually reinforcing.

In regard to the framing of issues and modalities, the first issue highlighted was the defining of security arrangements between the EU and NATO to govern information exchanges and access by designated officials of the EU and its member states to NATO planning structures. The second issue was to ensure that the Helsinki Headline Goal and NATO's Defense Capabilities Initiative were mutually reinforcing. The third issue was the need to agree arrangements to enable the EU to have guaranteed access to NATO assets and capabilities by the time the EU became operational. The final issue to be dealt with was defining the permanent arrangements that will govern EU-NATO relations.[32] The proposed method for tackling these issues was to be the establishment of an EU-NATO ad hoc working group for each of the four issues and for any new issues that may arise, coordinated on the EU side by the interim PSC.

By the time of the Nice European Council, based on the deliberations of these ad hoc working groups, the permanent arrangements for relations with NATO had been drawn up by the EU. The proposed arrangements for consultation "outside times of crisis" were:

- Meetings between the PSC and the North Atlantic Council (NAC) and ministerial meetings at least once during each EU Presidency, with either organization able to request further meetings.
- Meetings between the NATO and EU Military Committees to be held as required at the request of either organization, with at least one such meeting during each EU Presidency.
- Meetings between subsidiary groups in the form of ad hoc EU/NATO groups or expert groups, where there is a need for NATO expertise on specific subjects.
- When necessary, in particular where the capabilities and expertise of the Alliance are concerned, the dialogue will be supplemented by inviting appropriate NATO representatives to meetings (e.g., inviting the Secretary-General of NATO to ministerial meetings).
- Regular contacts between the secretaries-general, secretariats, and military staffs of the EU and NATO as a contribution to transparency and exchanges of information and documents.[33]

In line with these arrangements, the newly established PSC and the NAC met for the first time in February 2001, shortly after Nice, under the new permanent NATO-EU consultation arrangements,[34] though they had met before under the interim arrangements. The first formal ministerial meeting between the new permanent EU bodies and their respective NATO counterparts occurred on May 30, 2001, when the EU and NATO foreign ministers met in Budapest. This meeting was followed on June 12 by the first formal meeting of the EU Military Committee and the NATO Military Committee, where they discussed the future development of EU-NATO military cooperation.[35] The PSC and the NAC met again on June 26, 2001. The NATO structures that the EU is interacting with are illustrated in Figure 4.3.

The Nice summit also saw the arrangements for EU-NATO relations in times of crisis and the proposed arrangements for the implementation of "Berlin Plus" (Paragraph 10 of the Washington Communiqué) detailed. Berlin Plus was the idea to build upon the 1996 Berlin NATO summit decision to develop the idea of Combined Joint Task Forces (CJTFs) so that

Figure 4.3 NATO Structural Organization, 2002

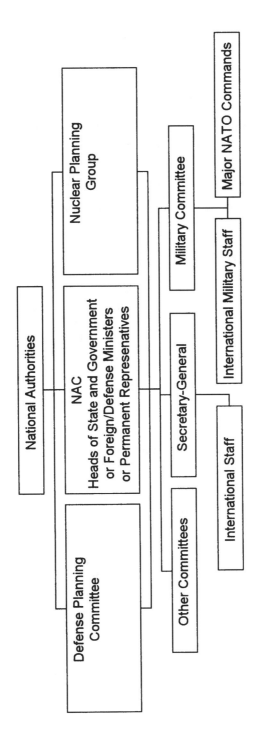

Notes: The NATO Secretary-General meets with the EU Council Secretary-General, the NAC meets with the PSC (both in ministerial and representative formation), the EUMC with NATO's Military Committee, the EUMS with the International Military Staff (IMS), and there can be ad hoc group meetings at the military committee and staff level.

some or all of the European members of NATO could undertake an operation without the United States. This concept was to be strengthened and subsequently became the Berlin Plus arrangements.

The Presidency Report proposes that as a crisis emerges, EU-NATO contacts and meetings should be stepped up, so that the two organizations can discuss their assessments of the crisis and how it may develop. The PSC will ask the EUMC to instruct the EUMS to determine and prioritize the strategic military options. Once the EUMS has its initial options, it may call on external planning sources, in particular the guaranteed access to NATO planning capabilities, to analyze and refine these options.[36] This contribution will be evaluated by the EUMS, which may commission any additional work. The matter of guaranteed access to NATO planning capabilities was the major issue that Turkey used to try to exert leverage on the EU in its case for greater representation within ESDP.

The EU Presidency's proposals for the implementation of the Berlin Plus arrangements, in the event of an operation calling on NATO assets and capabilities, caused controversy within some NATO member states, notably Turkey. Berlin Plus covers the issues of access to NATO planning capabilities, availability of preidentified assets and capabilities, and the identification of a series of command options available to the EU.[37] The proposal stated the following:

1. The EU will have "guaranteed access to NATO's planning capabilities" without case-by-case authorization by NATO.
2. Preidentifying the collective assets and capabilities of the Alliance for EU-led operations will be carried out by the EU and NATO experts and validated by a meeting of the military committees of the two organizations. If the EU considers an in-depth study of a strategic option calling for NATO assets, the PSC will inform the NAC.
3. EU and NATO experts will discuss and attempt to identify a range of options for the selection of part or all of a chain of command. These will again be validated by a meeting of the two military committees. Once selected, while the entire chain of command will remain under the political control and strategic direction of the EU throughout the operation, NATO will be informed of developments by the appropriate bodies (the PSC and chairman of the EUMC).[38]

No actual agreement was reached between the EU and NATO on these issues, although consultation arrangements have been put in place. The primary reason for this, as alluded to above, was Turkey's position, which blocked most negotiations while it tried to ensure it had satisfactory representation on ESDP matters, despite its not being a member state of the EU. If Turkey were to contribute militarily to an operation, it would sit on the

Committee of Contributors that manages the operation on a day-to-day basis and would have the same rights and obligations as other contributors. However, ultimately, it is the PSC that retains overall control, and the PSC is made up of the fifteen EU member states and therefore excludes Turkey. Under the arrangements outlined earlier, the PSC would consult extensively with the Committee of Contributors, but at the end of the day it makes the final decisions and does not have to guarantee to include the contributors' suggestions.[39]

It was very difficult to satisfy the concerns of Turkey and once these had been resolved in late 2001, Greece objected to the agreement with Turkey. Then in spring 2002 the situation was reversed again, with Turkey objecting to a compromise position. Finally the situation was resolved at the Copenhagen European Council and the Berlin Plus arrangements were agreed upon, but only after extensive political pressure by various EU states and the United States (the details of this dispute are elaborated in Chapter 6).

Planning and Conduct of Operations

The planning of operations is the most sensitive issue for many states and is one that the EU is unlikely to resolve swiftly among its own member states and with NATO. Instead, an informal and variable pattern is likely to emerge in the operational planning aspects of ESDP.

The original ideas on the planning and conduct of operations were outlined at an informal meeting of EU defense ministers in Sintra, Portugal, on February 28, 2000. The document presented at this meeting describes the proposed arrangements for the planning and conduct of EU-led operations, both including and excluding the use of NATO assets. It outlines a framework for two levels of planning, strategic and operational, and briefly covers procedures during the conduct of an operation. At the strategic planning level, during the emergence of a crisis, the EUMS would provide an initial military assessment to the PSC, through the chairman of the EUMC. The PSC, together with the PPEWU and other relevant parts of the European Council secretariat, would develop a political-military framework. Once agreed by the member states (in the Council), the PSC would, through the chairman of the EUMC, then task the EUMS to develop and prioritize military strategic options.[40] This framework is illustrated in Figure 4.4.

Operational planning and command arrangements were also outlined, with the EUMC and EUMS confirmed as the permanent military components of the CFSP decisionmaking structure, as illustrated in Figure 4.4. Below the EUMS the chain of command would have three more levels: operation commander with a strategic-operations headquarters, a force

Figure 4.4   Planning and Conduct of Operations: With or Without NATO?

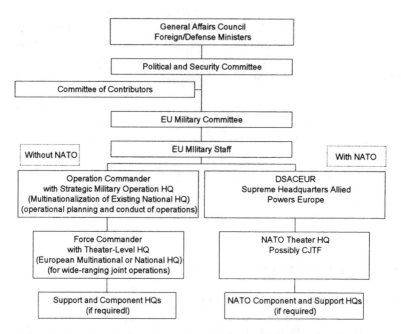

Notes: The upper levels of the command chain are identical whether or not the EU uses NATO assets, ensuring EU political control of an operation. The difference occurs below the military staff level, when operational planning is needed (something the EU currently eschews); then either NATO or a national or multinational asset is used to plan and conduct operations.

commander with a theater-level headquarters, and possibly supporting and component headquarters (made up from existing European multinational forces and commands).[41] The origin and structure of the command arrangements would depend on whether NATO assets (e.g., Supreme Headquarters Allied Powers Europe [SHAPE]) were to be used. Where NATO command structures were not used, the national assets of a participating state would be used, augmented by the other participating states. Once an EU-led operation was under way, the chairman of the EUMC and the operation commander would report to the EU political authorities, which would keep NATO informed.[42] These detailed plans go a long way toward establishing the procedures for running an operation. However, they do not touch upon the sensitive issue of leadership within ESDP. Although it has been suggested that a single figurehead should speak for ESDP, it has also been acknowledged that such a position may take some time to achieve. Until that time, and especially during operations, it is more likely that certain states will be the driving force behind the development of ESDP and the conduct of operations.

Leadership

If NATO assets and capabilities were not used for an EU operation, then a national headquarters would need to be utilized. If a national asset was to be used to coordinate an EU operation, that state would naturally expect to play a leading role in the operation. Since only two states, the UK and France, really have a national headquarters capable of running a multinational military operation on a reasonable scale (e.g., Stabilization Force [SFOR] or Kosovo Force [KFOR]), it seems logical that one or both of these two states would form the core of the leadership. This argument is further bolstered by the fact that these same two states have been the main manpower and equipment contributors in various military operations during the last ten years. For example, in the 1991 Gulf War, the UK supplied as many forces as the rest of non-U.S. NATO combined, roughly 35,000 troops, while France provided about 15,000, as many as the four other non-U.S. NATO contributing members combined.[43] Meanwhile, today the UK and France are providing about half of the ground troops for KFOR, approximately 14,500,[44] and the UK provided half of the NATO force in Macedonia for Operation Essential Harvest.

It is apparent from these brief examples that the UK and France have been leading, and continue to lead, the drive toward the implementation of a successful ESDP. They are also the ones who have invested the most in making sure any future operation linked to ESDP is run effectively and achieves the desired outcome, as evidenced by their St. Malo Declaration, their troop commitments in the Balkans and elsewhere, and their defense reform programs.

The issue of leadership, however, cannot solely be determined by who commits the most troops, most regularly, although this is a significant factor. Political, diplomatic, and economic factors should also be taken into account, and in this respect Germany also has an important leadership role. Despite its problems in reforming its defense establishment, it still has the third largest defense expenditure in the EU and the largest armed forces in Europe. Second, its history since World War II as a "civilian power," eschewing traditional power politics, sets it apart from the postimperial nuclear powers of France and the UK. Germany's status as a civilian power parallels the EU's history as a civilian power; as such, it could act as a mediator within the EU to help develop consensus and ease fears of the UK's and France's more interventionist nature in dominating security matters and decisions.

However, even this trio of states should not hold exclusive rights to leading the formation of ESDP, reforming defense structures and policies, and commanding operational activities, if and when they occur. Other states, such as Italy, have recently been closely involved in military operations on Europe's periphery, especially in the Balkans (e.g., Albania, Kosovo, and Macedonia) and should also be able to take the lead or form part of the leadership when contributing. Second, other states may have a greater stake in a particular crisis than those mentioned above. Their links with and knowledge of the states or issues involved may set them out as the more useful leader of an operation. Third, within the envisaged ad hoc Committee of Contributors that would be established on the decision to launch an operation, all parties can contribute to the decisions regarding that particular operation. This indicates that the EU has already tried to avoid the establishment of a permanent leadership group or "directoire."

Despite a rigid directoire not being advisable, some form of leadership from the more experienced states will help ensure that ESDP, and the steps needed to make it effective, move in the right direction. For example, the reform of the UK's armed forces and its defense policy during the 1990s, especially in the wake of its Strategic Defense Review (SDR) and Kosovo experience, are a reasonable framework for other states to apply to their defense policy. In fact, some French defense officials stated as much themselves. Second, these states, having the largest militaries and associated budgets, are also in the best position to lead by example in encouraging cooperative procurement projects. Such projects, like the strategic transport aircraft, the A400M, are critical if the EU is to plug the capability gaps that currently exist within the armed forces of the EU member states.

In effect, an informal and unacknowledged directoire has already emerged involving the UK, France, Germany, and to a lesser extent Italy. The other states are not in favor of a formal directoire but appear to realize that an informal leadership grouping is almost inevitable and even necessary for policies to progress, and those with the most experience in a particular field will end up driving its developments.

Besides the states being involved, the High Representative for CFSP should also be involved as the main coordinator within the EU, keeping all parties informed of what is happening. He/she should also be able to coordinate any pre- or postintervention mediation and assistance and coordinate between the military and civilian aspects of an EU operation.

Returning to the command arrangements, the chairman of the EUMC and the designated operation commander would report to the EU political authorities. If NATO assets were involved, it is likely that the operation commander would be the DSACEUR (currently a German four-star general). Below the level of operation commander, there would be a theater commander and, depending on the nature and scale of the operation, other subordinate commanders.

Hence the necessary arrangements are in place for the EU to undertake a military operation, at least on paper. It is now critical to undertake exercises, such as the EUMS exercise in spring 2002, to develop a good understanding and working procedures for turning these paper plans and wiring diagrams into a functioning structure.

Additional Developments

Absorbing WEU Functions

The final significant changes to the institutional structures are the inclusion of the appropriate WEU bodies and functions in the EU. The Nice Presidency Report noted the WEU Ministerial Council's Marseilles Declaration of November 2000 that saw the end, or the suspension, of most of the WEU's activities in anticipation of the EU taking over these functions.[45] In that vein, the Presidency Report stated that "the European Union has confirmed its intention of itself assuming the crisis management function of the WEU," thereby making the WEU largely redundant.[46] It went on to specify that the Council had adopted decisions to establish an EU Satellite Center and an Institute for Security Studies, which would incorporate the existing WEU structures (i.e., the EU takes over the WEU's satellite center and security studies institute). This was confirmed on July 20, 2001, when two Council joint actions were agreed on the establishment of the satellite center and security studies institute, both operational as of January 1, 2002.[47] On an operational level, the Council agreed to take over the WEU-organized Multinational Advisory Police Element (MAPE) in Albania.[48] The WEU's residual functions and structures would focus on enabling the member states to fulfill the commitments of the modified Brussels Treaty, particularly in relation to Article 5 (collective defense) and Article 9 (relations with the WEU Assembly).[49] The structures, to enable these residual functions to be carried out, were put in place in July 2001.

Nice Treaty Amendments

The formal Nice Treaty made amendments to a few articles pertaining to security and defense. The main changes were in relation to the WEU, developing the notion of enhanced cooperation and widening the use of qualified majority voting. Article 17 saw references to the WEU being used to elaborate and implement the decision of the EU being dropped (since it was agreed that most of the WEU's functions would be absorbed into the EU). Article 23 had a line added that specified the appointment of a CFSP special representative as a decision to be made by qualified majority voting. Article 24 also introduced new areas for the use of qualified majority voting in the conclusion of international agreements, where unanimity is not required for internal decisions. This was perhaps evidence of further attempts to streamline and "communitize" the CFSP decisionmaking process. The section on enhanced cooperation was detailed in Articles 27(a)–27(e). This attempted to allow EU member states to develop closer relations on matters of security and defense and move forward together in this field, without prejudicing or creating inconsistencies in the values and interests of the EU in CFSP.[50] Finally, in a declaration attached to the Treaty of Nice, it was made clear that the intention was to make ESDP operational as quickly as possible in 2001 and a decision was to be taken by the Laeken European Council by the end of December 2001.[51]

As expected, at the Laeken European Council summit in December 2001, the ERRF was declared operational, but only partially. The EU declared itself able to "conduct some crisis management operations" and to be "in a position to take on progressively more demanding operations, as the assets and capabilities at its disposal continue to develop."[52] The crisis management operations that the EU declared itself operational for were the low-end Petersberg tasks of humanitarian assistance operations and national evacuation operations. In essence, these were operations that EU member states were capable of prior to the ESDP project being initiated. Hence, declaring an initial operational capability was no great surprise, especially since such an operation is likely to be run from a national headquarters. Nevertheless, it is still another step toward an effective ESDP.

Conclusion

The EU has come a long way in a very short period of time in establishing the institutional framework and structures deemed necessary to implement its desire to undertake crisis management operations, as defined by the Petersberg tasks. It has the PSC, EUMC, and EUMS to plan and manage an operation, linked to the High Representative and his PPEWU to ensure coherence. These bodies are overseen by the Council, which will ultimately provide the political leadership, direction, and decisionmaking needed for military operations. The EU has established institutional procedures for consultation and cooperation with NATO and absorbed the relevant functions and structures of the WEU to complement what it had established itself.

However, a number of institutional issues remain unresolved. There are still calls for the Council of the EU to meet in session with defense ministers so that their expertise could become a formal part of the EU's defense and security policymaking system. The defense ministers of the EU states already meet informally on a semiregular basis and it seems sensible to incorporate these meetings formally into the overall ESDP structure. There appeared to be more agreement on this in 2002 than there was in 1999–2000, and this resulted in the first formal meeting of the General Affairs Council in defense ministers session taking place on May 13, 2002.

Second, there is the issue of whether or not the bodies within the Council secretariat need to be rationalized so as to produce even greater coherence and reduce, or even eliminate, the overlap in the work the numerous bodies are undertaking. Currently, it appears that there are overlapping institutional structures within ESDP—for example, the apparent overlaps between the PSC and Coreper in preparing work for the General Affairs Council. The PSC would appear to be the natural choice for a lead role in ESDP, but the political rivalries between member states and within the EU mean that a solution will be neither swift nor simple.

Third, there remains the unresolved issue of which personality within the EU takes the lead on ESDP. It is still unclear to many within and outside the EU whom they should contact on ESDP matters. The options are the High Representative for CFSP, the Commission President (the figurehead of the EU), the External Relations Commissioner, the EU Presidency (i.e., the head of state in possession of the six-month rotating presidency), or a possible new position of an EU President of the European Council (possibly in place of the rotating presidency). However, the addition of yet another prominent figurehead would merely add to the confusion currently undermining the leadership of ESDP. A single, clear leadership position is essential in the field of security and defense.

This leads to a fourth institutional challenge, the division of responsibilities between Pillar I and Pillar II of the EU, between the Commission and the Council. The Commission has previously handled the Pillar I CFSP issues of trade, aid, and economic sanctions; now it also handles the civilian aspects of crisis management. Meanwhile, the Pillar II issues of CFSP, which now focus on ESDP, are handled by the Council secretariat. This division of labor produces tensions and reduces coherence, and a solution needs to be found.

These obstacles to organizational integrity need to be resolved to ensure that a credible, effective, and coherent security and defense policy can be created and implemented, allowing the EU to play an effective role in international security affairs.

Notes

1. *Consolidated Version of the Treaty on European Union* (Luxembourg: Office for Official Publications of the European Communities, 1997), art. 26.

2. Council of the European Union, *Presidency Conclusions: Cologne European Council,* Bulletin of the European Union 6-1999 (Luxembourg: Office for Official Publications of the European Communities, 1999), sec. 2, par. 4.

3. Council of the European Union, "An Effective Council for an Enlarged Union: Guidelines for Reform and Operational Recommendations," in *Presidency Conclusions: Helsinki European Council,* Bulletin of the European Union 12-1999, annex 3, sec. B, par. 5.

4. Ben Soetendorp, *Foreign Policy in the European Union* (London: Pearson Education, 1999), p. 73.

5. *Declaration on the Establishment of a Policy Planning and Early Warning Unit,* in *Consolidated Version of the Treaty on European Union.*

6. European Commission, *Communication from the Commission: A Project for the European Union* (Brussels, May 22, 2002), p. 14.

7. Council of the European Union, *Presidency Report on the Strengthening of the Common European Policy on Security and Defence,* in Council of the European Union, *Presidency Conclusions: Cologne European Council.*

8. Ibid., sec. 3.

9. Council of the European Union, General Affairs, *Draft Presidency Report on the European Security and Defence Policy* (Brussels, December 13, 2000), 14056/3/00 REV 3, annexes 3–4.

10. Ibid.

11. Council of the European Union, General Affairs, *Presidency Report to the Gothenburg European Council on European Security and Defence Policy* (Brussels, June 11, 2001), 9526/1/01, p. 7.

12. Council of the European Union, General Affairs, *Draft Presidency Report on the European Security and Defence Policy,* p. 38.

13. Council of the European Union, General Affairs, *Military Bodies in the European Union and the Planning and Conduct of EU-Led Military Operations* (Brussels, February 29, 2000), 6215/1/00, p. 4.

14. Ibid., p. 5.

15. Council of the European Union, General Affairs, "Chairman of the Military Committee" (Brussels, April 9, 2001), press release, 7833/01.

16. Council of the European Union, General Affairs, *Presidency Progress Report to the Helsinki European Council on Strengthening the Common European Policy on Security and Defence,* in *Presidency Conclusions: Helsinki European Council,* annexes 1–4, p. 21.

17. Council of the European Union, General Affairs, *Military Bodies in the European Union,* p. 9.

18. Council of the European Union, General Affairs, *Draft Presidency Report on the European Security and Defence Policy,* p. 45.

19. Taken from "Remarks by Dr. Javier Solana, High Representative of the EU for CFSP on the Occasion of the Official Launching of the Political and Security Committee" (March 1, 2000); "Remarks by Dr. Javier Solana, High Representative of the EU for CFSP at the Inaugural Meeting of the Interim Military Body" (March 7, 2000); and "Appointment of the Head of the Military Experts Seconded by Member States to the EU Council Secretariat" (March 8, 2000). See http://ue.eu.int/newsroom.

20. Council of the European Union, *Presidency Conclusions: Cologne European Council.*

21. Council of the European Union, General Affairs, *Draft Presidency Report on the European Security and Defence Policy,* p. 49.

22. Council of the European Union, General Affairs, *Presidency Report to the Feira European Council on "Strengthening the Common European Policy on Security and Defence"* (Brussels, June 15, 2000), 9149/00, app. 1.

23. Council of the European Union, General Affairs, *Draft Presidency Report on the European Security and Defence Policy,* p. 50.

24. Ibid., p. 52.

25. Ibid.

26. Ibid., p. 53.

27. Ibid.

28. Ibid.

29. Council of the European Union, General Affairs, *Presidency Report to the Feira European Council,* p. 20.

30. Council of the European Union, General Affairs, *Draft Presidency Report on the European Security and Defence Policy,* p. 54.

31. Council of the European Union, General Affairs, *Presidency Report to the Feira European Council,* p. 22.

32. Ibid., pp. 22–23.

33. Council of the European Union, General Affairs, *Draft Presidency Report on the European Security and Defence Policy,* pp. 55–56.

34. Terry Terriff, Mark Webber, Stuart Croft and Jolyon Howorth, *European Security and Defence Policy After Nice,* briefing paper, New Series no. 20 (London: Royal Institute of International Affairs, April 2001), p. 2.

35. Luke Hill, "EU Military Staff Goes Operational," *European Voice* 35, no. 25 (June 20, 2001): 2.

36. Council of the European Union, General Affairs, *Draft Presidency Report on the European Security and Defence Policy,* p. 56.

37. North Atlantic Council, "Washington Summit Communiqué," NATO press release, NAC-S (99) 64, April 24, 1999.

38. Council of the European Union, General Affairs, *Draft Presidency Report on the European Security and Defence Policy,* pp. 58–60.

39. Sharon Riggle, "The Fuss About Turkey," *European Security Review* no. 5 (April 2001): 2.

40. Council of the European Union, General Affairs, *Military Bodies in the European Union,* p. 11.

41. Ibid.

42. Ibid., p. 14.

43. Michael O' Hanlon, "Transforming NATO: The Role of European Forces," *Survival* 39, no. 3 (Autumn 1997): 9.

44. Ministry of Defense (UK), *Kosovo: NATO Forces: Facts and Figures: The Kosovo Peacekeeping Force, KFOR* (London, 1999).

45. Western European Union, Council of Ministers, *Marseilles Declaration* (Marseilles, November 12, 2000).

46. Council of the European Union, General Affairs, *Draft Presidency Report on the European Security and Defence Policy,* p. 10.

47. Council of the European Union, General Affairs, *Council Joint Action of 20 July 2001 on the Establishment of a European Union Satellite Centre* (2001/555/CFSP) and *Council Joint Action of 20 July 2001 on the Establishment of a European Union Institute for Security Studies* (2001/554/CFSP).

48. Council of the European Union, General Affairs, *Draft Presidency Report on the European Security and Defence Policy,* p. 10.

49. Western European Union, Council of Ministers, *Marseilles Declaration.*

50. Conference of the Representatives of the Governments of the Member States, *Treaty of Nice* (Brussels, December 12, 2000), SN 533/00.

51. Ibid., p. 7.

52. Council of the European Union, *Declaration on the Operational Capability of the Common European Security and Defence Policy,* in *Presidency Conclusions: Laeken European Council,* Bulletin of the European Union 12-2001, annex 2, p. 10.

5

Military Capability: Aspirations and Reality

C urrently, the armed forces of many of the EU states are still founded on the standing armies that were needed for territorial defense during the Cold War era. This legacy is wholly unsuited to the operations that may be required under the European Security and Defense Policy (ESDP), or even within the Combined Joint Task Force (CJTF) concept of the North Atlantic Treaty Organization (NATO). These potential operations, based on the Petersberg tasks, require modern force projection capabilities, which EU member states currently either do not possess or do not have in sufficient quantities. Although a few states, notably the Netherlands, have undergone a wholesale transformation, and others, such as the UK, have made significant progress in reform, the changes under way in many of the other states, such as Spain, have been slow and in some cases, like Germany, somewhat halfhearted.

Transformation is needed due to the changing nature of potential operations. During the Cold War, the principal role of the armed forces of almost all the EU states was to contribute, through NATO, to the protection of Western Europe from a Soviet invasion from the east. This dictated all levels of doctrine, planning, training, and procurement, stressing the need for large defensive forces with heavy armor to protect the states of Western Europe. The situation today is that, for the foreseeable future, Western Europe, and indeed most of Central and Eastern Europe too, no longer face a threat of invasion. Nevertheless, there are still threats to the security of the EU states and their citizens, predominately from terrorist organizations, there is insecurity and instability on the periphery of the EU, and there are threats to the interests and values of the EU states.

In light of the tragic events of September 11, 2001, the EU states cannot rule out the possibility of a large-scale terrorist strike on one of its cities, militaries, or a critical part of its infrastructure. This possible threat, in itself, requires a reorientation of the armed forces. Indeed, the UK has again taken the lead in this matter with proposals to use the reserve forces for so-called "homeland defense." However, there is also the possible need to take action overseas to prevent a terrorist strike, requiring high-quality intelligence, both electronic and human, and a range of capabilities, including precision munitions, special forces, rapid reaction forces, transport, force protection, and combat search and rescue. Although this possibility of preemptive action does not sit comfortably with many EU states, it is an avenue that would have to be explored, as a last resort, if irrefutable evidence was uncovered and all other measures to foil the strike failed.

There are also the security concerns that have troubled Europe since the end of the Cold War, principally the areas of instability, conflict, and failed states that occupy the regions surrounding the EU. These matters need to be resolved, first by political, diplomatic, and economic pressure and assistance. But if these measures fail and conflict and disintegration look likely, then the use of force to maintain stability or, in a worst-case scenario, restore stability, is an important option to have. Once again, for these types of operations intelligence is the first critical capability the EU states will need to improve, followed by transport, communications, rapid reaction forces, and logistics. All of these capabilities are areas that need to be improved, either qualitatively, quantitatively, or both, across the EU.

Finally, there are the interests and values of the EU and its member states, which they will want to protect and promote. Some of these are clearly expressed in the treaties, while others are less explicitly documented. The treaty objectives for the Common Foreign and Security Policy (CFSP) include safeguarding "the common values, fundamental interests, independence and integrity of the Union"; "preserving peace and strengthening international security"; and to "develop and consolidate democracy and the rule of law, and respect for human rights and fundamental freedoms."[1] These objectives are wide-ranging and ambiguous, but they do illustrate some of the interests and core values that CFSP, and hence ESDP, aim to protect and promote. The other, less often articulated interests include continued access to affordable energy supplies, nonproliferation, and illegal immigration. The external instabilities that may threaten any or all of these interests and values should be resolved before they create internal instabilities within the EU. For example, stabilizing a state undergoing conflict or internal collapse may prevent other states from becoming embroiled and may limit the exodus of refugees who always accompany such events, in turn reducing tensions and instabilities within the EU.

Hence it is apparent that these new threats, risks, instabilities, and interests require the full range of foreign and security policy instruments. This perception entails a military dimension to the EU. As suggested earlier, this military dimension requires a different foundation for the armed forces in order to match the different strategic environment. It requires more flexibility in all areas of the military that may be relevant for Petersberg tasks, so that location, timing, and type of forces required do not hinder any prospective action. The reforms undertaken so far, and those still under way, have made some progress toward creating this new balance of capability within the armed forces of the EU states.

Although the EU declines to put any territorial limit on the potential areas of operation, it seems apparent that, for the near future, these are more likely to be around the periphery of the EU through the Mediterranean, up through the Caucasus, and on through the eastern limits of Europe. There will also be interest in Africa and the Middle East for historical, political, and economic reasons. Operations further afield are not completely excluded, but they are likely to be undertaken through the UN or in partnership with the United States and other interested parties. One important point to note, in the context of areas of operation, is that transport (deployability) will be a vital capability.

Thus the main focus of this transformation is on restructuring the militaries to make them smaller, but more flexible, deployable, and sustainable, so that they can respond rapidly to emerging crises. These changes can be seen in both military personnel and equipment priorities. The states committed to the most significant changes were initially the Netherlands and the UK, but now France, Italy, and several others are well under way with their reorganization. As these changes take effect, they should contribute to an overall improvement in the combined pool of forces and capabilities available to the EU for crisis management operations.

National Restructuring

European forces need to change in order to provide the increased "deployability, flexibility, mobility, sustainability, and interoperability" necessary for an effective force projection capability.[2] Hence, for most EU states, if not all, defensively positioned standing armies are now redundant. If the armed forces of the EU states are to engage in conflict, it will almost certainly be outside the territorial limits of the EU and NATO (though possibly within the Organization for Security and Cooperation in Europe [OSCE]). Therefore, any EU military and security policy will need to have the capability to know what is happening in its areas of interest (intelligence) and need to be able to get there with sufficient military power when needed (force projection).

This process of change is now under way in several EU states. Over the past few years defense reviews have been held in most states, and their defense White Papers indicate a move toward smaller, more mobile forces. Several reform programs have been under way in EU member states since the mid-1990s. The most significant include the 1998 British Strategic Defense Review (SDR), the 1997–2002 French reform program, the German restructuring proposals of 2000, the Spanish Defense White Paper of 2000, the Dutch Defense White Paper of 2000, and the Italian Defense White Paper of 2000. These White Papers and defense documents, and some earlier ones in the UK and the Netherlands, are the basis for many of the restructuring and reform programs under way today. They all aim to move these states toward the acquisition of a rapid and flexible force projection capability.

The UK's foreign policy–led SDR announced fundamental changes in the focus and structure of the UK's armed forces over a fifteen-year period. The SDR built significantly upon previous reforms that began the restructuring process earlier in the 1990s and took a significant step in reorienting the focus of the British armed forces. It increased the emphasis on "joint" operations to enhance the coordination between all three services in peacetime and in time of conflict. The most important development in this respect is the creation of the Joint Rapid Reaction Forces. These forces will benefit from the second major focus of the SDR, improving deployability. The speed and efficiency of deploying these and other forces will be greatly improved by the acquisition of new strategic airlift (four C-17s) and sealift capabilities (four roll-on/roll-off ships).[3] Clear evidence of the shift toward force projection and rapid deployment is the plan to acquire two larger aircraft carriers capable of handling up to fifty aircraft and helicopters, to replace the three small carriers now in service.[4] The SDR had a new chapter added to it during 2002 regarding the changes and capabilities required in the wake of the terrorist attacks of September 11, 2001. This chapter outlines plans to use the UK's reserve forces as the foundation of a homeland defense force to protect against terrorist attacks within the UK. This new priority may further squeeze the resources available for the other changes planned in the SDR. Even with the current levels of resources continuing, many of these equipment projects are still several years from entering service, and in the meantime some shortfalls in the force projection capability will remain.

Nevertheless, the traditionally expeditionary nature of the UK military in general, and the SDR in particular, are useful models for other European states to follow if they are to provide the EU with an autonomous military capability. However, given national preferences and defense traditions of using their own system, this will be a difficult, though not unfeasible, change for some states to make. Both France and Germany, with very strong military ideas and traditions, have shown similarities to UK concepts in their more recent reforms.

The major changes in the armed forces of other West European states tend to follow a similar pattern. France's 1997–2002 reform program has led to a major restructuring of its armed forces, including the abolition of conscription and the move to an all-professional military. This program included significant cuts in French army, navy, and air force personnel from the 1997 level of 430,500 to a target of 228,071 by the end of 1999.[5] One of the key features of the program's four major aspects of defense strategy was the concept of "projection." Projection requires the armed forces to be capable of deploying significant resources outside the national territory and sustaining them there. The plan for the French army is to be able to have a rapidly deployable force of 50,000 troops for operations within the North Atlantic Alliance or 30,000 troops in a main theater outside NATO and 5,000 in a secondary theater.[6] The French Ministry of Defense has stated that projection is to become *the* priority mission of the army. Additionally, to give the French army a more expeditionary role and allow more active participation in a NATO or EU military force, the army's nine divisions will be entirely restructured around four divisions—an armored force, an engineering force, a rapid reaction armored force, and an assault infantry force—and complemented by a balanced armored force using tanks and helicopters.[7] The 1997–2002 reform program was one of the most sweeping restructuring efforts in the French armed forces and the new 2003–2008 program hopes to consolidate and build upon the changes made to date.

In July 1994, as part of a major restructuring process, the German federal government fixed the future peacetime strength of the armed forces at 340,000, including up to 135,000 conscripts. This was down from an interim ceiling of 370,000 and a Cold War figure of 600,000.[8] The other significant development in 1994 was the Constitutional Court ruling of July allowing (on a case-by-case basis) German participation in multinational peace support operations. This was followed in June 1995 by a document outlining the restructuring of the armed forces into a main defense force, reaction forces, and the "basic" military organization.[9] This resulted in the establishment of a Crisis Reaction Corps (KRK) of approximately 50,000 troops. The KRK, coupled with the court ruling, allows a potentially much greater role for Germany in any future EU defense and security policy. In 2000 several reports were produced, outlining proposals for a further, more fundamental reform of the Bundeswehr. The defense minister's report became the primary basis for further reform. It advocated reducing the size of the armed forces to 255,000, but increasing the size of reaction corps to 150,000 troops, again moving further in the direction of force projection.[10]

The German armed forces have also been much more involved in military action, both within and outside Europe. Operations in the Balkans, and more recently in Afghanistan, have seen a gradual but definite shift in German security policy. Chancellor Gerhard Schröder has spoken of a "new form" of self-defense that, despite the dominance of civilian factors, must not have any taboos against military interventions.[11] Subsequent

German deployments to Afghanistan are a sign that Germany's concepts and capabilities are being transformed.

One state that has undergone a wholesale transformation of its forces is the Netherlands. A review shortly after the end of the Cold War decided on a new set of objectives for the armed forces. First, the Dutch military should be capable of participating in four peacekeeping operations simultaneously. Second, it should maintain rapidly deployable assets in peacetime for the protection of NATO territory and for peace enforcement. Finally, it should maintain the capacity to generate sufficient forces to contribute to the defense of NATO in case of a major threat.[12] The changes led to large-scale restructuring and significant reductions in personnel, including the suspension of conscription. The emphasis is on qualitative changes in terms of equipment, readiness, and availability in order to improve mobility and flexibility. In November 1999 the Dutch published the Defense White Paper of 2000, which continued to emphasize the need for force projection, stating that "flexibility, combat readiness, mobility, combat power, sustainability, security, inter-operability and quality" must feature strongly in the future armed forces.[13] The restructuring in the Netherlands has gone so far toward international cooperation that the Dutch now only foresee taking part in military operations as part of an international alliance and thus have placed strong emphasis on participating in multinational formations, such as the UK/Netherlands Amphibious Force.

These are just four examples of a general trend in the restructuring of the armed forces of the EU states. Other states undergoing significant change include Spain, Italy, and Portugal, which have all decided to move to an all-volunteer, fully professional military in the coming years. The other EU states, perhaps with the exception of Greece, are also, to varying degrees, refining their policies and reforming their capabilities to better suit the new strategic environment. An important common thread that should be highlighted with regard to the restructuring of these militaries is the ever-increasing move toward joint and multinational formations. These will become ever more important as the burden of providing full-spectrum military capabilities becomes too much for many EU member states. Currently only the UK and France are close to having a true full spectrum of capabilities. There are now many bi- and multinational formations within Europe upon which further cooperation could be founded, allowing greater practical military cooperation to take place "on the ground" between EU states.

The Combined Result

The objectives of ESDP are centered on improving the military capabilities of the EU member states, to allow them to undertake a wide range of potential operations that may be required under the Petersberg tasks, or in other operations in support of CFSP. These capabilities require modern, mobile, rapidly deployable, and sustainable force projection capabilities, which EU member states do not currently possess in sufficient quantities or quality. The ability to project force involves, primarily, two components: personnel and equipment. These have to be utilized effectively by careful planning and appropriate command and control (headquarters) capabilities, which are critical to a successful operation and for which a number of issues remain unresolved. The military personnel component has two important parts in relation to ESDP: availability and training. The equipment component as well can be divided into two parts: deployability, or having the capabilities to transport personnel to theater, and providing personnel with the required operational support once in theater, namely communications, intelligence, and air power. Without these components an EU designated force will be ineffective in its crisis management operations and will therefore risk damaging the credibility of the EU, its CFSP, and its ESDP. It is therefore vital to look at the present and future capabilities and assets of EU member states' armed forces, with specific reference to these components.

Personnel

The foundation for many European militaries through much of the twentieth century was conscription. This was well suited to the defense of national territory, the principal objective of European armed forces during the Cold War, but is unsuitable for the types of missions envisaged by ESDP in the current international environment. Today's potential crises and operations will need smaller, more mobile, and rapidly deployable forces for operations outside the national territory of the EU member states. For the most part this means that conscripts are unsuitable for the operations that may be encompassed by the Petersberg tasks. In the early 1990s, just the UK and Luxembourg had all-volunteer (professional) armed forces, but through the decade they were joined by two more states, Belgium and the Netherlands, and on November 30, 2001, by France. All of the other EU member states still have a percentage of conscripts within their militaries.

There are a number of reasons why conscripts are unsuitable for crisis management operations, as envisaged in ESDP. First, conscript militaries are generally not appropriately or sufficiently trained for overseas crisis management or peacemaking operations, which are often complex and highly volatile. Second, some states (notably Germany) have impediments to their conscripts operating outside of their national territory. Indeed, until the Constitutional Court ruling of 1994, Germany could not send any military personnel into combat overseas. Future military operations envisaged for the EU will almost certainly occur outside of current EU member states' territory and most probably outside of EU territorial limits. Third, having conscripts makes deploying units overseas even harder because the units are often made up of a mix of both conscripts and volunteers. This means that the units have to be rearranged to contain just volunteers, adding to the amount of time needed to prepare and then deploy the force. Fourth, having large sections of the armed forces made up of conscripts entails high manpower levels, leading to higher personnel costs in the long term, which in turn leaves less financing available for equipment procurement and research and development. For example, the personnel costs for the UK in 2001 were estimated at 40 percent of total defense expenditure, while in Germany they were 61 percent. Meanwhile, the spending on equipment in Germany is 13 percent of total defense expenditure, as compared to 25 percent in the UK.[14]

The late 1990s saw a trend toward reforming the personnel policies of many of the EU member states and a restructuring of their armed forces. Several of the EU member states are now in the process of eliminating or suspending conscription, including France, Italy, Spain, and Portugal, and are moving toward all-volunteer, professional militaries. However, the shift toward all-volunteer militaries has been more expensive than planned, resulting in less cost savings and a slower transition period.[15] The most significant state to make this change so far has been France. It set out in the 1997–2002 Loi Programmation Militaire (LPM) the aim of abolishing conscription by the end of 2002, but actually abolished it at the end of November 2001. It no longer has conscripts in its military ranks, but it still has some conscientious objectors performing civilian duties. Italy aims to complete the abolition of conscription by 2006, Spain by 2003, and Portugal in 2003. Of the major military powers in the EU, Germany is the one state that has not moved toward the complete abolition or suspension of conscription. However, it is reducing the number of conscripts and developing a much larger, fully professional rapid reaction corps, which should benefit any future EU operation.

There are historical and societal reasons behind Germany's decision, and it is unlikely to change its policy in the near future. After two world wars the Germans followed a largely nonmilitary policy during the Cold War and their military was developed within NATO. They found the use of military power for anything other than self-defense difficult to justify, a position still deeply ingrained in the German populace. Second, on a more pragmatic level, Germany is now so reliant on the conscripts who opt out of military training and perform civilian duties that many services, such as health care, now rely on this source of labor. Other states with strong traditions of conscription, for very different reasons, include Austria, Finland, Greece, and Sweden. Table 5.1 shows the status of moves toward all-volunteer forces.

Table 5.1 Status of Conscription in the Fifteen EU Member States, August 1, 2002

	Status	Term of Service	Conscript Percentage
Austria	Discussing future policy	7 months and 30 days over 8 years; or 8 months total	49.71
Belgium	No conscription	N/A	0
Denmark	Conscription	4–12 months, 24 months in some ranks	25.11
Finland	Conscription	6, 9, or 12 months (12 for officers, noncommissioned officers, and special duties)	48.66
France	Last conscripts left November 30, 2001	Used to be 10 months	0
Germany	Conscription remains, in lower numbers	10 months, can be extended to 12–23 months voluntarily	36.15
Greece	Conscription	Army up to 18 months, air force and navy up to 21 months	55.36
Ireland	No conscription	N/A	0
Italy	Conscription to end December 31, 2004	10 months	32.38
Luxembourg	No conscription	N/A	0
Netherlands	No conscription	N/A	0
Portugal	Conscription to be suspended in 2003	Army 4–8 months, air force and navy 4–12 months	18.65
Spain	Last conscripts left December 31, 2001	Used to be 9 months	0
Sweden	Conscription	Army and navy 7–15 months, air force 8–12 months	44.25
United Kingdom	No conscription	N/A	0

Sources: National documentation and International Institute for Strategic Studies, *The Military Balance 2002–2003* (Oxford: Oxford University Press, 2002).

The significance of abolishing conscription is that it will increase the level of training for all personnel in the armed forces, the number of personnel available, and the speed at which they can be deployed. These are all critical elements in making the European Rapid Reaction Force (ERRF) effective and credible. The increase in the number of available personnel for EU operations is very important because, at present, despite the large number of active armed forces in the EU, it will not be a simple task to assemble a force of 60,000 troops and sustain them for a year. This is because the figures of a maximum 60,000-troop deployment, as envisaged by the EU, and a total active armed forces strength of 1,583,350 for EU member states (not including Denmark, which has opted out of ESDP), do not convey the complete picture.[16] If these figures were the actual situation, a full-scale ERRF operation would need just 3.8 percent of EU member states' armed forces. In reality, the actual demands on EU member states' armed forces are much more challenging. Table 5.2 shows the number of active military personnel within the EU, the number of conscripts, and the number of deployed troops.

This table hints that there are a number of reasons why the demands on the armed forces of the EU states are more challenging than first appears. First, to sustain a force for a year (or for any long duration), the general rule applied by military analysts is to multiply that figure by three.[17] This is done to take account of the need to earmark not just those forces that are

Table 5.2   EU Member States' Armed Forces: Active, Conscripts, and Deployed, August 1, 2002

	Active Armed Forces	Number of Conscripts	Deployed Forces[a]
Austria	34,600	17,200	938
Belgium	39,260	0	3,475
Denmark[b]	22,700	5,700	1,211
Finland	31,850	15,500	999
France	260,400	0	34,987
Germany	296,000	107,000	8,887
Greece	177,600	98,321	3,239[c]
Ireland	10,460	0	451
Italy	216,800	70,200	7,783
Luxembourg[d]	900	0	49
Netherlands	49,580	0	5,731
Portugal	43,600	8,130	1,406
Spain	177,950	0	2,856
Sweden	33,900	15,000	873
United Kingdom	210,450	0	31,176
Total[e]	1,583,350	331,351	102,850

Source: Figures adapted from International Institute for Strategic Studies, *The Military Balance 2002–2003* (Oxford: Oxford University Press, 2002).

Notes: a. Using *Military Balance* definition of "overseas deployment," which includes permanent bases but not short-term deployments or operations in progress. Does include peacekeeping operations. These figures do not include forces deployed on overseas training assignments.

b. Denmark has opted out of participation in ESDP; hence its troops will not count toward final figures.

c. Including 1,250 troops seconded to Greek-Cypriot forces.

d. In addition, Luxembourg has "some" forces in KFOR.

e. Totals exclude Denmark, as it had opted out of taking part in ESDP.

deployed, but also those that are training and preparing to deploy and those just returned from deployment. So in the case of the maximum corps size deployment of 60,000 troops for an ERRF operation, the actual number of troops used over the course of a yearlong operation is more likely to be nearer 180,000.

Second, and related to the issue of conscription raised earlier, a significant though declining percentage of EU member states' armed forces are conscripts. As these are generally unusable for the operations envisaged for an ERRF, the number of available forces is actually less than the 1.58 million cited above. The total number of conscripts in the EU member states is approximately 331,000 (see Table 5.2), bringing the number of available troops down to 1.2 million.

Third, of these remaining troops, approximately 103,000 are currently deployed overseas. When the rule of three is applied to these, as it must be, the overall number of troops needed for current overseas deployments approximates to 309,000. While troops on deployment can be recalled by national governments under exceptional circumstances, and many troops stationed in Germany and elsewhere could be temporarily redeployed, these troops would eventually need replacing. Taking all these figures into account, the number of available forces for an EU operation falls to 940,000. So if the ERRF needs 180,000 troops to sustain a yearlong operation, and the available forces number 940,000, a total of roughly 19 percent of EU member states' forces could be used for an ERRF operation. This places a much greater burden on the armed forces of the EU member states, presenting a much more challenging, but not impossible, scenario for defense planners.

The challenge for defense planners is made even more complex by the problem of putting together a rapid reaction force for a crisis management operation. If these forces do not exercise and train together, there will be problems concerning how well different units can fit together, operate together, and communicate with each other. This is especially important in the command and control element of military operations. The interoperability problem is not just in terms of equipment, but also in terms of methods, strategies, and doctrine. Some of the EU member states that are also in NATO will exercise together and there will be a commonality in the methods and doctrine applied. However, there are four EU states that are not in NATO and do not regularly exercise with these states. They also need to be accommodated, through other exercise programs, for example, Partnership for Peace, and through their involvement in UN-authorized peacekeeping missions. Peacekeeping operations in the Balkans, involving both NATO and non-NATO states, have begun the process of informing non-NATO EU states (and other European states) of NATO practices, but only on a very limited scale. However, this process is not a one-way street. The four non-

NATO EU states can also bring useful methods and perspectives into some EU crisis management operations, from their extensive experience in UN peacekeeping operations. It should also be noted at this point that, even within NATO, the complete standardization of equipment and functions, attempted for fifty years, has failed to materialize. This suggests that the EU should not necessarily look for a complete standardization of command and control and other systems, but should, for effectiveness and efficiency, look to develop a high level of interoperability.

On a more positive note, however, as more EU member states transform their personnel policies to eliminate conscription, the number of available forces should increase. The overall size of EU member states' armed forces may well decrease, but the total number and percentage available for crisis management operations will increase. The elimination of conscription should also entail better and more appropriately trained armed forces free of any legal impediments to their deployment on crisis management operations outside of their national territory. If the personnel issue does develop positively, as it shows signs of doing, then as long as there are no major additional deployments, the real problems for the viability and credibility of an ERRF lie in the areas of planning and headquarters and equipment.

Planning and Headquarters

The issues of planning and headquarters have received a lot of attention in the last year, without being resolved. There are two key levels of planning: strategic and operational. Strategic planning has not been a particularly contentious issue and the arrangements were agreed at the Sintra meeting of EU defense ministers in February 2000 in the "Toolbox Paper." It has been agreed that the EU Military Staff (EUMS) will be responsible for identifying and assessing military options in an emerging crisis. As it develops the military strategic options, it may draw on NATO or national headquarters for planning support. The EUMS then makes a recommendation to the Political and Security Committee (PSC) through the EUMC chairman.[18] The relatively simple and quick agreement for the strategic planning arrangements has not been mirrored in the arrangements for operational planning, which took over two years to negotiate.

The arrangements detailed at Sintra appeared relatively straightforward, with an option for operations using NATO assets and capabilities and an option without the use of them. The first scenario is based on the arrangements made at the Washington NATO summit in March 1999, the "Berlin Plus" arrangements, which if fully implemented would provide the EU with assured access to NATO planning capabilities and the presumed availability of other preidentified common assets.[19] Hence, for EU-led operations using

NATO assets, Supreme Headquarters Allied Powers Europe (SHAPE) would be the main body carrying out operational planning and force generation. In this situation, the Deputy Supreme Allied Commander Europe (DSACEUR), always a European, would be the primary, though not only, candidate for operation commander.[20] Other NATO assets, such as theater and component headquarters, may also be requested. For EU operations without recourse to NATO assets and capabilities, "planning and command arrangements would draw on existing national and multinational HQs available to the EU."[21]

However, since these proposals were developed there has been a continuing impasse between the EU and NATO over the guaranteed access for the EU to NATO operational planning capabilities (i.e., SHAPE). The EU has requested guaranteed access to NATO's planning capabilities and the "presumed availability" of other NATO assets, assuming NATO is not using them. However, this has been slow to arrange. At Nice, the EU put forward a number of proposals on the issue of access, cooperation, and non-EU European NATO states participating in EU operations.[22] These suggestions were aimed at minimizing the duplication of assets and capabilities, a central aim of NATO, the United States, and the EU since this project started. However, key issues of access to capabilities are still not fully resolved and procedures for EU-NATO consultation and sharing are yet to be finalized.

As described earlier, Turkey and Greece have been the two principal stumbling blocks that have created this impasse. From December 2000, through most of 2001, Turkey proved to be the major obstacle to getting an EU-NATO agreement on access to planning capabilities. In December 2000, Turkey blocked the Berlin Plus and Nice proposals within NATO's North Atlantic Council (NAC) that would guarantee the EU access to NATO's planning capabilities.[23] It wanted participation in the EU's decisionmaking process when operations in its region were being considered, in return for the use of NATO's planning capabilities.[24] This is simply not possible. A state cannot have guaranteed participation in the decisionmaking process of an organization of which it is not a member. Turkey continued to threaten to veto the guaranteed and unrestricted EU use of NATO planning capabilities through most of 2001 if its concerns were not addressed. It preferred to provide access on a case-by-case basis and demanded to be involved in all EU military operations, even those not involving NATO assets.

Turkey's main concern was that the ERRF may be used in its direct area of interest, especially in Cyprus and the Aegean Sea, to the detriment of Turkish interests and in support of Greek interests.[25] During most of 2001 the UK and United States held discussions with the Turkish administration to try to resolve the dispute and, in December 2001, a year after its

NAC veto and two years after the original impasse, Turkey agreed to a deal on EU access.[26] Turkey had reportedly received assurances that ESDP would not affect its security interests in its region (Cyprus and the Aegean) and that it would be consulted on a case-by-case basis.[27] However, almost as soon as Turkey had accepted the deal, Greece objected to the agreement at the Laeken European Council. Greece claimed the agreement undermined the autonomy of the EU and did not address Greek security concerns (again referring to Cyprus and the Aegean).[28] Despite the pressure put on Greece to accept the agreement at the Laeken summit, and since, the impasse was not resolved until December 2002.

Without an agreement being reached, which guarantees the EU access to SHAPE for operational planning, the EU had to seriously consider the alternative of national or multinational headquarters for operational planning. For this purpose, the EU could call on the planning staffs within the member states' national headquarters, such as in the UK and France, both of which have been offered to the EU and which could plan military operations at the scale envisaged by the Petersberg tasks. Alternatively, the EU could also use the EUMS as the basis for a planning staff and integrate national contributions when a crisis emerges and intensive operational planning begins. A final option, creating much consternation in the United States and other non-EU NATO states, is for the EU to establish its own permanent operational planning capability along the lines of SHAPE. This would likely create a lot of anger in Washington, which, since former secretary of state Madeleine Albright's "three Ds" (discrimination, decoupling, duplication), has stressed the importance of no unnecessary duplication. One of the main concerns in the U.S. Department of Defense is that, if an operation were to go wrong, it would inevitably fall to the United States to shore up or rescue a EU force in theater.[29] On this basis, the United States wants to have some input at the planning level to make sure the EU planners have not overlooked anything that may create problems during an operation. They also believe that the EU should focus its spending efforts on equipment capabilities, rather than re-create a second SHAPE solely for EU planning purposes.[30]

With regard to headquarters capabilities, a 1999 report to the Western European Union (WEU) Council by the Defense Committee of the WEU Assembly identified three command levels, operational, force, and component headquarters, and defined their roles:

- Operational headquarters (OHQs) are a combined joint formation, located in one of the member states, working at the strategic level to provide the overall command and undertake the operational planning.
- Force headquarters (FHQs), also a combined joint structure, operate

at the operational level and must be capable of deploying into or close to the theater of operations; they are the equivalent of NATO's CJTF headquarters concept.

* Component command headquarters (CCHQs) are multinational formations deployed in theater to oversee a single force component (land, air, or sea) of an operation.[31]

The Council's statement on improving European military capabilities indicates that the EU may have sufficient capabilities, asserting that "member states are offering a sufficient number of headquarters at the levels of operation, force and component, as well as deployable communication units."[32] However, later in the same declaration, the Council does make the critical point that a qualitative analysis of these headquarters has still to be made. General Klaus Naumann is less optimistic, believing that "the European Union has, at this point in time, no real appropriate command and control capability."[33] Therefore, once again, the EU will have to rely on NATO or on national capabilities (the framework nation concept). If access to NATO capabilities and assets has been assured, then SHAPE is the likely, though not the only, option to operate as the operational headquarters (the force and component headquarters within NATO could also be requested). In such a scenario, the primary choice of operational commander would be the DSACEUR. The principal problem with this arrangement is that it appears to detract from the autonomous nature of ESDP, making it reliant on the acquiescence of non-EU states.

If NATO assets were not being used, the EU would have to utilize the framework nation concept, whereby the core of a national headquarters is turned into a multinational headquarters as personnel from participating states are added on. There are currently just two national joint headquarters capable of acting as the framework nation, providing operational headquarters and overseeing an entire ERRF operation. The UK's Permanent Joint Headquarters (PJHQ) at Northwood and France's Joint Operational Command at Creil are the most capable existing facilities within the EU.[34] Even these will need additional resources and possibly expansion to become a combined (multinational) headquarters, as it will be necessary to accommodate officers from other EU member states (and possibly other states) that are participating in the military operations. There are signs that additional assets may become available as EU states restructure their armed forces for joint operations and follow the example set by the British and the French by establishing joint commands to manage all aspects of a deployment as part of an EU operation. In this respect, both the Germans and Italians have established joint operations headquarters in recent years.[35]

However, two potential problems exist when using a national operational headquarters for EU operations. First, given the importance and potential leverage of being the framework nation, there may be political competition to acquire the lead role, delaying the decisionmaking as the disputes are resolved.[36] It also has the potential to create divisions within the EU at the very time it needs to show consensus. Second, incorporating officers from other states into a national headquarters is only likely to be done when a crisis emerges and planning and force generation begin, which could cause delays and disrupt the effectiveness of the headquarters.[37] This would slow the process of detailed operational planning and force planning at precisely the moment when it needs to work at its most swift and efficient pace.

To circumvent these two problems, and the problem of EU autonomy, it appears that the EU should have its own permanent multinational headquarters for planning and commanding an operation. This would, however, create serious concerns within the U.S. defense establishment, which wants to be involved in the planning of operations, as discussed earlier. The other problem with a permanent EU operational headquarters is that it would require, among other capabilities, an autonomous satellite intelligence capability, something the EU member states are unlikely to be able to afford in the foreseeable future.

At the level of force headquarters, there is again the option of proceeding with or without recourse to NATO assets. If NATO assets were to be used, then the CJTF headquarters concept would be utilized, as set out at the NATO summit in Berlin in 1996 and elaborated upon in Washington at the 1999 NATO summit (Berlin Plus). The problem of using CJTF headquarters is that the principal formations these would be developed around are Allied Forces Northern Europe (AFNORTH) and Allied Forces Southern Europe (AFSOUTH). Both of these "parent" headquarters contain a wide range of nationalities, which naturally include U.S. personnel.[38] This may create problems if the United States, or other states, did not want to participate, because these officers would then have to be replaced, causing further delay and disruption. On the other hand, if the United States did participate, it would once again raise questions about the autonomy of EU decisionmaking and action.

If an operation were to be undertaken without recourse to NATO assets, there are several assets within the EU member states that are designed to command multinational forces in the theater of operations. As the EU has taken over the crisis management role of the WEU, a reasonable starting point for identifying potential force headquarters is the list of multinational formations designated as "forces answerable to the WEU" (FAWEU). These formations are military units and headquarters that could be made available on a case-by-case basis, as designated by the then-WEU states. In total there are seven formations: the Eurocorps, the Multinational Division (Central), the UK-Netherlands Amphibious Force, the Eurofor, the

Euromarfor, the German-Netherlands Corps, and the Spanish-Italian Amphibious Force.[39] Despite this array of potential force headquarters, just three have the potential to manage an operation involving tens of thousands of troops: the Multinational Division (Central), which is also part of NATO's Allied Rapid Reaction Corps (ARRC), the Franco-German-based Eurocorps, and Eurofor.[40] The Multinational Division (Central) and Eurofor are highly mobile and deployable, but being only division-sized headquarters they are slightly undersized. Meanwhile, the Eurocorps is a better-sized, corps headquarters and has good staff and capabilities, but it is slightly less mobile.[41] The problem with all of these options is that, at present, none of them are joint structures. They are all predominately single-service formations. Of the three, the Eurocorps appears to have the most potential, especially as it was placed at the disposal of the EU for crisis response operations in June 1999 and is being transformed into a rapid reaction corps.[42] Second, it already has air and naval liaison officers and this is a solid foundation on which to expand and further integrate the aerial and naval elements of the Eurocorps headquarters.

The potential and the limits of a purely European force headquarters have been highlighted by the deployment of Eurocorps to command the Kosovo Force (KFOR) in April 2000. This decision was a positive step, in that it indicated a determination among several EU states to start to assume more responsibility and control over security and crisis management within and around the European continent. However, in practice, it has also created worries, because it has only managed to supply 350 officers of the 1,200 currently present in the KFOR headquarters and also needed extensive support from NATO (command and control assets) to perform its role effectively.[43] Overall, the use of the Eurocorps to command the KFOR operation will be of benefit to ESDP. It will alert the EU member states to new and continuing problems in the command capabilities of European-based headquarters and allow them to find solutions and test them in the complex realities of a large-scale peace support operation.

At the final level, component command headquarters, the EU member states' only deficiency is a naval component command headquarters. Ideally, for a landing operation from the sea followed by a land-based element, it would be necessary to have a joint headquarters with 200 staff based on a command ship. The EU member states do not have such a capability at the moment, although the UK and France do have some capability in this field. For example, the UK's HMS *Ocean* and France's *Foudre* are both capable of housing a headquarters of about 100 personnel.[44]

Equipment

Given the transformation in personnel policy, it is not surprising that the number of units deployable within the EU member states has, in principle, increased in recent years. However, the equipment needed by these armed forces is still lacking in several critical areas, particularly the means for transporting them to a theater of operation, sustaining them there, and providing them with the full range of equipment and intelligence to successfully complete a mission. The equipment issue is subdivided into three groups, transport, in-theater support, and strike capabilities.

The first significant equipment problem the armed forces of the EU member states face is the means for transporting them to a theater of operation (deployability). In general, the transport capabilities for getting armed forces into a specific region quickly, and in sufficient numbers, are inadequate, in terms of both air and maritime capabilities. This is a critical capability for the ERRF because it will be an expeditionary force with, according to EU officials, the potential to operate globally in support of CFSP (although it is more likely that it will be in regions surrounding Europe).[45] Indeed, it is probably safe to assume that, if an ERRF were to engage in conflict, it will almost certainly be outside of the geographical limits of the EU and NATO (though possibly within the OSCE). This "near abroad" idea has been further endorsed by media references to an operational radius of 4,000 kilometers from Brussels.[46] While EU officials and documentation decline to put any limits on the operational reach of the ERRF, they are using these sorts of distances as part of their planning assumptions. These distances entail the need for strategic air- and sealift and this is precisely the capability that is largely missing from the inventories of the armed forces of the EU's member states.

The airlift that the EU member states do have is principally only suitable for short-range, lightly equipped units. Michael O'Hanlon argues that deploying the initial several thousand troops to the crisis zone is possible for the Europeans.[47] This would be based on the transport aircraft they do have and the ability to refuel them at bases or in the air en route. Table 5.3 details current EU airlift assets. There appear to be a sufficient number of transport aircraft for the EU states to draw on. However, many of these aircraft cannot carry the heavier and larger-sized equipment, the C-160s and G-222s cannot travel the distances envisaged in the planning assumptions (up to 4,000 kilometers), and the C-160s belonging to France and Germany are now aging aircraft in need of replacement.[48]

The real problems arise in the period from two weeks to three months after a crisis starts. It is then that EU states would need large amounts of support troops, logistical equipment, and heavy armor, but be unable to deploy them because of the lack of large transport aircraft, fast sealift, and dedicated cargo and tanker vessels.[49] Without strategic air- and sealift improvements, the personnel improvements currently under way in several EU states, which aim to increase the availability of troops and develop a rapid reaction capability, will be of little consequence. For the rapid reac-

Table 5.3   Medium and Heavy Military Transport Aircraft Available in the EU, 2001

	C-130	C-160	C-17	G-222
Belgium	11	—	—	—
France	14	67	—	—
Germany	—	84	—	—
Greece	15	—	—	—
Italy	15	—	—	38
Netherlands	2	—	—	—
Portugal	6	—	—	—
Spain	12	—	—	—
Sweden	8	—	—	—
UK	51	—	4	—
Total	134	151	4	38

Source: A. Dumoulin, Raphael Mathieu, and Vincent Metten, "Introduction to the Comparative Survey of the White Papers, Official Documents and General Policy Papers Related to the Security and Defence Policy of the Fifteen Member States of the European Union" (Unpublished Paper, Brussels, Royal Defence College, 2001).

tion element of an EU force, strategic airlift will be critical. The need for strategic airlift, the long-haul transportation of troops and equipment, including a large capacity for loading vehicles and other large cargoes into a large, versatile cargo bay by a ramp,[50] has been highlighted in numerous capability studies. The EU member states have recognized the requirement and have been attempting to find both national and multinational solutions to provide them with an effective and long-term capability.

The long-term solution to the lack of strategic airlift appeared to have taken a major step forward in December 2001, when the Organization for Joint Armaments Cooperation, known by its French acronym of OCCAR, signed a contract on behalf of eight European states (seven from the EU plus Turkey) with the Airbus Military Company for the production of the A400M military transport aircraft. The contract is for 196 aircraft: Germany has ordered 73, France 50, Spain 27, the UK 25, Turkey 10, Belgium 7, Portugal 3, and Luxembourg 1 (to be based in Belgium). However, Germany has yet to secure funding for all 73 aircraft and its 2002 defense budget allows for only 40 aircraft.[51] At the end of January 2002, the Bundestag voted to secure the additional funds from the 2003 budget, but the opposition parties (who abstained from the vote) immediately lodged a claim with the Constitutional Court to declare the ratification void.[52] This, in turn, has forced the government to postpone the funding approval until 2003. In December 2002 Germany announced serious cuts in its defense budget and that as a consequence it would only be able to buy 60 of the A400M aircraft, 13 fewer than originally planned.[53] However, this still ensures that the order number will not fall below the minimum required to make the project viable, namely 180 aircraft. This is not the first problem for the project. In autumn 2001, Italy withdrew from the project with the loss of 16 orders. While it retained the right to rejoin the program, this is the most significant problem yet encountered. It is all the more significant because, instead of spearheading the development of EU defense capabilities and fulfilling the Helsinki Headline Goal, this project looks increasingly like it may become the ultimate sign of a weak commitment to the ERRF in some EU member states. In turn this could result in a loss of credibility for ESDP as a whole.

There are alternatives to the A400M, such as Boeing's C-17, the Russian An-124, and the Westernized Ukrainian An-70.[54] Nevertheless, a project designed, procured, built, and deployed by European states would signal a clear and strong commitment by the major EU members to fulfill the Helsinki objectives. It would also illustrate how the EU states can develop and implement innovative and cooperative programs to overcome their military shortfalls. This project, if successful, could provide a model by which other capability shortfalls could be overcome, providing both a European-based solution to a European deficiency and a massive boost to the European defense industry. If the A400M project does succeed, first deliveries are scheduled for 2008, though given the delay in Germany's funding for this project, this date is likely to slip, perhaps to 2010 or later. In the interim period, other EU states should follow the UK's lead in leasing four C-17s from the United States, for up to seven years, to meet its demands for strategic air transport prior to delivery of the A400M.[55]

Some states have made plans to upgrade, renovate, and extend the life of their existing transport aircraft, for example the C-130 Hercules of Belgium, Italy, Portugal, and Spain, the C-160 Transalls of France, and Italy's G-222.[56] In addition, both Italy (22 aircraft) and the UK (25 aircraft) are procuring the C-130J transport aircraft, an upgraded version of the current C-130 but with greater range. However, this does not solve the problem of "strategic" lift, as illustrated by the capability of the A400M, which can transport double the volume and almost double the weight compared to a C-130J. Until the A400M comes into service, the UK is the sole potential source within the EU for a very limited number of strategic (long-range, heavy-lift) transport aircraft. The scale of the task to transport troops rapidly, in sufficient numbers, and with their necessary equipment is clearly illustrated by the fact that transporting a brigade of 7,000 troops and their equipment 4,000 kilometers would take a rotation of 50 A400Ms two weeks to complete.[57] It should be noted that even if the A400M does become operational, the EU states would still have to lease very large "outsized" transport aircraft, such as the An-124, for carrying very large or heavy equipment. This is because the specifications of the A400M do not allow the transportation of a main battle tank, a less critical capability for the envisaged operations, relying instead on light and medium armored fighting vehicles and other key support elements.[58] EU member states already charter such aircraft and efforts should be made to formalize these arrangements and guarantee access to them.

Airlift is critical for getting troops and their vital equipment rapidly into the theater of operations, to secure airports and ports if necessary and to indicate the determination of the EU to act. Nevertheless, sealift is also a vital capability for force projection and is a major priority for the EU states, as it is another area where the EU's military transport capabilities are severely deficient. Sealift was vital to the deployments to the Gulf in 1990–1991 and to Kosovo in 1999, accounting for 95 percent and 90–95 percent respectively of all equipment deployed.[59] Both France and the UK had to charter merchant ships at commercial rates to deploy to Kosovo. The only state in the world to have a significant and dedicated sealift capability, designed for military transport, in its inventory is the United States, with a combined total of 53 vessels in its prepositioning and sealift programs and a further 70 vessels in its ready reserve force on notice of four to twenty days.[60] The U.S. built up these capabilities in the wake of the Gulf War, when it too had to charter commercial vessels to transport all the required equipment into the Middle East.

At present in the EU, only Italy (one), Spain (two), and the UK (two) have shipping vessels of over 1,000 tons designed for strategic military transport, and these are all chartered from the private sector.[61] Ad hoc chartering (leasing), such as that undertaken to deploy forces to Kosovo, could also be utilized for the deployment of future EU operations. The problem with this system, as demonstrated during the deployment of KFOR, is that arranging the lease and acquiring the ships is expensive and, more important, takes time, as the vessels are recalled from their commercial assignments and reassigned to their military role. This slows down the deployment of troops and makes a mockery of the notion of a rapid reaction force. For example, it took five months to complete the deployment of 40,000 troops to Kosovo.[62] The difficulties of acquiring vessels for the commercial sector rapidly was highlighted when the French deployment was delayed by at least ten days of waiting for the first chartered vessel to arrive at Toulon, the departure port for French forces.[63] The French deployment of 4,500 troops and accompanying equipment to Kosovo required the chartering of twelve roll-on/roll-off (RoRo) vessels from the commercial sector, in addition to its 4 specialist amphibious ships.[64] In principle, chartering is fine, but in addition to cost and availability, there are also significant problems with the suitability and quality of the vessels used. Many RoRo vessels are not suitable for transporting the very heavy equipment, and the shrinking number of commercial RoRo vessels means that even those of dubious quality and flag are forced into action.

Given the sealift problems encountered in deployments to the Balkans throughout the 1990s, several EU states, in their recent defense documents, recognized the need to improve their capabilities in this field. The UK has decided to build six new RoRo vessels (four additions and two replacements),[65] each capable of transporting about 10,000 tons of cargo, while Belgium, the Netherlands, Luxembourg, and France are investigating the possibility of joint procurement projects to enhance their sealift capabilities. Again, if plans are realized, these are steps in the right direction, but more states need to take action to bolster the military sealift capacity of the EU member states.

The figures for sealift improve marginally when amphibious transport vessels are taken into consideration. However, this is another important asset that the EU has in only limited quantities. Table 5.4 illustrates the current amphibious capability of the EU states. An amphibious capability is crucial for the swift and direct insertion of troops and equipment into a theater of operations, particularly when port facilities are limited or unavailable. Together, the EU states at the moment could transport around 10,000

Table 5.4   EU Member States' Amphibious Transport Capabilities, 2001

	Amphibious Platforms	Total Capacity
France	9 (4 LPD, 5 LSM)	2,340 troops, 115 tanks, 6–8 helicopters
Greece	7 (LST)	2,300 troops, 36 tanks
Italy	3 (LPD)	1,050 troops, 90 trucks, 6 helicopters
Netherlands	1 (LPD)	600 troops, 4–6 helicopters
Spain	4 (2 LPD, 2 LST)	2,040 troops, 6,000 tonnes of vehicles, 10 helicopters
United Kingdom	6 (1 LPH, 1 LPD, 4 LSL)	2,510 troops, 79 tanks, 25 helicopters
Total	30	10,840 troops, 230 tanks, 90 trucks, 6,000 tonnes of other vehicles, 51–55 helicopters

Sources: Figures adapted from International Institute for Strategic Studies, *The Military Balance 2001–2002* (Oxford: Oxford University Press, October 2001); and national defense documents.

Note: LPD = landing platform dock, LSM = landing ship medium, LST = landing ship tank, LPH = landing platform helicopter.

troops using current amphibious capabilities.[66] This is likely to increase in the coming years as several states have undertaken plans to improve amphibious capabilities. The UK already has a new landing platform helicopter (LPH) in service, capable of transporting up to 830 troops and several helicopters. This vessel will be joined in 2003 by two new landing platform docks (LPDs) and in 2005 by four large landing ships, carrying 245 and 350 troops respectively.[67] Meanwhile, other EU states are also improving their amphibious capabilities. Two of France's four existing LPDs are to be replaced by new, larger LPDs in 2004–2005; the Netherlands is to acquire a second LPD with CJTF headquarters facilities; Spain is building two additional LPDs; and even Germany is looking at acquiring three multirole sealift ships.[68]

Returning to aerial assets, the third element of strategic deployment is air-to-air refueling. Currently the EU lacks sufficient tanker aircraft to extend the "reach" of an EU force by enabling the in-flight refueling of its aircraft. This problem was crystallized during the Kosovo campaign. Just three EU member states, the UK, France, and the Netherlands, provided tanker aircraft to Operation Allied Force (OAF), supplying a total of 14 between them, as compared to the 170 refueling tankers provided by the United States at the peak of the campaign.[69] In addition to these three states, Italy and Spain also have four tankers each. Table 5.5 details the current aerial refueling capabilities within the EU member states. These numbers of tanker aircraft are insufficient to aid the deployment to, and maintain air patrols over, a theater of operations at any distance from the EU's territorial limits. There are plans in several EU states to upgrade or replace their existing tanker fleets, but there will also be a need for these fleets to be expanded and for other EU states to acquire this sort of capability.

Of the states that currently have this capability, France is planning to

Table 5.5   Aerial Refueling Capabilities in EU Member States, 2001

	Aerial Refueling Capabilities
France	11 C-135 FR, 3 KC-135
Italy	4 Boeing 707-320
Netherlands	2 KDC-10
Spain	4 Boeing 707, 5 KC-130H
United Kingdom	6 L-1011 Tristar, 20 VC-10
Total	55

Sources: International Institute for Strategic Studies, *The Military Balance 2001–2002* (Oxford: Oxford University Press, October 2001); and national defense documents.

procure two additional aerial tankers, Spain is to modernize its four Boeing 707 tankers, and Italy is to acquire four new tanker/transports. Meanwhile, the UK is proceeding with its Future Strategic Tanker Aircraft (FSTA) program to replace its existing aircraft.[70] The FSTA program, along with the A400M project, is part of the Air Transport and Air Refueling Exchange of Service (ATARES) agreement, signed by European Air Group participants Belgium, France, Germany, Italy, the Netherlands, Spain, and the UK in February 2001, which enables states to share airlift and tanker capabilities in operational conditions.[71] This is the sort of collaboration and cooperation the EU will need in all areas if ESDP is to be a success. In addition, Germany is to integrate an in-flight refueling system into the Airbus A-310 and Greece is planning to procure a new fleet of tankers, giving the EU two more potential sources of aerial refueling capability.[72] The in-flight refueling capability will not just enhance the projection of the ERRF, but will also be vital in maintaining the option of constant combat and electronic warfare aircraft operations.

Once an ERRF has arrived in the area of operations, it will immediately require a number of key operational and support capabilities, including communications; intelligence, surveillance, target acquisition, and reconnaissance (ISTAR); and aerial combat capabilities, ranging from suppression of enemy air defenses (SEAD) to precision strike and close air support. All of these capabilities have been identified as shortfalls in the Capabilities Catalog.

One of the most fundamental capabilities necessary once in theater is effective and secure communications, the third element in the C^3 field (command, control, and communications). The ability to communicate, both with other units in theater and with the different headquarters, is vital to an operation. Three EU states, France, Italy, and the UK, possess satellite communications capability for the military (*Syracuse III, Sicral,* and *Skynet-4* respectively)[73] and this should be sufficient to provide the ERRF with what it needs. In addition, both France and the UK are examining replacements for their systems.

The remaining problems for the EU states are addressing the continuing, though improving, shortfall in deployable communications modules and significantly improving the interoperability of the different national communications systems. During OAF there was a lack of interoperable, high-volume secure communications capability, which affected all levels of the operation.[74] There were major disparities in the numbers and types of secure telephones at various headquarters and secure radios aboard aircraft.[75] The lack of encryption technology and keying material resulted in information being passed through open channels, severely compromising operation security.[76] The only communication system NATO had, the Limited Operational Capability for Europe (LOCE), was used, but it was overwhelmed, requiring some orders and targets to be hand-delivered and then transmitted though each state's communication system, causing severe delays and reducing flexibility.[77] Both on the ground and in the air, the lack of secure communications meant that sensitive information was vulnerable to interception by Yugoslav forces. The UK also had difficulties in supplying man-portable satellite communications equipment for ARRC headquarters personnel (the UK is the framework nation for the ARRC) and NATO had to assist to remedy the shortfall.[78] Therefore, the priority for the EU member states would appear to be to acquire interoperable, secure communications systems to allow the rapid and secure dissemination of information, intelligence, plans, and targets during an operation. These can even be bought "off-the-shelf" from commercial suppliers to reduce the costs.

The next group of support capabilities that the ERRF will need is ISTAR. Both prior to and during a moderate to high-end Petersberg operation, the ERRF will need to have large amounts of intelligence on which to base very difficult decisions and take action. There is a lot of debate as to what sort and how extensive the intelligence capability for ESDP should be. At one end of the spectrum, it seems logical that, if the EU is to have the capacity for autonomous action and the capacity for analysis of situations and sources of intelligence, it should have its own full range of intelligence capabilities, up to and including satellite intelligence. The EU member states currently have a limited capability in this field, with both satellite imagery and signals collection technology in the list of shortfalls disclosed at the Capabilities Improvement Conference. At present, the EU member states' capability for information gathering by satellite relies on commercial images purchased by the Torrejon Satellite Center, the *Helios 1* military satellite, and bilateral agreements primarily with the United States. The reliance on commercial satellites is fine when relations are good or interests converge, but when there are diverging interests or priorities, this access cannot be guaranteed. The *Helios 1A* and *Helios 1B* observation satellites, the product of a French, Italian, and Spanish program, are a useful start, but they can only operate in daytime and clear weather. Finally, reliance on bilateral agreements with the United States has its difficulties, as the EU itself has no agreement and the member states have differing levels of access to U.S. intelligence. The UK has the best access to U.S. intelligence, through its "special relationship" and the U.S.-UK information-sharing agreement. Other states do not receive nearly as much information and this can create situations where different states develop different situation assessments, depending on the amount and level of intelligence they have.

Hence, for an autonomous European defense capability, satellite intelligence and the ability to process, interpret, and securely disseminate that information will have to be further developed. The WEU audit of assets and capabilities stressed the need for "improved WEU Satellite Center access to commercial—and, above all, military—high resolution satellite imagery."[79] There are three principal types of observation (imagery) satellites, each able to operate in different conditions. Optical satellites operate in daylight and clear conditions, infrared satellites can operate day and night in clear weather, while radar satellites can operate in all conditions but produce a different type of image that is harder to interpret. Ideally, to cover a larger geographical region, twenty-four hours a day and in all weather conditions, several types of satellites should be used.

There are a number of observation satellite projects currently under way within the EU member states that may fulfill this objective. The most determined EU state in developing satellite capabilities is France, which is developing, together with Belgium and Spain (each with a 2.5 percent stake), the *Helios 2* military satellite, which has optical and infrared capabilities, to replace *Helios 1*. Meanwhile, Germany is working on the *SARlupe* radar satellite constellation, Italy is developing the *Cosmo-Skymed* radar satellite constellation, and Spain is developing *Ishtar,* an optical satellite system.[80] The UK has forgone the option of developing observation satellites, relying instead on the United States for its imagery intelligence.

These are all national programs, but there is a degree of cooperation between them. In January 2001, France and Italy signed an agreement to share images developed from their respective programs, thus complementing each other's capabilities. The French will give the Italians their optical images and the Italians will share their radar images. The various satellites, six in total, will be launched between 2003 and 2006.[81] The French also reached agreement with Germany in June 2000 to share satellite images. These developments should give some of the major EU member states an enhanced satellite imagery intelligence capability that could prove vital to ESDP.

To make use of these forthcoming capabilities at an EU level, some form of agreement between the states developing the satellites and the EU to expedite the transfer of information in times of crisis would be beneficial. The processing, interpreting, and disseminating of intelligence for EU purposes could be based at the Torrejon Satellite Center, which the EU has taken over from the WEU. However, this facility will also require personnel highly trained in *military* intelligence analysis (currently most of the imagery is civilian related) as well as secure communications to disseminate the information to the necessary parties.

Some analysts, senior military officers, and civilian personnel in the ministries of defense across the EU and within the EU structures believe that the expense of developing even more sophisticated satellite systems is too high.[82] They do not believe that the EU and its member states need to develop a truly autonomous satellite intelligence capability similar in scope to that of the United States. They argue that the money could be better spent to provide a whole host of other capabilities for the ERRF. They also believe that, for the types of operations envisaged for the ERRF, satellite intelligence may not be the most useful, arguing that the use of human intelligence and manned and unmanned aerial assets will provide more accurate and timely intelligence.[83]

The use of unmanned aerial vehicles (UAVs) in Kosovo and even more extensively in Afghanistan has reinforced this line of thinking. The problem is that the EU states lack the most capable and modern UAVs, the HALE/MALE (high/medium altitude long endurance) versions.[84] These are predominately U.S. owned, and it was the United States that provided most of those used in Kosovo and more recently in Afghanistan. The UAVs that the EU states do possess are primarily older systems, which are slow, low-altitude, short-range, short-duration vehicles that cannot transmit information in real time.[85] Hence their utility as an intelligence-gathering device is limited, especially as they are more vulnerable to being shot down. Recently, however, France has improved this situation with the acquisition of four of the more advanced MALE UAVs.[86] However, France's UAV capability is still only a fraction of that of the United States.[87] In particular, the EU states do not have any HALE UAVs, such as the Global Hawks of the United States, which fly at even greater altitude and have better range and endurance. The better these capabilities are, the better the intelligence gathering should be, and this could improve the chances of preventing a conflict/escalation or provide vital information if a military operation was deemed necessary.

A number of national studies on these more modern and capable UAVs are under way across the EU, but no cooperative projects have yet followed. This may change now that the Capabilities Improvement Conference identified UAVs as a shortfall area and assigned France responsibility for directing the study on UAVs.[88] A UAV capability is not critical in the immediate future, as the low-end Petersberg tasks (e.g., humanitarian operations) that the EU has declared itself operational for are not dependent on satellite or UAV capability. However, for larger, more difficult operations, UAVs will be vital to operational planning and in-theater support.

The ability to locate, identify, and if necessary target enemy units and positions will be provided by the assets discussed above, but there is also a need for further battlefield surveillance, coordination, and target-acquisition technology. During the Kosovo campaign the European contributions to manned as well as unmanned airborne surveillance were limited. In total, just three E-3 Sentry aircraft (Airborne Warning and Control System [AWACS] aircraft) and one Nimrod aircraft were provided by the UK and six reconnaissance Tornado aircraft were provided by Germany. In comparison, the United States contributed twenty-nine reconnaissance and surveillance aircraft, twelve surveillance drones,[89] and presumably its vast satellite resources. For the ERRF, the UK and France have committed to providing one or two AWACS aircraft each.[90] These aircraft will be important for both their battlefield surveillance and their command and control capability, but depending on the size of the operation they may not be enough. NATO also has a fleet of AWACS aircraft, which, if the EU-NATO agreements on access to capabilities are ever fully resolved, could prove extremely useful to the EU. The sharing of this type of capability will also avoid duplication of an expensive asset, a central aim of NATO. On a more positive note, in the late 1990s European states declined to buy the U.S. JSTARS system, for surveillance and target acquisition, even at a reduced cost,[91] yet today there are two programs to develop a similar capability within the EU states. The two major procurement projects, to improve battlefield surveillance and target acquisition, are the SOSTAR-X program involving France, Germany, Italy, the Netherlands, and Spain, and the UK's ASTOR/RISTA initiative.[92] In addition to these programs, France's Horizon all-weather heliborne battlefield reconnaissance system is already operational and played a role in the Balkans. The development of these surveillance systems is a benefit to both the Europeans and the United States. Long-term reliance on the United States for these capabilities would become increasingly frustrating for the Europeans, while eventually causing resentment in the United States.

Overall, the EU states do have some useful ISTAR capability, but they need to purchase or develop some of the more modern and technologically advanced systems to provide the extensive real-time intelligence critical to the higher-end Petersberg tasks. Hence the current ISTAR capability should not impede an ERRF from living up to the initial operational status declared at the Laeken European Council. This should not, however, lead to the neglect of improvements in intelligence-gathering capability, as without it the EU will not be able to develop a real, effective military capability and may be caught short when more arduous tasks are undertaken. Instead, a genuine attempt to collaborate on developing these expensive capabilities should be undertaken, thereby spreading the costs. ISTAR is one of the areas where collaboration to improve capabilities, while preventing duplication and keeping costs as low as possible, has the greatest potential.

The final group of assets required to meet the headline goal comprises various aerial combat capabilities, including SEAD, precision-guided munitions (PGMs), air superiority, and maritime air power. In all but one of these areas, air superiority, the EU member states have severe capability deficiencies. In Operation Allied Force the U.S. Air Force and U.S. Navy carried out the majority of strike sorties, supplying over 80 percent of the aircraft. Meanwhile, the U.S. Navy accounted for nearly all of the cruise missile launches, apart from an undisclosed but relatively small number fired by the UK submarine HMS *Splendid*.

The most severe limitation in air power for EU member states is the SEAD capability, with just fifty Tornado electronic combat and reconnaissance (ECR) aircraft from Germany and Italy and a fleet of ground attack aircraft for destroying radar sites with antiradiation missiles.[93] During the air campaign over Kosovo, only Germany and Italy from the EU states provided substantive SEAD capabilities. These two states provided ten German and four Italian ECR Tornado aircraft, which flew just 8 percent of SEAD sorties but delivered a much more significant 35 percent of the munitions in SEAD operations.[94] So although the EU assets in the realm of SEAD are somewhat limited, they are an effective and critical element to military operations. Without these sorts of capabilities the risk to air forces increases greatly. An alternative to simply acquiring more SEAD aircraft was raised in the UK's report on lessons learned from the Kosovo crisis, which suggested examining the possibility of improving SEAD capability by improving intelligence, surveillance, and reconnaissance (ISR) and sensor-to-shooter links.[95] This would improve the location and identification of enemy air defense assets and allow the rapid transmission of that information to an aircraft in theater, in order for it to disable that capability. Whichever method is used, an increase in SEAD capability for the EU states is desirable to improve the protection of EU assets and personnel.

The second severe aerial combat capability deficiency for the EU member states is the availability of all-weather PGMs. Among the EU states, this capability is largely limited to the French and UK air forces, with their laser-guided bombs, while the UK is the only state with a potent but limited cruise missile capability, with the Tomahawk TLAM launched from its submarines. Cruise missile capability is becoming increasingly attractive to several states, as their stand-off firing ability reduces the risk to a state's own air crews or troops and increases the options available in shaping a crisis by heightening the possibility for coercive diplomacy. The situation regarding stand-off firing missiles will improve with the introduction of a new air-to-surface cruise missile, the SCALP EG/Storm Shadow, in France, Greece, Italy, and the UK.[96] In addition, France will procure a naval version of the missile and is also developing the Apache antirunway missile.[97] Germany has decided to procure the Taurus air-to-surface missile. This is another example of how fifteen different defense budgets and procurement policies end up producing less capability for the money spent, when compared to the United States.

The effectiveness of PGMs, first hinted at during Operation Desert Storm in 1991, became more apparent during Operation Allied Force. General-purpose munitions outnumbered precision-guided munitions two to one during OAF, but 70 percent of the confirmed hits were allocated to the PGMs. However, there were limitations and problems with some PGMs. One of the problems with the laser-guided bombs was their inability to be utilized in adverse (cloud and fog) weather conditions. The more advanced PGMs, principally using global positioning satellite (GPS) guidance systems, were more effective. A particular success was the U.S. joint direct attack munition (JDAM), which was highly effective even during cloud cover.[98] The other problem that PGMs could not solve was strikes on mobile targets. These were far more difficult to locate and positively identify, which is primarily a problem of the ISR capability and illustrates the need to develop numerous parts of the armed forces simultaneously to make effective use of a newly acquired capability. Having additional precision weaponry options will maximize the chance of success against a given target,[99] require fewer sorties, and prevent the relocation of a target, thereby reducing the risk to the armed forces.

The final important element of air power for the ERRF is maritime air power, namely aircraft carriers. This capability gives states the ability to project air power into a theater of operations without cooperation from friendly neighboring states, which cannot be guaranteed in all regions of the world. Without the use of air bases and ports of a friendly state in or near the theater of operations, the projection of coercive power becomes heavily reliant on aircraft carriers. Currently, EU states' capabilities in this field are limited to three relatively small STOVL (short takeoff vertical landing) carriers operated by the UK, with one in extended refitting, the slightly larger, nuclear-powered carrier launched by France in 1999, and one small carrier each for Italy and Spain. This capability will have to be significantly improved, not necessarily in quantity but at least in quality, if ESDP is to be taken seriously. An expeditionary carrier force group will need to be central to ESDP's development, as such a capability is useful in both conflict prevention and crisis management operations. The mere presence of such a carrier force may dissuade a state from further escalating tensions and moving toward military action, while the aerial firepower and support assets it carries can play a critical role if combat operations are necessary. A major development in this area is the UK's plan to build two new, larger carriers of 50,000 tons (twice the size of their current carriers).[100] These new ships would provide a major boost to the pool of forces within the EU (though their use is not guaranteed). In autumn 2002 this capability of maritime air power was given a further boost by France's announcement in its military program law (LPM 2003–2008) that it will be building a second aircraft carrier.[101] Nevertheless, it may be beneficial if perhaps one or two other states also developed this capability. Aside from procuring the ships, there is also the need to procure the air power to go with them. In the case of the UK, the carriers it is proposing will need about 150 aircraft to fill capacity (likely to be filled by a naval variant of the JSF) and this again will be an expensive program.[102] The French are to equip their carrier with naval versions of their Rafale combat aircraft.

One aerial asset for which EU states do have an advanced and comprehensive capability is air superiority. Here, these states are already capable of countering all but the most advanced of potential adversaries. This capability is likely to be further enhanced by the acquisition of the EF-2000 Typhoon (the Eurofighter), the Rafale, the JSF, and a new range of BVR (beyond visual range) missiles.[103]

The End Result

In summary, the EU member states currently have the necessary equipment capabilities to make the initial operational capability a reality and will be able to carry out the lower-end Petersberg tasks if needed. They could also carry out various peacekeeping roles if pressed to do so. For this, they would need access to NATO planning and other capabilities and would probably have to charter, borrow, and even purchase additional assets. The real problems in equipment capability terms arise at the upper end of the Petersberg tasks, especially peacemaking involving the use of combat forces, and in the definition of an autonomous capability. For upper-end Petersberg tasks, the EU member states are likely to require capabilities that NATO does not possess and cannot be chartered or leased from the United States or elsewhere. If the EU wants a truly autonomous capability, there will have to be an even greater investment in the whole range of capabilities discussed above, up to and including a full satellite intelligence capability. These capabilities will have to be acquired one way or another by the EU states and added to the Force Catalog. In turn, this will require even greater investment, quite possibly at a level that no single state can afford, which raises the need for more collaboration in setting the requirements, design, development, procurement, and maintenance of equipment programs and even some form of common funding for the most costly capabilities.

At present the EU's autonomous military capability (and the European contribution to NATO) is only being remodeled where no increase in defense expenditure is necessary. The restructuring of the armed forces into more flexible and rapidly deployable units is a vital step forward, as is the development of multinational formations. However, in order for a truly effective military capability, there needs to be more consultation, cooperation, and integration in defense policy, procurement, and planning. Initial steps have been taken, but if the EU is to afford a high-capability military backbone to support the fledgling CFSP, then much of the current duplication should be overcome and investment levels should be raised.

Notes

1. *Consolidated Version of the Treaty on European Union* (Luxembourg: Office for Official Publications of the European Communities, 1997), art. 11.1.

2. George Robertson, "The Alliance and Military Capabilities for European Security," presentation to the Royal United Services Institute NATO Fiftieth Anniversary Conference, London, March 8, 1999.

3. Ministry of Defense (UK), *The Strategic Defence Review* (London: HMSO, July 1998).

4. Ibid.

5. Ministry of Defense (France), *Defense and the Armed Forces of France* (Paris: Service d'Information et de Relations Publiques des Armées, June 1998), pp. 28–29.

6. Ibid., p. 8.

7. Stanley Sloan, "French Defence Policy: Gaullism Meets the Post Cold War World," *Arms Control Today,* April 1997, pp. 3–8.

8. Federal Ministry of Defense (Germany), *German Security Policy and the Bundeswehr* (Bonn: Press and Information Office of the Federal Government, October 1997), p. 36.

9. Federal Ministry of Defense (Germany), *The Bundeswehr and Its Mission* (October 1997), www.bundesregierung.de/english/02/0205/index12.html.

10. Federal Ministry of Defense (Germany), *The Bundeswehr: Advancing Steadily into the Twenty-First Century: Cornerstones of a Fundamental Renewal* (Bonn, May 2000), par. 58.

11. Gerhard Schroder, "A New Form of Self-Defence," interview given to *Die Zeit,* October 18, 2001.

12. Lorenzo Forcieri, *NATO Forces: Preparing for New Roles and Missions,* North Atlantic Assembly Committee Reports, Defense and Security Committee, Subcommittee on the Future of the Armed Forces (Brussels: North Atlantic Assembly, November 1998), p. 11., www.naa.be.

13. Ministry of Defense (Netherlands), *Framework Memorandum for the 2000 Defence White Paper* (The Hague, March 1999), p. 20.

14. North Atlantic Treaty Organization, "Financial and Economic Data Relating to NATO Defence: Defence Expenditures of NATO Countries (1980–2001)," press release, M-DPC-2(2001)156, December 18, 2001, www.nato.int/docu/pr/1998/p98-147e.htm.

15. U.S. General Accounting Office, *European Security: U.S. and European Contributions to Foster Stability and Security in Europe* (Washington, D.C., November 2001), p. 73.

16. Total active armed forces figure adapted from International Institute for Strategic Studies (IISS), *The Military Balance 2002–2003* (Oxford: Oxford University Press, October 2002).

17. See IISS, *The Military Balance 2001–2002;* G. Andréani, C. Bertram, and C. Grant, *Europe's Military Revolution* (London: Center for European Reform,

2001); and King's College London et al., *Achieving the Headline Goal*, Discussion Paper, November 2001.

18. Council of the European Union, *Military Bodies in the European Union and the Planning and Conduct of EU-Led Military Operations* (Brussels, February 29, 2000), 6215/1/00.

19. North Atlantic Council, "Washington Summit Communiqué," press release, NAC-S(99)64, April 24, 1999, par. 10.

20. Council of the European Union, *Military Bodies in the European Union*.

21. Ibid.

22. See Council of the European Union, *Annex VI: Arrangements Concerning non-EU European NATO Members and Other Countries Which Are Candidates for Accession to the EU; Annex VII: Standing Arrangements for Consultation and Co-operation Between the EU and NATO;* and *Appendix to Annex VII: Annex to the Permanent Arrangements on EU/NATO Consultation and Co-operation on the Implementation of Paragraph 10 of the Washington Communiqué*, in Council of the European Union, *Draft Presidency Report on the European Security and Defence Policy* (Brussels, December 13, 2000), 14056/3/00.

23. Douglas Hamilton, "Turkey Blocks Deal to Share NATO Force," *Washington Post*, December 16, 2000, p. A22.

24. Joseph Fitchett, "Turkey Puts Roadblock in EU Force Negotiations," *International Herald Tribune*, January 26, 2001.

25. Ian Black, "Turkey Blocks NATO Deal on EU Force," *Financial Times*, December 15, 2000.

26. Leyla Boulton and Judy Dempsey, "Turkey Lifts Objection to EU Rapid Reaction Force," *Financial Times*, December 4, 2001.

27. Ibid.

28. Judy Dempsey, "Greece Blocks EU Accord with NATO," *Financial Times*, December 10, 2001.

29. Interviews with officials in the U.S. Department of Defense, March 2002.

30. Ibid.

31. Benno Zierer, *A European Crisis Reaction Force: Reply to the Annual Report of the Council*, document no. 1668 (Paris: Defense Committee of the Assembly of the WEU, November 10, 1999), pp. 5–6.

32. Council of the European Union, General Affairs, *Statement on Improving European Military Capabilities* (Brussels, November 19, 2001), par. 5.

33. House of Lords, European Union Select Committee, *Eleventh Report: The European Policy on Security and Defence* (London, January 29, 2002), par. 68.

34. Ibid., par. 29.

35. U.S. General Accounting Office, *European Security: U.S. and European Contributions to Foster Stability and Security in Europe* (Washington, D.C., November 2001), pp. 73–74.

36. Zierer, *A European Crisis Reaction Force*, p. 11.

37. Ibid.

38. Ibid.

39. Western European Union, *Multinational Forces Answerable to WEU*, www.weu.int/eng/info/faweu.htm.

40. IISS, *The Military Balance 2001–2002*, p. 287.

41. Rachel Anne Lutz, *Military Capabilities for a European Defence* (Copenhagen: Danish Institute of International Affairs, 2001), p. 57.

42. Eurocorps, *History*, www.eurocorps.org.

43. François Heisbourg et al. *European Defence: Making It Work,* Chaillot Paper no. 42 (Paris: WEU Institute for Security Studies, September 2000), p. 88.

44. Zierer, *A European Crisis Reaction Force,* p. 12.

45. Interviews with EU civilian and military officials in the Council secretariat, November 2001.

46. "Die EU Plant eine Super-Armee," *Die Welt,* November 17, 2000, www.welt.de/daten/2000/11/17/1117eu203210.htx.

47. Michael O'Hanlon, "Transforming NATO: The Role of European Forces," *Survival* 39, no. 3 (Autumn 1997): 9.

48. John Wilkinson, *European Strategic Lift Capabilities: Reply to the Annual Report of the Council* (Paris: Assembly of the Western European Union, Interim European Security and Defense Assembly, November 5, 2001), p. 9.

49. O'Hanlon, "Transforming NATO," p. 9.

50. Wilkinson, *European Strategic Lift Capabilities,* p. 7.

51. J. A. C. Lewis and Craig Hoyle, "A400M Group Facing Tough Decision," *Janes Defence Weekly,* March 27, 2002, p. 5.

52. Defence Systems Daily, "A400M Project Under Threat Again as German Funding Stalls" (January 30, 2002), http://defence-data.com/archive/page13409.htm.

53. John Hooper, "Germany Forced to Cut Defence Spending," *The Guardian,* December 6, 2002.

54. IISS, *The Military Balance 2001–2002,* p. 287.

55. Ministry of Defense (UK), "Short Term Strategic Airlift Contract Announced," press release, 221/00, September 4, 2000, www.mod.uk/index.php3?page=2&nid=1059&view=724&cat=0.

56. A. Dumoulin, Raphael Mathieu, and Vincent Metten, *Introduction to the Comparative Survey of the White Papers, Official Documents, and General Policy Papers Related to the Security and Defence Policy of the Fifteen Member States of the European Union.* Unpublished paper. (Brussels: Royal Defence College, 2001).

57. Wilkinson, *European Strategic Lift Capabilities,* p. 9.

58. Craig Hoyle, Richard Scott, and Christopher Foss, "The Long Haul," *Jane's Defence Weekly,* February 6, 2002.

59. IISS, "The 'European Rapid Reaction Force,'" in IISS, *The Military Balance 2001–2002,* p. 286; and Wilkinson, *European Strategic Lift Capabilities,* p. 10.

60. IISS, "Military Sealift," in IISS, *The Military Balance 2001–2002,* p. 293.

61. Ibid., pp. 294–295.

62. IISS, "The 'European Rapid Reaction Force,'" p. 287.

63. Wilkinson, *European Strategic Lift Capabilities,* p. 5.

64. Ibid.

65. Ministry of Defense (UK), "Outcome of the Strategic Sealift (RoRo) and Alternative Landing Ships Logistics (ALSLs) Competitions," press release, October 26, 2000, www.mod.uk/index.php3?page=2&nid=1059&view=724&cat=0.

66. IISS, "The 'European Rapid Reaction Force,'" p. 286.

67. Royal Navy, "Future Ships," www.royal-navy.mod.uk/rn/print.php3?page=1969.

68. Hoyle, Scott, and Foss, "The Long Haul."

69. John E. Peters et al., *European Contributions to Operation Allied Force* (Santa Monica, Calif.: RAND, 2001), pp. 20–23, 33.

70. Dumoulin, Mathieu, and Metten, *Introduction to the Comparative Survey of the White Papers,* p. 128; and Craig Hoyle, "European Air Forces," *Janes Defence Weekly,* September 19, 2001, p. 38.

71. Hoyle, "European Air Forces," p. 38.

72. Dumoulin, Mathieu, and Metten, *Introduction to the Comparative Survey of the White Papers*, p. 128.

73. IISS, "The 'European Rapid Reaction Force,'" p. 287.

74. Peters et al., *European Contributions to Operation Allied Force*, p. 56.

75. U.S. Department of Defense, *Report to Congress: Kosovo/Operation Allied Force After-Action Report* (Washington, D.C., January 31, 2000), pp. 73–74.

76. Nicoll Alexander, "NATO Inhibited by Europe's Military Flaws," *Financial Times,* February 9, 2000.

77. Peters et al., *European Contributions to Operation Allied Force*, p. 57.

78. Ministry of Defense (UK), *Kosovo: Lessons from the Crisis* (London, June 2000), chap. 8, www.mod.uk/news/kosovo/lessons/chapter8.htm.

79. Western European Union, Council of Ministers, *Audit of Assets and Capabilities for European Crisis Management Operations: Recommendations for Strengthening European Capabilities for Crisis Management Operations* (Luxembourg, November 23, 1999), www.weu.int/eng/mini/99/luxembourg/recommendations.htm.

80. Georges Lemoine, *The New Challenges Facing European Intelligence: Reply to the Annual Report of the Council* (Paris: Assembly of the WEU, April 2002), C/1775, p. 15.

81. Ibid.

82. Interviews with officials of the EU Council, November 2001.

83. Interviews with EU and Ministry of Defense (UK) officials, June 2000 and November 2001.

84. IISS, "The 'European Rapid Reaction Force,'" p. 288.

85. Lemoine, *The New Challenges Facing European Intelligence,* p. 17.

86. Ibid., p. 18.

87. For example, an older UAV (the CL-289) could remain airborne for 30 minutes at an altitude of 600 meters. The new French UAVs can remain airborne for up to 6 hours at an altitude of 4,500 meters, relaying video images and identifying targets for laser-guided munitions. Meanwhile, the U.S. Predator drone is capable of 24-hour missions at an altitude of 7,600 meters and the Global Hawk is capable of 35-hour missions up to a distance of 2000 kilometers at an altitude of 20,000 meters. For more detail, see Lemoine, *The New Challenges Facing European Intelligence,* and Alan Meale, "Defence Equipment for European Crisis Management: Reply to the Annual Report of the Council" (Paris: Assembly of the WEU, November 2001), C/1760.

88. Ibid.

89. Tim Youngs, Mark Oakes, Paul Bowers, and Mick Hillyard, *Kosovo: Operation Allied Force,* House of Commons Library Research Paper no. 99/48 (London: House of Commons Library, April 29, 1999), pp. 69–72.

90. Lemoine, *The New Challenges Facing European Intelligence,* p. 17.

91. William Drozdiak, "Air War Exposed Arms Gap Within NATO," *Washington Post,* June 28, 1999, p. A1.

92. IISS, "The 'European Rapid Reaction Force,'" p. 288.

93. Ibid., p. 289.

94. Peters et al., *European Contributions to Operation Allied Force,* pp. 21–22, 32.

95. Ministry of Defense, *Kosovo: Lessons from the Crisis,* chap. 7.

96. Dumoulin, Mathieu, and Metten, *Introduction to the Comparative Survey of the White Papers,* p. 131.

97. Ibid.

98. William Cohen and Henry Shelton, *Joint Statement of William Cohen, Secretary of Defense, and General Henry Shelton, Chairman of the Joint Chiefs of Staff, Senate Armed Services Committee Hearing on Kosovo After-Action Review* (Washington, D.C., October 14, 1999), p. 13.

99. Ministry of Defense, *Kosovo: Lessons from the Crisis,* chap. 7.

100. Ministry of Defense, *The Strategic Defence Review,* p. 38.

101. Ministry of Defense (France), *Project de loi de programmation militarie 2003–2008* (Paris: Delegation a l'Information et a la Communication de la Defense, 2002).

102. Defense Procurement Agency, *Future Carrier Borne Aircraft* (May 2001), www.mod.uk/dpa/projects/fcba.htm.

103. IISS, "The 'European Rapid Reaction Force,'" p. 289.

6

U.S. and
NATO Responses

U.S. Support for Europe?

European integration has been a success story, and right from the time of the Truman Doctrine and the Marshall Plan, the United States deserves much of the credit for supporting it. It helped plant the seed, provided succor, and defended Western Europe from an external threat. The success of European integration fulfills a commitment made at the inception of the North Atlantic Treaty Organization (NATO).

Some in the United States were frightened that Western Europe would eventually clash with U.S. ambitions, that European ambitions were to build a state that would attain geopolitical equality with the United States, with the suggestion that the original framers wanted a European bloc, apart from the United States and USSR. For them, the United States supported European integration, but only conditioned by the framework of the Atlantic community and U.S. leadership. For them, a truly equal Europe was bound to lead to a threat to U.S. preponderance. However, Presidents Harry Truman and Dwight Eisenhower, and Secretaries of State Dean Acheson and John Dulles, supported European integration because they believed a U.S. presence in Europe should only be temporary, not permanent. Eisenhower, serving as Supreme Allied Commander for Europe (SACEUR), noted: "If in ten years, all American troops stationed in Europe for national defense purposes have not returned to the United States, then this whole project will have failed."[1] Dulles believed that the United States should not make life so easy for Europeans that they would depend on the United States.

Forty years later, after 1998, instead of there being only one major security organization in Europe, there were going to be two. No one was entirely sure how they would fit (or not fit) together, and how far European need for greater independence would go. The George W. Bush administration has needed to look at questions regarding the nature of the transatlantic relationship, about U.S. grand strategy, and about NATO itself, especially since the events of September 11, 2001.

Given the success of the European project, the United States has become aware that there are pressing threats from other quarters, so that Europe will receive less U.S. power and attention in the years ahead. Indeed, a pressing question may be whether there can be U.S. internationalism without an ongoing U.S. presence in Europe, and whether the United States will become more selective.

Stanley Sloan has perceptively written of three contrasting positions of how the United States should respond. He also makes the point that these views are shaped by overarching views of the U.S. role in the world, especially by U.S. worldviews.[2] For some, the United States has no choice but to assume the mantle of global leadership, but since it cannot do everything, it must have allies whom it can lead. Others, whom some might term "unilateralist," believe in the "do it our way" principle and wish that the United States would concentrate on its own perception of its national interest and pursue that rigorously. The three schools are:

- Traditional—those in the center of domestic politics support European integration and the transatlantic community of shared interests.
- Domestic interest—those who see the European Union's development as allowing the United States to respond to its own internal agenda, leading to a reduction in U.S. international commitments and, perhaps, to a U.S. exit from Europe.
- U.S. security interests—those who are skeptical of the benefits of European integration, believing that the United States should focus on and defend its own interests and, if necessary, disrupt the EU.

Given the new debate, the domestic and U.S. security interests are receiving more attention than previously. Sloan's three schools also had to contend with a variety of other themes.

Issues

Developments and debates since 1998 mean that the United States now has to confront directly its traditional ideas of a "twin pillar" NATO alliance, composed of a European and a U.S. pillar. This raises the question of whether U.S. officials really believed in or wanted such an alliance. Indeed,

Henry Kissinger observed in 1965 that the United States would pay a price if Europe achieved political and economic unification, since it would not want to be subservient and would wish to have its own distinctive views, so that it could challenge U.S. hegemony in Atlantic policy.[3] If Europe were in that position, why would the United States be willing to offer it security at a knockdown price?

In the William Clinton administration the principle was that there could be a European pillar of a strong transatlantic alliance, but not competing entities. As George Robertson (NATO Secretary-General) has said, the United States suffers from a "sort of schizophrenia . . . on the one hand saying, 'You Europeans have got to carry more of the burden.' And then, when the Europeans say, 'OK, we will carry more of the burden,' they say, 'well, wait a minute, are you trying to tell us to go home?'"[4] The United States believes in a fair and equitable sharing of the full range of security responsibilities and a proper balancing of costs and benefits, yet clearly it is still unsure of the mix of the political, military, and economic elements and what it means for U.S. hegemony.

If the EU becomes an economic, political, and military giant, the United States will need to give up its hegemonic pretensions and tutelage. This causes some problems for those in the United States who take U.S. leadership for granted. Some have spoken of NATO working so well because U.S. leadership "calls the shots, keeps recalcitrant members in line," and provides resources.[5] West Europeans still seemed to prefer U.S. leadership and protection to a real European alternative in the defense area, especially if that alternative might entail giving up some sovereignty in the defense field and spending more money. For the United States, NATO is still the preferred option. In December 2000 the U.S. Department of Defense declared that "a fundamental point of U.S. strategy is to maintain NATO as the pre-eminent organization for ensuring transatlantic security and the anchor of American engagement in Europe." However, it went on to say that, too often, this is equated with "leadership," which for the United States is simply a statement of facts, but for many Europeans can be seen as domination or overbearance. The Defense Department says that the United States must be prepared to share responsibility.[6] However, as Robert Hunter (former U.S. ambassador to NATO) explained before the House Committee on International Relations in November 1999: "While we supported a strong European pillar, we wanted it to be very much subject to our own leadership and the recognized primacy of NATO over WEU [Western European Union] or any other European-only security arrangements. As late as 1992, this led various U.S. administrations to express misgivings when WEU, or individual European governments, showed an inclination to take actions that could be at variance with our own central direction of the Alliance."[7] This theme could be seen, for example, in the speeches by William Taft IV (U.S. ambassador to NATO) early in 1991 and the so-called Bartholomew memorandum of February 1991.[8]

For many years kept secret, the Bartholomew memorandum laid down the law as far as the United States saw it. It reinforced messages that the Pentagon was becoming worried about any long-term rivalry to the United States. Having mentioned key developments—the Gulf, decline of the USSR's power, responsibility sharing, and economic tensions across the Atlantic—the Bartholomew memorandum went on:

> [T]his is not a time for Europeans to be sending a message however unintended to the US public suggesting that they want to reduce or marginalize the US role in Europe. We know that this is not the intention of our European allies, but we want to stress the danger that positions which seem to emphasize European over transatlantic solidarity or institutional changes which diminish the centrality of the Alliance could pose for American opinion. . . .
>
> While we understand that the logic behind political integration leads to a union that ultimately encompasses security affairs, we believe that the primary yardstick against which proposals and institutional innovations need to measured is whether they actually enhance Alliance defensive capabilities and make Europe more secure. . . . In our view, efforts to construct a European pillar by redefining and limiting NATO's role, by weakening its structure, or by creating a monolithic bloc of certain members would be misguided. We hope that such efforts would be resisted firmly.
> . . .
> Subordinating the WEU to [the European Community (EC)] would accentuate the separation and independence of the European pillar from the Alliance, weaken the integrity of our common transatlantic security and defense which . . . remain crucial.

The EC was "clearly not 'within the Alliance.'"[9]

This position began to change in the Clinton years, but now, under Bush, the question is whether the United States is going back to the Bartholomew mind-set. For some, the question is not whether Europe can achieve parity with the United States, but whether a mutually agreed devolution of power, with the United States in the lead, can be agreed. At what point will Europeans resent U.S. efforts to force the Alliance into particular courses of action? What is the difference between U.S. leadership and U.S. hegemony?

Part of the answer is that the smaller (and some of the bigger) European states could not do without the United States, especially given its power. The Bush administration tends to the view that there needs to be effective U.S. leadership to ensure that NATO remains at the center of a European security system and is responsive to U.S. interests.[10] Part of the

U.S. problem is how to avoid leadership looking like a policy of divide and rule.

The question of U.S. leadership has caused some to say that the EU should "accept the reality of the U.S. presence as a non-member member state within the EU."[11] It could be argued that the United States was the invisible guest at the meetings of the EU in 1998–1999, with some attempt to take U.S. interests and attitudes fully into account. Others argued that Washington was "justified in arguing that NATO have the right of first refusal and that the EU act independently only when the United States chooses not to engage."[12] This would have made the EU dependent on a U.S. decision and a junior junior partner, and would have left the EU to deal with either difficult issues or residual issues. It would not be a giant or even an independent player.

A particular U.S. worry, expressed by Hunter, was that the "EU might create a 'European Caucus' within NATO, in which all 10 WEU Members in NATO, today, and more later, would take the same positions and have to refer back to the European Council to change their views. I think that would be very dangerous for the effective working of NATO, and we have to oppose. . . . I think this point needs to be made very, very forcefully to the Europeans."[13]

Some of Bush's aides, after the December 2000 Nice summit, argued that the European Rapid Reaction Force (ERRF) was a "dagger pointed at NATO's heart."[14] The Pentagon may have thought that now was the time to plan to withdraw the U.S. military presence from Europe, since the ERRF could be seen as a desire by some Europeans (especially France) to distance themselves from the United States or to pave the way for anti-Americanism.

Some of the U.S. leadership are concerned that a more autonomous European capability will prove an excuse for the United States to bring its troops back home, or as Peter Rodman put it before the House Committee in 1999: "If the Europeans act as if they regard the alliance as dispensable, some Americans will welcome the opportunity to wave the Europeans goodbye."[15] In addition, House Representative Douglas Bereuter stated: "It needs to be clear to our European allies that the creation of competing institutions in Europe, that detract from NATO's capabilities and solidarity, would endanger public and congressional support for its commitment to the North Atlantic Alliance."[16] This could become increasingly important, given that the EU's economic power is now roughly equal to that of the United States. Increasingly Americans are asking why a fiscally challenged U.S. Congress should support a prosperous Europe. How can U.S. support for Europe's security be explained to the citizens of Iowa?

Americans want a bigger military and budgetary effort on the part of their European partners, but are not keen on seeing any transfer of power and influence. It is the word "autonomy" that causes the friction. Immediately after the St. Malo Declaration and the European Council meeting in Cologne, members of the House of Representatives International Relations Committee complained about European actions. Their chairman, Benjamin Gilman, asked whether the United States could "stop" such European developments, although he thought not.[17] The greater the stress on "autonomy," the greater the U.S. fear and the greater their concerns about its becoming a threat to U.S. policy leadership.

Part of the problem for the United States is that it has accepted that the Europeans are, or were, working toward European integration. For some Europeans, the Common Foreign and Security Policy (CFSP) and European Security and Defense Policy (ESDP) are part of a natural progression in that process, a complement to Europe's deepening economic and political progress. The coming of age of ESDP, at that moment of the successful launch of the Economic and Monetary Union (EMU), showed how much Europe was changing. From the standpoint of Eisenhower and Dulles this was a triumph, but now the United States must face the reality.

This raises the issues of how common the common interests across the Atlantic are and what the specific interests of the United States in Europe are. Until now, it was widely accepted by most in the United States that U.S. well-being depended in large measure on what happened in Europe, and that the United States needed an economically vibrant and peaceful Europe. This has been supported officially with the belief that transatlantic security is indivisible, and that the United States has permanent and vital national interests in Europe.

It is nearly always asserted that Americans and Europeans have common interests: democracy, human rights, and the rule of law; a zone of stability with strong economic ties, wealth, prosperity, open markets, and investments opportunities; and security, including the more than fifty-year-old NATO. NATO includes the integrated military structure, through which NATO forces can train and plan, create a degree of interoperability (which it does share with most other forces), and have the ability to conduct high-intensity joint and combined operations. U.S. allies contribute bases, infrastructure, and overflight and transit rights, allowing the United States to project its forces, if necessary, beyond Europe.

In a document on U.S. security strategy for Europe and NATO published in 1995, the Department of Defense was adamant not only that the U.S. European Command (USEUCOM) contributed to the essential security of Europe, but also that it "supports our efforts to extend stability . . . deters adventurism and coercion by potentially hostile states [and gives] the ability to conduct high-intensity joint and combined military operations with our NATO allies both in Europe and in other areas of common interests."[18] As well as during Desert Storm in 1991, the report says that between 1991 and 1995 USEUCOM was deployed over fifty times, to thirty states. By 2000 the number of USEUCOM operations had increased by a factor of twenty over the previous decade. The U.S. administration says that these forces can deploy more easily in certain cases from Europe and reduce the cost of deployments. It argues that this was true with the deployments to Bosnia in 1995 and Kosovo in 1999. Of the thirteen en route airbases that facilitate the rapid deployment of forces from the continental United States to areas of conflict overseas, six are in Europe. It is claimed that, without these, it would be "impossible to meet wartime requirements in Europe, the Middle East, and Southwest Asia."[19]

Not all agree, however, arguing that "US participation in NATO makes it more difficult for Washington to meet security challenges outside Europe. . . . [T]he alliance does not add to U.S. capabilities outside Europe, and never has. Since the Korean War, with the *partial* exception of the Persian Gulf War, NATO and the Western allies have either opposed, or refrained from supporting U.S. strategic and military interventions outside of Europe." NATO is therefore seen as a yoke that hinders the United States.[20] At the moment, this is a minority voice, but as the environment changes this charge is likely to become louder.

Apart from government ties, the transatlantic relationship has occasioned a thick network of economic ties and dialogues, which is likely to continue. Transatlantic trade is relatively balanced. Europe is the largest investor in forty-three U.S. states, and is either first or second in export markets for forty-two states. Forty percent of world trade is conducted between the United States and the EU. The United States and the EU are each other's largest single trading partners, accounting for 20 percent of each other's trade in goods and 33 percent of each other's trade in services. More than 7 million U.S. jobs depend on European investment in the United States, including 3.6 million Americans directly employed by European-owned companies. Twenty-five percent of all U.S. exports go to Europe and those exports support 1.6 million jobs. Fifty percent of U.S. direct investment abroad is in Europe and over 60 percent of foreign direct investment in the United States is from Europe. Europe was the second-largest customer of the United States, taking 30 percent of U.S. exports, and its second largest supplier.[21] There is a notion that extending the "zone of stability" will further enhance U.S. economic interests in Europe. Thomas Pickering was confident that the EU would help "ensure that United States trade, investment, and political interests are preserved and protected."[22]

About 60 percent of Americans claim European ancestry or ethnic origin. There are also the intellectual and philosophical ties. The United States claims to be a European power, and wants a close relationship with the greatest concentration of like-minded peoples and with one of the world's greatest centers of economic power and its growing market. For many, such as Simon Serfaty, U.S.-European common interests and values make it imperative for the link to remain, given that "US interests are now too significant to be left to others, a disengagement has become neither possible nor meaningful."[23] Americans are part of the European and global economy. While some may not like it and some want to lead the world and Europe, they cannot abstain. However, there is perhaps a growing concern that too many economic issues are beginning to have too much of an impact across the Atlantic, as trade disputes are increasingly mentioned in transatlantic discussions, for example, bananas and steel.

Although increasingly it is being pointed out that there have been, and are, differences stemming from geopolitics, history and culture, economic interests, and competition for sales, among other factors, many Americans now believe that the trade, economic, and financial disputes across the Atlantic are at least as important as the politico-military ones. They become concerned that the EU is moving toward protection and economic autarky. Some worry that without the glue of external threat (and September 11, 2001, has not helped), classic trade issues might spill over into the area of security and defense. Are some of the recent problems over bananas and steel part of a longer-term secular trend or mere blips? Small economic issues can begin to poison the atmosphere, especially in the area of competition. Increasingly, at the beginning of the twenty-first century, trade was being raised on nearly every visit between the EU and the United States. As will be seen in Chapter 7, there is also the question of whether the United States is willing to take the blame for the lack of a "two-way" street of defense procurements, and would be willing to allow licenses for the transfer of advanced technology to allied states.

Part of the problem is that the United States is the only superpower left in the world and has a global point of view, while most Europeans are profoundly regional. With the notable exceptions of France and Britain (and the former colonial powers of Portugal until 1974, and Belgium from 1960 to 1964), most West European states have not maintained military forces or engaged in large-scale military actions outside of Europe since 1945. Instead, they have acted individually or within the UN and EU, relying almost exclusively on political and economic levers to advance their interests outside of Europe—apart from Iraq in 1990–1991. Europeans generally see their principal threats coming from closer to home.

Even after September 11, many EU member states are considerably less comfortable than the United States with what has been seen as NATO's "out-of-area" operations, partly because of profound policy and philosophical disagreements with the United States. Germany and others have either no, or a limited, vision of the use of military instruments of power.

As noted above, the United States has to make up its mind as to what role it would like to see its allies fulfilling. The United States is still trying to work out the mind-set of the British. Given that ESDP is primarily a British idea, does this mean that there will be a greater British reluctance to stand behind U.S. initiatives in the future, and weaken the link? At the moment, with Afghanistan in 2001–2002 and the unqualified support of the British during the March 2003 Iraq war, this appears unlikely, but there is a doubt about the future. The United States needs Europe to become more outward-looking and less preoccupied with itself.

The real concern is that some in the EU, especially France, want to build the EU into a genuine counterweight to the United States. The United States has a historical suspicion of France, believing that France has a different vision of the future. The United States has a strong resistance to the alleged neo-Gaullist character of the ESDP proposal. There is enormous hostility to France's alleged intentions, its behavior, and its attempt to marginalize the influence of the United States. While the United States took some comfort from the fact that the French vision was a minority view, it believed that France wanted to increase the degree of European military independence from NATO and perhaps compete with the United States. This notion implied closer cooperation of the armed forces of Western Europe, separate from NATO structures. In particular, some statements by President Jacques Chirac and French ministers angered the United States, particularly the stress they placed on the concept of autonomy. Chirac had stressed that the EU cannot be fully effective until it possesses a completely autonomous capacity for action, especially in the area of defense. He wanted a completely all-European chain of command, with Europe having its own military committee that would give orders to a European military staff, to be carried out by European national or joint forces, bypassing NATO. Chirac, on October 19, 1999, stated: "The European Union must be able to act on its own, either utilising its own means, or making use of those made available to it by NATO. It must therefore have its own arrangements for the provision of advice, analysis and military leadership, which it currently lacks."[24] He also said that it was premature to discuss these matters with NATO.

Of particular sensitivity to the United States has been French talk of a unipolar world, describing the United States as a being a "hyperpower" *(hyperpuissance)*. Former French foreign minister Hubert Vedrine argued, "We cannot accept either a politically unipolar world, nor a culturally uniform world, nor the unilateralism of a single hyperpower. And that is why we are fighting for a multipolar, diversified, and multilateral world."[25] The French hoped that Europe might have the courage to go further than was currently envisaged. The debacle of French behavior over Iraq in the winter of 2002–2003 confirmed all of the worst fears of the United States, and for some confirmed that France was beyond the pale in respect to NATO and the United States.

Peter Rodman is not alone in seeing that Europe was the continent where the idea of balance of power was invented. Representative Brad Sherman notes that "Europeans, by reflex, see the imbalance of power across the Atlantic as a problem."[26] Some others in Europe seem to think in the same way as the French, for example, former Dutch prime minister Wim Kok and Helmut Schmidt. Many Americans remain suspicious that France will be able to seduce Tony Blair and Germany into its vision and seek to pursue its alleged objective of pushing the United States out of Europe. The French refusal to overcome the final barriers to a full reintegration into the NATO command structure also annoyed Washington.

What upset the United States was its perception that the French were militarily ineffective. Even French hostility to the U.S. national missile defense system angered the United States, given that it believed that the French had done so much to make sure that "rogue states get nuclear weapons and ballistic missiles. . . . [T]he French have been most critical of us protecting ourselves from a risk that they have done so much to create."[27]

The United States over the next few years has to make up its mind whether it trusts the EU or not—does it see the EU as a partner or a competitor? There are some Republicans in the United States who have long been suspicious of European integration and the European agenda. John R. Bolton, appointed undersecretary of arms control and international security in 2001, was vehement in his objections to what the EU was doing. He pointed to European objections to U.S. hegemony, claiming that the State Department was failing to see that "deeper European economic integration has advanced so far beyond its Marshall Plan roots that U.S. interests are now challenged, rather than advanced by 'ever closer union.' Indeed, 'ever closer union' already threatens NATO."

He went on to ask, "What makes a policy 'European' as opposed to 'Western' or 'Atlanticist'?" He gave a catalog of policy concerns where the Europeans were "undercutting" not just NATO, but the whole Alliance: the breakup of Yugoslavia, Kosovo, relations with Turkey and Cyprus, the Middle East, trade and finance, the attitude toward EU enlargement (where he argued that some applicants had been told that they needed to have closer ties with the EU than with the United States), and the political baggage of the euro. For most U.S. officials, there was also the concern with Europe's bête noire, the Common Agricultural Policy (CAP). The real issue was whether a European identity, including defense, might define itself as something different than the defense interests of the United States.

Bolton concluded that "everything wrong with the EU's internal decision-making process has now infected NATO."[28]

Others, like Robert Hunter, have been more supportive, arguing that European developments have promoted political support for defense, helped the arguments about not renationalizing defense, offered a stronger partner to the United States, allowed Germany to play a full role, and could be fully compatible with NATO. Hunter talked of an "effective bargain" being struck between the Europeans and the United States in 1996 from which everyone gained—the bargain ensured the supremacy of NATO and that the European Security and Defense Identity (ESDI) would be built within NATO, with the formula of "separable but not separate." Hunter also said: "I never have been able to identify any such major operation, supported by the Europeans, in which we ourselves would not wish to be engaged—and that means NATO."[29] The official position is that, in any significant action, the United States would support a NATO role and would be a part of it. Conversely, it is highly unlikely that the EU would ask the United States to step aside and not participate. If this is true, the United States can actively support ESDP. Some Europeans might say that, given U.S. and EU hesitations over Yugoslavia and Bosnia, the question will become whether either can agree.

When Tony Blair and Jacques Chirac developed the notion of an ESDP in 1998, many U.S. officials were initially hostile. On November 8, 1999, the Senate unanimously passed a resolution that claimed that NATO was the "only military alliance with . . . real defense capabilities," that NATO structures were the "basis for ad hoc coalitions of willing partners among NATO members," and that European NATO members must possess military capabilities that could "operate jointly with the United States."[30] It noted that military operations against the former Republic of Yugoslavia in 1999 had highlighted European shortcomings in command, control, communications, and intelligence resources, combat aircraft, precision-guided munitions, airlift, deployability, and logistics, and the "overall imbalance between the United States and European defense capabilities," which undercuts transatlantic burden-sharing. The Senate argued that "NATO should remain the primary institution through which European and North American allies address security issues of transatlantic concern." All should improve their defense capabilities, particularly through NATO's Defense Capabilities Initiative (DCI). The Senate also noted that the EU wanted to have "the capacity for autonomous action . . . when the Alliance as a whole is not engaged," but it went further by saying that, on matters of common transatlantic concern, the EU should "undertake an autonomous mission through the European Security and Defence Identity *only after* the North Atlantic Treaty Organization had declined to undertake that mission" (italics added). The original motion had carried a connotation that NATO should "assign" tasks to Europe, that the EU was subservient to NATO. However, that was fixed by an agreed amendment. The Senate espoused "improved European capabilities," not "new institutions." It addressed discrimination and duplication by name and decoupling by implication.

The House resolution said much the same thing, although being more vociferous in the praise of NATO, past and present, and adding ground surveillance, readiness, mobility, sustainability, survivability, armaments cooperation, and effective engagement to the list of shortfalls.[31] It also said that CFSP should "complement, rather than duplicate NATO's efforts and institutions, and be linked to, rather than decoupled from NATO structures, and provide for full and active involvement of all European Allies, rather than discriminating against the European Allies that are not members of NATO." The resolution was passed by a vote of 278 to 133, with both the majority and minority being bipartisan.

Both the Senate and the House were reflecting a growing bipartisan concern. In the House the opponents were not so much concerned with specifics, but represented misgivings about the cost of the U.S. role in NATO and NATO's role in 1999. A minority U.S. view was expressed by Representative Brad Sherman of California, who called the European-U.S. relationship, when it came to burden-sharing, the "biggest rip-off in history that the United States has been forced to bear the burden of defending democracy and freedom around the world while a block of countries richer than ourselves does so little."[32]

Since November 1999 the concerns expressed in the Senate and House resolutions have been echoed in the administration, and have continued to be a problem. U.S. legislators have continued to complain about the capabilities of the Europeans, and for some, rebalancing of the transatlantic cost is the only solution. What Congress and the administration will decide in the future is a matter of debate.

Within the administration it may be that the civilian staff tend to downplay the negative aspects of ESDP and the military-minded are looking at the capabilities issues, the relationship with NATO, and residual suspicion of the French. Among leading Republicans a wide difference of opinion has existed, ranging from encouragement of ESDP to the opposition of John Bolton, particularly to the notion of an autonomous European defense capability. At the moment, the administration is supporting ESDP, but it does want ESDP to ensure U.S. leadership and to ensure that NATO remains supreme. Even solid supporters of ESDP do have concerns and there is some hesitation as to whether it is "yes" or "yes but" and where the emphasis should lie. It is unlikely to become "yes yes." Most of the concerns cannot be put to rest in the immediate future.

A major U.S. concern has been that Europeans would put their energies into institutional developments and frameworks, but would neglect capabilities and spending, which could become a distraction from the real problem. In February 2000, Secretary of Defense William Cohen expressed concern that the EU might end up establishing a new bureaucracy without any new military capability.[33] This might convince the Europeans that real progress was being made when it was not. No new structures will change things unless there is an increase in capability that will require an increase in defense spending. To make matters worse, from a U.S. perspective the Europeans might end up with a force that they believe would be able to take independent military action when it cannot and that also complicates NATO efficiency. The question is which comes first—institutions or capabilities?

In some respects the significance of the air campaign over Kosovo in 1999 is ironic. The disparities that were revealed between the capabilities of the United States and the capabilities of the Europeans were a turning point for ESDP. In reviewing Kosovo, William Cohen and the chairman of the Joint Chiefs of Staff, General Henry Shelton, told the Senate Armed Services Committee that "the operation highlighted a number of disparities between U.S. capabilities and those of our allies. . . . The gaps in capabilities that we confronted were real, and they had the effect of impeding our ability to operate at optimal effectiveness with our NATO allies. . . . Such disparities in capabilities will seriously affect our ability to operate as an effective alliance over the long term."[34] Even those sympathetic to ESDP were aware that such a relationship, based on such disparities, would be unhealthy and potentially corrupting. The United States clearly believed in 1999 that having to carry the lion's share of the mission was unhealthy. A similar preponderance of U.S. manpower, firepower, equipment, and resources might not be sustainable in the future, for either the United States or the Europeans. Many U.S. officials accepted that Europeans would not want to feel so dominated again and would want a greater say in conduct of operations. For that reason, despite the objectors, an ESDP is not just tolerable from a U.S. administrative perspective, but essential to maintaining the viability and vitality of the transatlantic link if the burdens can be shared more equally. In an ideal world an ESDP might lessen European resentment of U.S. hegemony, but a problem for the United States was whether the EU was really united on Kosovo and whether it might have a problem on conflicts within states.

Given the technological gap, the fear was that, if Europe did not modernize, the United States would not be able to work with the EU even if it wanted to. If interoperability was to continue to be important, then improvements were necessary. That is why many spoke of the need to make NATO's DCI effective so that the allies could work together.

The DCI was launched at the 1999 Washington NATO summit. It

addressed the need to improve military capability in five key areas: (1) deployment and mobility, (2) sustainability and logistics, (3) command and control information systems, (4) effective engagement (i.e., capabilities to achieve objectives with the lowest possible risk to NATO forces and the lowest possible collateral damage), and (5) survivability of forces and infrastructure.[35] These were translated into fifty-eight short- and long-term objectives, under the leadership of a High-Level Steering Group to coordinate, prioritize, and harmonize the work.

The Alliance has made modest progress in some DCI areas, but in many respects the results have been disappointing, especially with regard to the time scales involved, airlift, command, control, and communications (C^3) capabilities, and the amount of money involved. The most difficult objectives, such as those involving acquisition of expensive platforms or expensive research and development, are years from completion.

For many U.S. officials, the DCI was crucial for NATO. However, they were also critical as to whether the EU was serious about ESDP. The United States took the view that the ESDP headline goal involved medium- and long-term commitments that will take a decade or more to fulfill. While the lower end of the Petersberg tasks might be accomplished, shortfalls in major defense systems and equipment would prevent the EU from leading sustained, higher-intensity military operations. Some hope that, because ESDP is a European initiative, the Europeans will have a greater incentive to strengthen their defense capabilities. As a result the headline goal is a more realistic objective than the DCI, which has too many objectives for most states to consider.

If Europeans were to do more, it might relieve the United States from some of its defense burden, especially if the EU can take on board lower-level conflicts. The United States would then support the new EU defense entity, provided that the relationship with NATO is clarified and that real military effectiveness is achieved. Whether the Europeans build the capabilities will be the real litmus test for many U.S. officials, as well as whether the improvements are in areas that matter in modern warfare. In December 2000 the Department of Defense said that the "'jury is still out' on Europe's willingness, as a whole, to follow through on all agreed DCI objectives,"[36] and this remains the case. For some, the main threat is not that the EU will do too much but that it will do too little.

Resources have been and remain a big issue, partly because European budgets have fallen or remained flat, even if the fall has been generally arrested. Even where there have been European increases, they have been modest and future projections suggest that defense budgets will remain fairly constant over the next four to five years. In 2000 the average NATO share of gross domestic product (GDP) on defense was 2.4 percent, 2.9 percent for the United States, and 2.0 percent for European NATO states. It is not necessarily the size of the budget that is the problem, but the fact that weapons procurement funds will continue to be squeezed as a high proportion of the budget goes to troops and very little, by comparison, goes to equipment. Of nineteen NATO states, seven spent 60–80 percent of their defense budgets on personnel in 2000.[37] There are also disparities between the defense expenditures of the EU states, with Britain and France spending above 2 percent of GDP and Germany and Spain less than 1.5 percent. Germany's annual real growth rate in defense expenditure is projected to be −1.6 percent from 2000 to 2004, with the UK's increasing by slightly less than 1 percent. While Britain spends 40 percent of its defense budget on procurement and research, Germany, Italy, Belgium, and others spend less than 15 percent. Some U.S. officials suggested that, if the EU states were serious about ESDP, they should adopt "convergence criteria" on defense spending, similar to the convergence criteria for the EMU, with research and development and procurement being among the criteria. While many states have conducted defense reviews aimed at reducing force numbers, creating more rapidly deployable forces, and moving toward all-volunteer forces, some of the gains have been slow to come, because of the costs of the transformation.

In addition, the big four in the EU—France, Germany, Italy, and Britain—spent about 25 percent of GDP on social programs, while the United States spent 16 percent.[38] This is one reason why the United States is concerned about the new A400M cargo airlift, as other spending puts pressure on it. Spending has also affected the movement to end conscription and move to an all-volunteer force, which it is hoped will be better trained and more highly skilled. While nearly 70 percent of NATO allies have moved to an all-volunteer force, some have found that the shift has been more expensive than originally planned and has resulted in less savings than expected.

A failure to spend would hurt NATO and ESDP. The Europeans give every indication that they are unwilling to increase their defense expenditure. As in the past, the Europeans are strong on rhetoric but short on results. A European defense dimension will not happen with present military budgets. Indeed, with over 2 million men, Europe was hard-pressed to deploy and maintain 40,000 troops in Kosovo.

Reducing the gaps will demand more money, more political will, more policy cohesion, more efficiency in procurement, better research and development, or "more of everything, and better in everything."[39] One problem is that the United States and the EU will never agree on what an appropriate level of defense spending should be, since they have different threat perceptions and a number of different demands on their budgets, such as pensions, health care, and welfare.

A big problem is getting the Europeans to agree on the new kinds of threats that they, NATO, and the United States are facing—economic inequality, environmental destruction, ethnic and national differences, migration, proliferation of weapons of mass destruction, terrorism (including cyberterrorism), religious conflicts, and resource conflicts, particularly over oil (as Europe may be more sensitive to the stability of oil supplies and prices than it was in the 1970s)—and how to deal with them. A significant part of the problem is missile defense, as the United States looks to Iran, Iraq, Libya, and North Korea. Clearly the United States sees missile defense as crucial, reinforcing the credibility of U.S. security commitments in Europe, and finds the European opposition unusual. For a while it looked as if missile defense could destabilize the relationship, but some of the heat now seems to have gone out of the issue.

The "Three Ds"

Many of the U.S. objections were expressed in the "three Ds"—discrimination, decoupling, and duplication, or as one commentator put it, the "five Ds"—the aforementioned three plus declining commitment to NATO (and competing military staffs) and defense expenditure remaining static.[40]

Apart from particular concerns about Turkey, discrimination was about the non-EU European members of NATO—Turkey, Norway, Iceland, Hungary, the Czech Republic, and Poland—being squeezed out of policy- and decisionmaking. The United States was advancing concern that the traditional mechanism of NATO consensual decisionmaking would be disrupted by the EU having a caucus before NATO meetings. Such discrimination would cause divisions in NATO. If the EU were to decide on military action in a crisis, the door should be open for non-EU members to take part (as was the case in the WEU) in the military intervention, on the basis of the autonomy of the EU decisionmaking under CFSP and ESDP being respected. The non-EU European NATO members would need to be consulted and brought into the process—the question became how. The reasons for involving the non-EU European members were threefold: (1) if the EU was involved, the crisis could escalate and could then involve NATO in an Article 5 commitment; (2) they would be willing to contribute NATO and national assets to EU-led operations; and (3) in any case they contribute to European security in their own right.

It was firmly believed that European NATO non-EU members could make a substantial contribution to an EU-led mission and that the EU would be acting against its own strategic interest if it excluded them. The key U.S. words for some sort of arrangement were "transparency" and "reciprocity" between NATO and the EU, and as a quid pro quo the United

States was willing to allow the four non-NATO EU members to gain transparency into NATO defense planning and access to NATO assets. Again the question became whether that access was to be assured or not. The other question was that, of the fifteen EU members, eleven were NATO states and four were not—Ireland, Austria, Finland, and Sweden—and it was far from clear how they would fit into the arrangement, or whether they would regard such an arrangement as a backdoor membership of NATO. They, and others, are not keen on one U.S. notion, that of EU/NATO membership being complementary.

The United States is worried about duplication, which for some is the most complex argument. The original U.S. line was "no duplication," but this changed to the more elastic "no unnecessary duplication." The catch is that what is unnecessary is in the eye of the beholder. As seen above, everyone agrees that the EU must improve its capabilities. Even the Combined Joint Task Force (CJTF) concept, with its "separable but not separate" forces, would have meant that Europeans were beholden to the United States if they wanted to act, that the United States would have a veto—which of course is what some U.S. officials wanted. However, as Charles Kupchan has said:

> The admonition against the duplication of military assets, while not without merit, is also overwrought. It would obviously make no sense for the EU to create an entirely new set of defence structures paralleling those of NATO. . . . At the same time, the very notion of autonomy implies a healthy measure of duplication. Without some redundancy, Europe will never be able to act without US assistance. . . . Europe will need to maintain its own basic infrastructure, forces and strategic lift. The US should discourage *unnecessary* duplication, but encourage the EU to procure the core assets needed to undertake autonomous action.[41]

However, the United States is worried about the duplicative EU military planning staff. William Cohen said in October 2000 that "what we don't want to see is a separate planning bureaucracy established that is independent and separate from that of NATO itself."[42] He also feared that NATO and the EU could become competing organizations, if there were "uncoordinated, inefficient, and ad hoc responses."[43] That same month, the Department of Defense, in its strategy for strengthening transatlantic security for the twenty-first century, also spoke about the dangers of unnecessary and costly duplication, but went on to say:

> This cooperation should extend to the creation of a common, coherent, and collaborative defense planning review process, a complex area where NATO has proven tools and is willing and able to assist the EU . . . if close consultation takes place at many different levels—political and tech-

nical, formal and informal—with an emphasis on full transparency between the two. The right kind of links will serve the mutual interests of all NATO and EU members.[44]

The United States did not want a second set of forces and commands. It wanted the EU to set up regular and reliable links between ESDP and NATO/the United States, particularly, so that there were no surprises. The key for the United States became having a mature and balanced relationship between NATO and the EU, but a problem emerged in the debate as to whether the United States wanted to say that NATO should have the right of first refusal and that the EU should only engage when the United States chooses not to. A House resolution of November 1999 was clear that CFSP (ESDP) should "complement, rather than duplicate NATO efforts and institutions,"[45] a view with which the Senate concurred, except in its statement that CFSP "should not promote unnecessary duplication."[46] Given the existence of CJTF and NATO, the United States wanted to know why the Europeans had to do their own thing. It might understand if this would harness political support for retaining defense capabilities, and prevent the renationalization of defense. If Europe were to develop an integrated capability able to plug into NATO/U.S. systems, but also able to operate on its own, that would be acceptable and should not lead to any basic incompatibility.

While some claim that "ten years after the Berlin Wall came down, the spectre of de-coupling is once again haunting trans-Atlantic relations,"[47] this does not so much concern ESDP as it does questions about whether NATO can identify a new role that will keep all of its members on board. In respect to ESDP, decoupling was more of a threat for the future, relating to claims and counterclaims about U.S. hegemony. Most accepted that the relationship would need to be rebalanced and that the traditional basis of the transatlantic relationship could not survive. It was also accepted widely (if not universally) that that EU was not about to go off on its own with 60,000 troops, since that capability would be modest and, probably in every conceivable mission, the EU would want U.S. help because of the critical assets that the United States would be able to bring to the expedition. If anything, some would argue that the EU would need to be worried about U.S. commitment—the old story—and perhaps particularly given Senate and House reservations about Kosovo.

Decoupling perhaps was not an immediate threat, because many U.S. officials were aware that the real obstacles to the fulfillment of ESDP were intra-European debates and doubts about capabilities. A reason against decoupling is that the United States knows that there is no Article 5 WEU or NATO guarantee in the EU. There is no formal, legal commitment for the fifteen EU states to defend one another, and without Article 5 of NATO a great deal of confusion would be sown.

One interesting thing about decoupling relates to Britain and Germany. Britain has always been traditionally Atlanticist, rather than European, in its orientation to security matters and it has denied that the ERRF would constitute an independent European army. However, ESDP was a British proposal and Britain maintains a pivotal position in shaping its evolution. This has raised the question of whether Tony Blair, at least in 1999–2000, was more inclined to the EU than to the United States and, given British self-exclusion from the EMU, wanted to put Britain back in the heart of the Europe debate by promoting ESDP. The United States clearly remembers his support over key issues such as Iraq, Kosovo, and September 11, but there remains a fear that he and Britain might be seduced by the EU, so that in the future Britain will look to the EU, and not the United States, for leadership. If Tony Blair, with an EMU referendum in mind, wants to resolve British doubts on membership in the EU, what will be the consequences? According to Stanley Sloan, the "Blair initiative was given the benefit of the doubt. The Administration thought that British motivations were solid," but between St. Malo and Nice the United States believed that the British "had not been 100 per cent transparent about the likely outcome" and that negotiations tended to follow French wishes on "autonomy."[48] In 2002–2003, Tony Blair clearly sided with the United States over Iraq and opened up a huge gulf with most of his European colleagues, particularly the French. That rift may only heal after the passage of several years. Similarly, the United States is watching the Germans to make sure that ESDP does not become too Gaullist. Perversely, it is reassured by German defense cuts, which seem to suggest that the Germans do not take ESDP too seriously. Some have noted the discrepancy between Germany's rhetoric and its actions. They remember too, however, the Germans pushing for a Conference on/Organization for Security and Cooperation in Europe (CSCE/OSCE) solution to the European security problem, their courtship with the French over the Franco-German brigade of 1991 and the Eurocorps of 1995, and German sentiments about U.S. hegemony. However, the United States knows that it is the primary security guarantor for Germany.

Some Europeans hoped that the language of George Robertson, Secretary-General of NATO, would ameliorate the "three Ds" concern. He enunciated the "three Is": improvement in European defense capabilities; inclusiveness and transparency for all Allies; and the indivisibility of transatlantic security, based on shared values. However, it is not clear whether this did ameliorate U.S. concerns, although Strobe Talbott, deputy secretary of state, did accept the redefinition.[49]

Concern with the three Ds has led some, in the U.S. Senate and elsewhere, to wonder whether there could be a new, rational division of labor between the United States and the EU, a more equal sharing of NATO's responsibility. During the 2000 presidential campaign, Condoleezza Rice, now Bush's national security adviser, argued for a new division of labor within NATO that would make the Europeans responsible for peacekeeping duties, such as those in the Balkans and as envisaged in the Petersberg tasks (which are now part and parcel of ESDP), while U.S. troops would give priority to meeting looming security challenges in East Asia, the Persian Gulf, and the Middle East.[50] Alternatively, the Europeans could look after European security and the United States could look after security beyond Europe. In such a scenario ESDP could take over some of the responsibilities that the United States was growing increasingly disinterested in. Of significance is the type of operation that the United States might wish to become involved in, given that Rice and Colin Powell have some reluctance about committing U.S. troops.

A question that emerges is whether the United States would let the EU take the lead and determine policy. Another is whether this would seriously erode the sense of common purpose that is supposed to be at the heart of NATO. The U.S. administration is aware that Europeans can make key military contributions—for example, from 1996 to 2001 Europeans contributed 56–70 percent of the NATO ground troops. It is also aware that multinational operations provide operational benefits of combining resources and capabilities, improving interoperability, shared responsibility, and risk, so that no one state carries the burden. It also appreciates the role of specialized forces, such as the British marines and Special Air Services (SAS).

The United States has noted that, as part of ESDP, there will be a civilian crisis response capability that could include the rapid deployment of 5,000 civilian police and is aware of how helpful this work has been in the Stabilization Force (SFOR) and the Kosovo Force (KFOR). The EU clearly does have skills in humanitarian issues and can perhaps play a role in that area. This leads to two key U.S. positions on ESDP: Will it work? And will it help to keep the Alliance together? It is important to remember that the EU's policy is at a formative stage, as is its relationship with NATO.

The Official U.S. Position
as Outlined in NATO Meetings

In the 1990s, through NATO, the United States also had to cope with EC/EU developments. Just after the EU came into existence on November 1, 1993, the North Atlantic Council (NAC) met in Brussels in January 1994. The NAC acknowledged that the transatlantic link was the bedrock of NATO, but also said that it wanted to further adapt the Alliance to reflect "the development of the emerging European Security and Defence Identity, and to endorse the concept of Combined Joint Task Forces." The CJTF was to give flexibility to respond to security requirements beyond attacks on NATO and to allow non-NATO partners to join in. Whatever the French and others saw in the CJTF, for the United States it was a way of making it possible for NATO to operate more flexibly.

NATO welcomed the Treaty on European Union (TEU), "which will strengthen the European pillar of the Alliance and allow it to make a more coherent contribution to the security of all the Allies," but confirmed that "the Alliance is the essential forum for consultation among its members and the venue for agreement on policies." It gave its "full support" to the development of an ESDI, which it believed would strengthen the European pillar of the Alliance, allow the European allies to take greater responsibility for defense, and reinforce the transatlantic link. It mentioned that the Europeans wanted the WEU to be the defense component of the EU and said that NATO would adjust to this and work in close cooperation with it, on the basis on "complementarity and transparency." Crucially it said:

> We therefore stand ready to make collective assets of the Alliance available, on the basis of consultation in the North Atlantic Council, for WEU operations undertaken by the European Allies in pursuit of their Common Foreign and Security Policy. We support the development of separable but not separate capabilities which could respond to European requirements and contribute to Alliance security. Better European coordination and planning will also strengthen the European pillar and the Alliance itself. Integrated and multinational European structures, as they are further developed in the context of an emerging European Security and Defence Identity, will also increasingly have a similar important role to play in enhancing the Allies' ability to work together in the common defence and other tasks.

To do this, the NAC "endorse[d] the concept of Combined Joint Task Forces as a means to facilitate contingency operations" and agreed that this concept should be developed, with the necessary capabilities established. NATO and WEU were to work on "implementation in a manner that provides separable but not separate military capabilities that could be employed by NATO or the WEU." The CJTF was to be part of NATO's integrated command structure, within which groupings of allies could take on a wide variety of missions outside the NATO area.[51]

Over the next two and a half years, the modalities of CJTFs were worked out by NATO and the WEU. In Berlin in 1996 a ministerial meeting of the NAC again reiterated the acceptance of the ESDI and argued for completion of the CJTF concept, again using the slogan "separable but not separate military capabilities." Berlin was about promoting greater burden-sharing by the Europeans in defense matters, particularly in crisis management.

For the United States, this was a basic bargain to ensure the primacy of NATO, by confirming that the ESDI would be within NATO and not outside it. It was agreed that the ESDI would use the CJTF for planning and the creation of militarily coherent and effective forces capable of operating under the political control and strategic direction of the WEU. NATO would identify the assets, headquarter elements, and command support. WEU operations would be subject to review by the NAC. No separate structures were required and CJTF staff were effectively to be double-hatted—that is, personnel had other responsibilities when not operating in CJTF mode. In effect, the CJTFs were combined national units to be used in contingency situations (notably what became the Petersberg tasks). NATO and the WEU were to have joint exercises to ensure that the CJTF worked. Collectively they were to identify the scope and requirements of WEU missions and submit them to the NAC.[52]

There were to be new CJTF headquarters, which could be transferred whole to the WEU; the assignment of certain NATO staff officers (for example, the Deputy SACEUR, who could become the WEU strategic commander); new capabilities for command and control; a planning function (so that WEU planning could be carried out at NATO's Supreme Headquarters Allied Powers Europe [SHAPE]); and assets such as satellite communications. Given this, for many U.S. officials the argument became what other things the Europeans wanted, since now there were opportunities for different coalitions of the willing to pursue different things. However, it must be said that there had been years of wrangling over the CJTF, especially over how and when Europeans might use U.S. military assets. For the United States, what was agreed in Berlin was an effective bargain and its bottom line. Part of the argument was to become the degree to which subsequent developments in CFSP/ESDP built on or deviated from Brussels and Berlin. It is noticeable that, while the United States supported the European development,

1. ESDI was within NATO,
2. the primacy of NATO and the transatlantic link was asserted,
3. NATO (and the United States) would control the CJTF,
4. the CJTF had to be "separable but not separate" from NATO, and
5. the relationship between ESDI and NATO had to be complementary and transparent.

It is also noticeable that these debates and decisions were taking place before the 1998 developments of ESDP, and, with a euroskeptic Conservative government in London, the United States believed that British opposition and veto would thwart French aspirations.

Before the real idea of ESDP, as opposed to ESDI, was launched, the NAC held another summit meeting in Madrid in 1997. It reiterated the previous NATO positions and welcomed the decisions made at the European Council and the intergovernmental conference (IGC) at Amsterdam. It welcomed the progress made on the internal adaptation of the Alliance's structures, the implementation of the CJTF for WEU-led operations, and the "development of ESDI within NATO, for European command arrangements able to prepare, support, command and conduct WEU-led operations." It also welcomed the adaptations of the command structure in NATO to give Europeans more say and the role of Deputy SACEUR covering ESDI-related responsibilities,[53] although the United States was not too happy about this development.

On the fiftieth anniversary meeting of NATO in April 1999 in Washington, the meeting of the now nineteen heads of state and government in the North Atlantic Council tried to provide an opportunity for NATO to set in motion concrete steps to deal with the future and to take on board the recent developments of ESDP. The United States acknowledged that a key requirement was capabilities and what came to be known as the "three Ds"—decoupling, discrimination, and duplication—and some of the communiqué acknowledged those concerns. The United States mentioned what had been agreed in Brussels and Berlin, talked about "building" ESDI within the Alliance, and launched the DCI. The NAC "welcome[d] . . . the strengthening of a common European policy in security and defence" as agreed at St. Malo and Vienna, believing that a stronger EU would help the "vitality" of the Alliance. Specifically the NAC agreed on the following:

- The EU could have capacity for autonomous action where the Alliance "as a whole" was not engaged.
- There was to be mutual consultation, cooperation, and transparency.
- The commitment of Europeans to improve their defense capabilities was welcomed.
- The commitment of avoiding unnecessary duplication and the commitment to avoid discrimination with non-EU European members of NATO were welcomed.
- There should be "the necessary arrangements for ready access by the European Union to the collective assets and capabilities of the Alliance," although the particulars were to be approved by the North Atlantic Council in permanent session. They would need to "respect the requirements of NATO operations and the coherence of its command structure."

In doing so, the following needed to addressed:

- Assured EU access to NATO operational planning capabilities for EU-led operations, to prevent the creation of an EU counterpart to SHAPE.
- The presumption of availability to the EU of preidentified NATO assets.
- European command options, especially the developing role for the Deputy SACEUR, so that he could be responsible for force generation for NATO and EU operations and would be double-hatted, as operational commander of an EU-led operation while retaining his NATO post.

The Alliance's Strategic Concept said much the same, although it also stated that the CFSP development "would be compatible with the common security and defense policy" established by NATO. It did say, in addition, that the ESDI "will assist the European Allies to act by themselves, as required, through the readiness of the Alliance, on a case-by-case basis and by consensus, to make its assets and capabilities available for operations in which the Alliance is not engaged militarily." This was to be under the WEU or as otherwise agreed as long as it took account of the "full participation of all European Allies if they were so to choose."[54]

The European Union and NATO

Two big controversies concerning EU-NATO relations, which partly involved U.S. concerns, were whether the new developments would be within or outside NATO, and Turkish and Greek tensions about EU assured access to NATO. The first controversy came to haunt debates. ESDI was a mechanism within NATO by which the European allies could gain access to NATO common assets and capabilities for operations led by the WEU. Its objective was a European pillar in NATO. ESDI did not give rise to much concern because of its Alliance framework.

ESDP, autonomous from NATO and within the EU framework, has been different. It was foreshadowed by the TEU inclusion of "defense" in the remit of CFSP, and was brought to the fore by the inclusion, in the Treaty of Amsterdam in 1997, of the Petersberg tasks as the focus of CFSP's defense instrument. For the United States, ESDI is about developments being "within NATO," under the U.S. umbrella, and ESDP is about developments being "outside NATO" and potentially a threat to the U.S. leadership and NATO. Part of the problem in the debate is that *ESDI* and *ESDP* are often used synonymously. Stuart Croft and others have argued that "from the outset . . . ESDI was always a *NATO military project,* essentially designed to solve a number of structural and political problems within the Euro-Atlantic community" but that, at Cologne and Helsinki, *ESDI* was rechristened *ESDP* and took on a new cast "as an inherent part of the EU's long-term political agenda," which was to establish an independent European security policy.[55] As Strobe Talbott said in London in October 1999, the United States "would not want to see an ESDI that comes into being first within NATO but then grows out of NATO and finally grows away from NATO, since that would lead to an ESDI that initially duplicates but that could eventually compete with NATO."[56] In March 2001 Donald H. Rumsfeld argued that "actions that could reduce NATO's effectiveness . . . by perturbing the transatlantic link would not be positive." He went on to say: "Weaken NATO and we weaken Europe, which weakens us all."[57] Put another way: Will ESDP lead to a better defense for Europe and the United States, or is it now heading in a direction that is likely to render the NATO alliance less powerful and less positive? Or even worse, as Senators Jesse Helms and Gordon Smith argued after Nice 2000, "European leaders should reflect carefully on the true motivation behind ESDP, which many see as a means for Europe to check American power and influence *within* NATO. . . . [I]t is in neither Europe's nor America's interests to undermine our proven national relationships in favour of one with a European super-state whose creation is being driven, in part, by anti-American senti-ment."[58] A further concern is that ESDI will lead to an inward view of Europe regarding its involvement and its obligations, both within NATO and more generally.

Many on both sides of the Atlantic would argue that nothing needs to be done beyond NATO. An example of this is the agreement at the meeting of heads of state and government of the North Atlantic Council in Prague in November 2002 to create a NATO Response Force (NRF), which some might see as a putative rival of the ERRF. At Prague it was decided that the new NRF would be "technologically advanced, flexible, deployable, inter-operable and sustainable . . . including land, sea, and air elements ready to move quickly to wherever needed." The NRF was to have "initial opera-tional capability . . . not later than October 2004 and its full operational capability not later than October 2006." Although Prague made reference to the EU Headline Goal, it is not clear what the relationship will be.[59]

The United States looks to NATO as the preferred organization to act wherever possible, in particular to understand the likely threats and decide on the doctrine and capabilities to meet them. U.S.-European relations are the most complete and the most important. The United States would also say that it has supported wider European participation in NATO's new com-mand structure, and that, for example, it has supported European command of operations where European forces predominate on the ground (KFOR) and has also supported EU-inspired operations by making available NATO transport, intelligence, and logistics assets. It would be happy if NATO has first call on forces, including the Eurocorps, and happy if, when NATO assets were transferred to the Europeans, NATO could have them back any time it wanted. The problem for the Europeans is that this represents a U.S. veto on operations. The United States has a veto in the North Atlantic Council about the initial commitment—but this would be more blunt. Even if not NATO, the United States assumes that the NATO framework and cooperation will allow effective cooperation, either through bilateral, regional arrangements, or coalitions of the willing. Officially, the United States can welcome either NATO- or EU-led operations, when NATO as a whole is not engaged, and is keen to nurture and sustain links between NATO and the developing military arm of the EU. Similarly, it sees EU and NATO enlargement as being complementary, with some thinking that EU states that are not members of NATO should become members.

Would it still be true that, faced with a significant international challenge, the first recourse of the United States and the EU would be to each other? The difficulty is that the EU never did see itself as a subset of NATO, or as just a checkbook for policies made elsewhere. Some were more virulent in this approach than others, and some of course thought that they had a special relationship with the United States. Indeed, one could say that the most significant obstacles to ESDP are not between the United States and the EU, but intra-EU debates. There is also concern that EU developments will cause divisions within NATO Europe, undermining NATO cohesion. As Stanley Sloan has said, there is suspicion that the "demands of its institutional creations will encourage 'we/they' distinctions. . . . [T]here are likely to be EU governments and officials who seek to promote the EU's or their own standing by distinguishing European or 'NATO' positions."[60] There have been, and always will be, situations where the U.S. and EU positions are not identical, and where, without their being close ties in NATO, these differences could escalate. Both the United States and the EU must take care to avoid surprises.

The United States hopes that armed forces will restructure and equip for NATO *and* EU missions, rather than for NATO *or* EU missions. They take comfort from the fact that eleven of the fifteen EU states are in NATO and that each state has "but one defense budget and one set of forces. No European country, for example, would be in a position to purchase one set of airlift assets for NATO collective defense purposes or NATO-led crisis response operations and a separate set of assets for EU-led crisis response operations. The same holds true for communications and surveillance equipment, precision guided munitions, and so on."[61] The EU will need U.S./NATO support for everything except for the smallest contingencies, and it is in the EU's interests that NATO and the EU should be complementary. That is one reason why NATO has taken a number of concrete steps to support and link into the development of European capabilities, and has also embarked on cooperation.

There is a counterargument in the United States, namely that if ESDP is about the projection of EU collective will and if the EU is better able to face up to its share of the burdens, then it preserves the Atlantic link and does not destroy it, especially if the current level of dependency between the United States and the EU is unsustainable. For many U.S. officials, there is concern that some Europeans want to withdraw from U.S. leadership or "hegemony" and fragment transatlantic cooperation. They point to "European correspondence" between officials and the extensive level of consultation that now takes place within CFSP as evidence that the EU is beginning to come to increasingly unified positions before consultations or bargaining begins with nonmembers.[62] As a result, they fear that EU machinery might undercut not just NATO but the entire Atlantic alliance.

The other big issue is that of consultation and participation modalities for the non-EU European NATO members. The central issue has been Turkey's demand for representation during all ESDP discussions on security matters and potential operations, regardless of whether or not it was contributing to the operation and despite its not being an EU member. What complicated matters was a series of suggestions concerning interim and permanent solutions. With regard to the latter, there was also the complication of different arrangements for noncrisis ("routine") and crisis ("operational phase") situations. The routine phase would see exchanges of security and defense policy between the EU and the six non-EU European members of NATO plus the applicants, and between the EU and the six non-EU members of NATO. When the EU makes a decision to launch an operation, an ad hoc Committee of Contributors will be established, with all (EU, non-EU NATO European states and applicants) having the same rights.[63] Turkey refused to accept this.

The EU wanted to have autonomy of decisionmaking, to make sure that both NATO and the EU dealt with one another on an equal basis and that it would have assured access to NATO planning structures and assets. It hoped to come to an agreement on the basis of discussion in a series of EU-NATO working groups. Some of this came to fruition. In February 2001 the newly established COPS (Political and Security Committee) of the EU met the North Atlantic Council for the first time under the new permanent NATO-EU consultation arrangements.[64] The first formal ministerial meeting between the new permanent EU bodies and the respective NATO bodies occurred on May 30, 2001, when EU and NATO foreign ministers met in Budapest. This meeting was followed on June 12 by the first formal meeting of the EU's Military Committee and NATO's Military Committee, where they discussed the future development of EU-NATO military cooperation.[65]

The matter of guaranteed access to NATO planning capabilities was the major issue that Turkey used to try to exert leverage on the EU, both in terms of its own application to the EU and for greater representation within ESDP, and given Turkish relations with Greece and the volatility of the area. Turkey was firm in its desire to participate in ESDP decisionmaking in return for access to NATO planning capabilities, and threatened to veto guaranteed and unrestricted EU use of NATO planning capabilities if its concerns were not addressed. It would prefer to provide access on a case-by-case basis. However, late in 2001, Turkey appeared to drop its objections to EU access to NATO planning capabilities, when it agreed to a deal, brokered by the UK, the United States, and the Netherlands. Although details were not made public, it appears that Turkey changed its position after receiving assurances that it would be consulted on operations affecting Turkish interests. Some sources said it was unlikely that any EU military operation will occur in the Aegean or Cyprus.[66] However, Turkey has not been given an actual veto over EU operations. From the EU's point of view, a Turkish veto over EU operations in regions with a security interest to Turkey (not an EU member) would impinge upon the autonomy of the EU. In spite of this apparent success in negotiations, Greece perpetuated the stalemate. It objected to the deal with Turkey and, despite pressure from its fellow EU members, did not approve it. The real crux of the issue was not ESDP, strictly speaking, but the rivalry between Turkey and Greece.

However, late in 2002 a deal was accomplished in two stages. On December 12, 2002, the European Council agreed a declaration that "Cyprus and Malta will not take part in EU military operations conducted using NATO assets once they become members of the EU" and they would not receive "classified NATO information."[67] A few days later a joint EU-NATO declaration on ESDP was issued that committed NATO to "giving the European Union, inter alia and in particular, assured access to NATO's planning capabilities, as set out in the NAC decisions on 13 December 2002."[68] Turkey and Greece appeared to be satisfied with this solution.

Getting It Right?

Maybe Peter Rodham was right when he said that "everything depends on *how it is done*."[69] The game has not finished and a number of complex issues have to be resolved, not least the future direction of Europe and European security and the period of change in transatlantic relationship. Given how much the world has changed since 1989, it is difficult to try to predict the future. It would be wrong to try to portray U.S./EU relations in the last fifty years as "us" or "them." Both the United States and the EU will need to work to ensure that partnership prevails over rivalry in the way that they approach relations with one another. Will the United States continue to be the "invisible guest" at the EU meetings or will the Europeans go it alone? Will the United States adopt a nuanced policy or try to lecture the EU on what it should do?

ESDP ought not to be about rivalry but about synergy and a more balanced transatlantic relationship. The flurry of talks across the Atlantic shows that many are nervous about the outcome, and the United States perhaps needs to come out of the closet. Done right, with close cooperation, maximum transparency, and practical working arrangements between NATO/the United States and the EU, ESDP could strengthen the transatlantic relationship and the ability to manage crises. Done wrong, it could end up wrecking the relationship and NATO. Neither NATO/the United States nor the EU must take each other for granted, just assuming that each will be there.

As Strobe Talbott said in 1999: "If ESDI is misconceived, misunderstood or mishandled, it could create the impression—which could eventually lead to the reality—that a new, European-only alliance is being born out of the old, trans-Atlantic one. If that were to happen, it would weaken, perhaps even break, those ties . . . the ones that bind our security to yours."[70] Part of the answer is for Europeans to take U.S. interests and attitudes fully into account, and to be influenced by their perception of what the United States wants and is likely to do in response.

Both need to try to ensure that "Europe's Headline Goals for 2003 . . . must not be allowed to emerge as America's Deadline Goal."[71] Part of the question, too, concerns what the end goal for this European trend is to be, what sort of governance the Europeans are set on, and in what situation ESDP will be used. One of the things for the United States and the EU to appreciate is that, at the moment, no one knows the end goal. Indeed, looking back over European integration, it is quite clear that while Europe mostly gets to where it wants to go, it usually does so some time later than planned; indeed the EMU took twenty years to come to fruition, and the original EDC Treaty was signed in 1952. Europe is still a work in progress. It must make up its mind about whether it is willing to pay the price for its ambitions.

Notes

1. Louis Galambos, ed., *Papers of Dwight David Eisenhower,* vol. 12, *NATO and the Campaign of 1952* (Baltimore: Johns Hopkins University Press, 1989), pp. 76–77.

2. Stanley Sloan, *The United States and European Defence,* Chaillot Paper no. 39 (Paris: WEU Institute for Security Studies, 2000).

3. Henry Kissinger, *The Troubled Partnership: A Re-appraisal of the Atlantic Alliance* (New York: McGraw Hill, 1965).

4. Karen Donfried and Paul Gallis, *European Security: The Debate in NATO and the European Union,* CRS report to Congress, April 25, 2000, p. 5.

5. Charles A. Kupchan, "In Defence of European Defence: An American Perspective," *Survival* 42, no. 2 (2000): 16.

6. U.S. Department of Defense, *Strengthening Transatlantic Security: U.S. Strategy for the Twenty-First Century* (Washington, D.C., December 2000), pp. 10, 61.

7. Ambassador Robert E. Hunter, senior adviser, RAND Corporation, *Hearing Before the Committee on International Relations,* House of Representatives, 106th Congress, 1st sess. (Washington, D.C., November 10, 1999), p. 80.

8. Catherine Guicherd, *A European Defense Identity: Challenge and Opportunity for NATO,* CRS report to Congress, June 12, 1991, pp. 57–61.

9. Cited in Willem van Eekelen, *Debating European Security 1948–98* (The Hague: Sdu, 1998).

10. Condoleezza Rice, "Promoting the National Interest," *Foreign Affairs* 79, no. 1 (January–February 2000): 45–62.

11. Simon Serfaty, Center for Strategic and International Studies, *Statement to the Subcommittee on Europe of the Committee on International Relations,* House of Representatives, 107th sess. (Washington, D.C., April 25, 2001), p. 39.

12. Kupchan, "In Defence of European Defence," p. 53.

13. Hunter, *Hearing Before the Committee on International Relations,* pp. 32 and 44.

14. John Bolton, *Sunday Times* (London), December 17, 2000.

15. Peter Rodman, *Hearing Before the Committee on International Relations,* p. 35.

16. Douglas Bereuter, *International Herald Tribune,* March 6, 2000.

17. Representative Benjamin A. Gilman, *Hearing Before the Committee on International Relations,* p. 38.

18. Office of International Security Affairs, *United States Security Strategy for Europe and NATO* (Washington, D.C., June 1995), p. 27.

19. U.S. General Accounting Office (GAO), *European Security: U.S. and European Contributions to Foster Stability and Security in Europe* (Washington, D.C., November 2001), p. 38.

20. Christopher Layne, "Death Knell for NATO?" *Policy Analysis* no. 394 (April 4, 2001): 10 (italics in original).

21. William M. Berry, president, European-American Business Council, *Statement to the Subcommittee on Europe,* pp. 60–71.

22. Thomas Pickering, undersecretary for political affairs, address to the Slovak Foreign Policy Association, Bratislava, Slovakia, February 4, 2000, www.state.gov/www/policy.

23. Simon Serfaty, *Hearing Before the Committee on International Relations,* p. 94.

24. Rodman, citing a speech by Chirac at the *Hearing Before the Committee on International Relations,* p. 90.

25. *New York Times,* November 7, 1999.

26. Rodman, *Hearing Before the Committee on International Relations.*

27. Brad Sherman, *Hearing Before the Committee on International Relations,* p. 3.

28. Bolton, *Hearing Before the Committee on International Relations*, p. 68.

29. Hunter, *Hearing Before the Committee on International Relations*, p. 82.

30. Senate Resolution 208, 106th Congress, 1st sess. (Washington, D.C., November 8, 1999).

31. House Resolution 59, 106th Congress, 1st sess. (Washington, D.C., November 2, 1999).

32. Sherman, *Hearing Before the Committee on International Relations*, p. 3.

33. *Financial Times,* February 7, 2000.

34. William Cohen and Henry Shelton, *Joint Statement of William Cohen, Secretary of Defense, and General Henry Shelton, Chairman of the Joint Chiefs of Staff, Senate Armed Services Committee Hearing on Kosovo After-Action Review* (Washington, D.C., October 14, 1999).

35. *Defence Capabilities Initiative,* issued at the North Atlantic Council meeting in Washington, D.C., on April 23–24, 1999, *NATO Review* no. 2 (Summer 1999): D16.

36. U.S. Department of Defense, *Strengthening Transatlantic Security,* p. 17.

37. U.S. GAO, *European Security,* p. 6.

38. Ibid., p. 39.

39. Serfaty, *Statement to the Subcommittee on Europe,* p. 14.

40. Serfaty, *Hearing Before the Committee on International Relations,* pp. 36–37.

41. Kupchan, "In Defence of European Defence," p. 24.

42. William Cohen, U.S. secretary of defense, Department of Defense news briefing, Birmingham, October 10, 2000.

43. William Cohen, NATO press conference, December 5, 2000.

44. U.S. Department of Defense, *Strengthening Transatlantic Security,* p. 21.

45. House Resolution 59.

46. Senate Resolution 208.

47. Ivo Daalder, *Wall Street Journal Europe,* December 10, 1999.

48. Sloan, *The United States and European Defence,* pp. 15–18.

49. Strobe Talbott, deputy secretary of state, address to the North Atlantic Council, December 15, 1999.

50. Rice, "Promoting the National Interest."

51. *Declaration of the Heads of State and Government,* North Atlantic Council, Brussels, January 10–11, 1994, *NATO Review* no. 1 (February 1994): 30–33.

52. Ministerial Meeting of the North Atlantic Council, Berlin, June 3, 1996, *NATO Review* no. 4 (July 1996): 30–35.

53. *Madrid Declaration on Euro-Atlantic Security and Cooperation,* issued by the Heads of State and Government, North Atlantic Council, Madrid, July 8, 1997, *NATO Review* no. 4 (July–August 1997): D1–D4.

54. *Washington Declaration, Summit Communiqué,* and the Alliance's *Strategic Concept,* issued by the Heads of State and Government, Washington, D.C., April 23–24, 1999, *NATO Review* no. 2 (Summer 1999): D1–D13.

55. Stuart Croft, Jolyon Howorth, Terry Terriff, and Mark Webber, "NATO's Triple Challenge," *International Affairs* 76, no. 3 (July 2000): 503–504 (italics in original).

56. Strobe Talbott, speech to the Royal Institute of International Affairs, London, October 7, 1999.

57. Donald H. Rumsfeld, U.S. secretary of defense, Munich Conference on European Security Policy, March 3, 2001.

58. *Daily Telegraph,* December 28, 2000.

59. NATO press release (2002) 127, November 21, 2002.

60. Sloan, *The United States and European Defence,* p. 44.

61. U.S. Department of Defense, *Strengthening Transatlantic Security,* p. 20.

62. Bolton, *Hearing Before the Committee on International Relations,* p. 69.

63. Council of the European Union, *Presidency Report to the Feira European Council on "Strengthening the Common European Policy on Security and Defence"* (Brussels, June 15, 2000), apps. 1–2.

64. Terry Terriff, Mark Webber, Stuart Croft, and Jolyon Howorth, *European Security and Defence Policy After Nice,* briefing paper, New Series no. 20 (London: Royal Institute of International Affairs, April 2001), p. 2.

65. Council of the European Union, *Draft Presidency Report on the European Security and Defence Policy* (Brussels, December 12, 2000), 14056/3/00, annex 7.

66. "Turkey 'Deal' on Rapid Reaction Force," *BBC News,* December 3, 2001, http://news.bbc.co.uk.

67. Copenhagen European Council, *Presidency Conclusions,* December 12–13, 2002, SN400/02, declaration of the Council meeting in Copenhagen on December 12, 2002.

68. NATO press release (2002) 142, December 16, 2002.

69. Rodman, *Hearing Before the Committee on International Relations,* p. 92.

70. Strobe Talbott, address to the Royal United Services Institute, November 3, 1999.

71. Serfaty, *Statement to the Subcommittee on Europe,* p. 33.

7

Sovereignty, Arms, and Industry

The Policy Environment

The events since 1998, especially St. Malo and Kosovo, have changed the policy environment in the development, production, and sale of weapons. As Pierre de Vestel argued: "Public policy, whether it be industrial and technological or concerning security and defence, contributes in profoundly affecting the technological, industrial and social dimensions of armaments production."[1] However, as the North Atlantic Treaty Organization (NATO) has discovered over fifty years, there is something special about armaments policy, as member states are unwilling to pool sovereignty in such an important strategic and political area.

Member states have been reluctant to go beyond an insistence on preserving national sovereignty in this area of policy and have been more hesitant about transferring power than in those other spheres of policy that have been the hallmark of half a century of European integration. In foreign policy and security, caution has reigned. Member states have been mindful of the fact that "foreign policy" and armaments touch directly on those factors that make a state a state—that is, the status of sovereignty.

Given contract-theory explanations of the origins and nature of the state—that it is to protect the lives and property of its citizens—and the role of external sovereignty in defining a state as a state, any encroachment upon the foreign, defense, and armaments policy by outside agencies threatens the very concept and existence of a state. The management of political relations between a state and other states is a criterion of statehood. Thus, member states of the European Union have always been extremely reluctant in practice to transfer any power of decision to another agency.

181

According to Keith Krause, there are three reasons why states wish to maintain a defense industry: pursuit of victory or survival in war, pursuit of power and identity, and pursuit of wealth.[2] The question now is whether these factors apply to the European Union. Will they accept that, "as a result of the growing internationalisation of security and defence issues, the European countries will progressively have to resort to more systematic or institutionalised forms of cooperation"?[3] Or will the EU member states maintain a situation whereby "there is no instance of integration in defence issues in Europe in the sense of a transfer of national sovereignty to an institution or supranational decision-making procedures"?[4]

EU member states seem reluctant to sacrifice their own independent balanced forces and to trust others by relying on them to provide armed forces. They prefer to have their own tastes and preferences for defense, with differing perceptions of manpower and equipment needs. Moreover, member states have remained caught in the tension between, on the one hand, wanting to both speed up the process for decisionmaking and enhance the prospect of decision, and on the other hand, wishing to safeguard their own capability to obstruct any proposed decision that they may object to. In Amsterdam, after much debate on the Common Foreign and Security Policy (CFSP), they agreed to make it more difficult for member states to obstruct the process, but nonetheless provided them with the facility, "for important and stated reasons," to oppose the majority.[5] However, they were also clear that there could be no question of the qualified majority vote for decisions that have "military or defence implications," and this has remained true on armaments.

Integration covering defense industries was excepted from economic integration, and the European Union has a smaller role in the regulation of the defense industry than in other sectors because of the old Article 223.1(b) of the European Economic Community (EEC/EC) Treaty, which said that

> any member state may take such measures as it considers necessary for the protection of the essential interests of the security which are connected with the production of or trade in arms, munitions and war material; and such measures shall not adversely affect the conditions of competition in the common market regarding products which are not intended for specifically military purposes.[6]

The question was asked over the years whether there could be a less restrictive interpretation than has been the case. While the above article is still in the EEC Treaty (296.1[b]), the Treaty of Amsterdam amendments to the Treaty on European Union (TEU) did introduce a new clause: "The progressive framing of a common defence policy will be supported, as

Member States consider appropriate, by cooperation between them in the field of armaments."[7]

But progress has been slow, as will be seen. The question now is whether there is sufficient pressure to bring about a less restrictive policy than in the past, especially since, for nearly fifty years, states in the EC/EU have been pursuing "ever closer union" and trying to construct some sort of political union. But the European Union is also composed of fifteen member states, with fifteen different legal systems that contribute to the continued existence of national citadels (particularly through laws on public-sector contracts),[8] and the complex pillar structure.

Spillover

There have been attempts to forge a common defense policy, and an integrated industrial policy, which at various times touched upon an armaments policy. In addition to that political aim, there has also been the functional aim of improving the economics and management of armaments development, production, and sales, especially given the idea that certain elements of this industry can no longer be managed at the national level. Over the years there have been arguments about which comes first: the political or the functional. Those arguments have now a new lease on life.

On the one hand, as has been shown in previous chapters, there is the movement to the European Security and Defense Policy (ESDP), whose political will and new institutional mechanisms might pave the way for an across-the-board rationalization. On the other hand, there are functional and industrial arguments that might lead to an industrial regeneration of European defense.

One such factor is the impact of the reduction in defense budgets in the 1990s and beyond, with world defense spending declining by a third, with a consequent reduction in markets both in Europe and overseas. Another factor is that as fewer European resources go into research and development and as defense inflation makes it more difficult for states to manufacture and acquire unilaterally a full range of high-technology weapons, there is a premium on longer production runs, more efficiency, and more competition. These have added to the pressure for rationalization and mergers among the European defense industry. There is recognition that a fragmented market makes the "internal functioning of transnational companies extremely complicated [and] creates costly duplication and weakens the governments' positions as customers *vis à vis* the new transnational champions."[9] While there has been a lowering of trade barriers and the establishment of the Single Market, this has not occurred in the arms trade, and there is no genuine free market in defense goods. Defense procurement has met national needs, but with the impossibility of states funding national solutions, the question now is whether the EU can hope to secure some of these national defense interests by action on the continental scale.

This may come about as the result of what William Wallace calls "informal integration": "intense patterns of interaction which develop without the impetus of deliberate political decisions, following the dynamics of the markets, technology, communications networks, and social change . . . a continuous process, a flow: it creeps unawares out of the myriad transactions of private individuals pursuing private interests."[10] As will be seen below, there is now an intense network of European relationships. This has been partly fueled by the fears of competition and hegemony from the United States, especially given U.S. industrial restructuring, so that a European industry would be able to compete and avoid Europeans becoming the "metal-bashers."

Some of these functional arguments were very important in the early theorizing about the EC/EU. Spillover, which was defined by Leon Lindberg as the process whereby "a given action, related to a specific goal, creates a situation in which the original goal can be assured only be taking further actions, which in turn create a further condition and a need for more action, and so forth," was regarded as the way forward.[11] A big question for the EU is whether this was and is true.

The founder of neofunctionalism, Ernst Haas, came to the "inevitable conclusion" that "functional contexts are autonomous. Integrative forces which flow from one kind of activity do not necessarily infect other activities, even if carried out by the same organisation."[12] Lindberg in turn argued that successful integrative steps might actually have a negative effect on the prospects for further integration.[13] So, while in the economic sphere there has been a step-by-step economic integration—a customs union, a single market, an economic and monetary union—there has been no beguiling automaticity leading to political integration or integration on armaments.

Even the Economic and Monetary Union (EMU) owed a lot to the political leadership of Helmut Kohl. Significant developments in the EU have depended upon political leadership by national elites and political agreements between states. The EC/EU is the victim of its own success— that is, it has partially or in some cases fully achieved most of its basic objectives, particularly in the economic sphere. Many have begun to feel that the need for radical solutions has passed, that a somewhat patched-up system of states could suffice. The EC/EU has done enough to satisfy its members—that is, they know that the current stage of development is not the optimal solution to Europe's problems and needs, but to many it is satisfactory and "good enough."

Twenty-five years ago Werner Feld and John Wildgen argued:

> Apparently, getting to know integration is not the same thing as getting to love it—at least in the political form. If we can think of experience with expert working groups as a socialisation exercise, then in the case of the political integration it is counter-productive. On the other hand, expert working group experience does seem somewhat productive of attitudes supportive of economic integration. This set of findings is largely consistent with trends in the literature on European integration downgrading expectations for spillover effects. The mere fact of having to work together does not uni-directionally impel integrative attitudes.[14]

This seems to be particularly significant in the field of armaments, given the notion of sovereignty and that defense has historically been set apart from the rest of European integration agenda. In the Single Market and EMU, the detailed consequences of policies are unpredictable, but in principle it is possible to make rational assessment of advantages and disadvantages.

Strategic Culture

Given this unpredictability, Alyson Bailes was probably right to ask whether there are self-evidently distinct "European models" or a "European set of values" in the organization and conduct of defense, or a common strategic culture.[15] At what point will member states be able to support a common defense policy or common defense, based on the Brussels Treaty obligation to "afford any Party so attacked all military and other aid in their power"?[16] Part of the problem here is that it must be questioned whether EU member states have ever seriously considered what is involved, whether there is a growing acceptance of a European frame of reference. The sorts of questions that have bedeviled a European frame of reference concern:

- different defense experiences and geopolitics situations of member states
- differences in size of member states and the conditions of their defense industries
- differences in ethics on weapons and exports
- failure to agree upon a genuine, viable, and common foreign policy
- lack of a common strategic culture
- lack of a common assessment of threats and risks, with agreed notions of where the EU is vulnerable
- lack of a common assessment of how to respond to such threats and risks

- no uniformity in manpower and training policy
- no or little movement toward common control, intelligence, and communications systems
- little movement toward proper funding of CFSP, ESDP, and armaments, even if this means significant increases in EU resources
- doubts about how many are willing to act on behalf of the Union
- doubts about how many are willing to accept casualties for the Union
- hesitations over the conditions under which capabilities should be deployed
- doubts over whether there exists a credible willingness to act when the agreed conditions exist
- reluctance to agree a division of responsibility or of labor
- failure to agree a customs barrier toward armaments import
- failure to establish a single authority responsible for armaments
- hesitations over deciding on a European preference in procurement

Before real progress can be made toward an ESDP, or a common defense industrial policy, solutions have to be found to these questions. Europeans have struggled to cope with these issues over the years—are they better able to cope now?

Particularly given the sensitivities of the "neutrals" and of NATO and the Western European Union (WEU) members, can such divisions be overcome? Do the Europeans share the same definitions of security? Can they agree on a strategic culture? Leaving aside the vexed question of the neutrality of Austria, Finland, Sweden, and Ireland during the Cold War, it is hardly surprising that they have a different attitude toward defense and security compared to, say, the British and the French. Will September 11, 2001, make them less keen on the soft view of security?

Is Jocelyn Mawdsley right to talk of the need to "reconcile national armaments policy cultures [given that] past national policy culture differences have caused collaborative projects to fail"?[17] Is it culture that partly explains the problems of homogeneity? Certainly, in the past, culture appears to have done so, with the French tending toward Colbertism and the British unable to decide between the Atlantic and Europe, and how to ensure value for money for every pound (£) spent.[18]

Despite this, particularly since the signing of the Single European Act (SEA) in 1986, the Tony Blair–Jacques Chirac initiative in 1998, and the altered domestic and international environments, the pressures of European integration and the internationalization of the defense industry have continued apace. The intensity of EU political and economic interdependence should not be underestimated. In May 1999 Blair said:

There is much talk of structures. But we should begin with capacities. To put it bluntly, if Europe is to have a key defence role, it needs modern forces, strategic lift and the necessary equipment to conduct a campaign. No nation will ever yield up its sovereign right to determine the use of its own armed forces. We do, however, need to see how we can cooperate better, complement each other's capabilities, have a full range of defence options open to us. This means greater integration in the defence industry and procurement. If we were in any doubts about this before, Kosovo should have removed them.[19]

The shortfalls of EU equipment were made even clearer at the Capabilities Commitment Conference in Brussels on November 20–21, 2000, and the follow-up Conference on EU Capability Improvement in Brussels on November 19, 2001. There is now, perhaps, a recognition that to be truly effective, defense policy must be independent and can only find its real expression through forces, personnel, and equipment that are its to command. Both in the last few years and before, there have been three types of response: the institutional, the industrial, and the transatlantic, although they all relate to each other.

Institutional Collaboration

One of the trickier parts of institutional collaboration is that it can be seen as forming a club or regime "with countries and firms joining so long as membership is expected to be worthwhile . . . governments create a club; they determine the rules for entry and exit, they set the entry fee and they distribute the benefits of membership through agreements to share the work between club members and their national producers . . . club rules will reflect the behaviour of 'actors' in each nation's political market place . . . votes, bureaucracies . . . and firms."[20]

Because of this, armaments procurement in Europe has seen something of an alphabet soup of different acronyms and institutions, and for most of the past fifty years the progress has not been very successful. There was no collaborative procurement strategy built into the original NATO, there has been competition between international collaboration and national citadels, there was imbalance across the Atlantic, and there have been the built-in restrictions on what the EC/EU could do. For all the talk in NATO about rationalization, interoperability, and standardization, until the mid-1980s, when costs began to rise exponentially, there was no good track record.

Groups within NATO, like the Conference on National Armaments Directors, established in the late 1960s, failed to produce or had a mixed record, and others outside NATO, like the Independent European Program

Group (IEPG—all the NATO European members except Iceland), founded in 1976 to promote European cooperation and to improve European competitiveness with the U.S. industry, did not greatly help either.

The role of the WEU had been extremely limited, although as part of the new energy to be put into armaments cooperation, in December 1991 in a declaration attached to the Maastricht Treaty the WEU did say that it would "examine further . . . enhanced cooperation in the field of armaments with the aim of creating a European armaments agency."[21] Following this, an armaments group was created in the WEU, the Western European Armaments Group (WEAG), which established in November 1996 the Western European Armaments Organization (WEAO), within which cooperation could be carried out. These WEU innovations, including the assumption of the responsibilities of IEPG and Eurogroup, had limited results. They became yet another forum for discussion. They lacked real decisionmaking powers (taking nonbinding decisions by consensus) and the members lacked political commitment.[22]

In the last few years, three European frameworks of armaments cooperation or organization have become more important: the European Union, OCCAR (Organisme Conjoint de Coopération en Matière d'Armement; Organization for Joint Armament Cooperation), and the Letter of Intent framework.

European Union

The EU has been constrained in armaments cooperation, and even what was agreed in Amsterdam only allowed the member states to cooperate together in ways and means of their own choosing—bilaterally or multilaterally and with or without the Commission. Competence was not given to European Union institutions nor was there to be a legally binding framework with jurisdiction by the European Court of Justice. Amsterdam rejected calls to repeal Article 223.

The Commission has had to use other competencies to try to influence outcomes: its powers over mergers and competition, control of exports of dual-use goods and technology, and the Common Customs Tariff (CCT), although on the latter two its role is restricted by member states. It can also try to use some of the EU budget for armaments-related issues, such as structural funds and research and technology, but the budget has to be approved by the European Parliament and Council. The Commission is well aware that closer cooperation on military purchases is an important and necessary element in developing a policy that will encourage industrial innovation and industrial policy. It also wishes to encourage European competitiveness globally (in both defense and technology-based goods) and to help secure a defense identity. In 1997 the Commission addressed these issues in a primarily economic manner in a report on implementing EU strategy in defense-related industries, which listed fourteen items that it would like to see the Community become more involved in: intracommunity transfers, the status of new European transnational companies, the openness of public contracts to all in the Community, research and development, customs duties de-regulation, innovation, technology transfer, competition, export promotion, structural funds as incentives, direct and indirect taxation harmonization, principle of access to markets, standardization of performance, and problems related to enlargement.[23]

The difficulty then and now is that the Commission is not master in its own house, and member states have wished to retain the right to procure military equipment in ways that best suit their own strategic and industrial interests. However, encouraged by the momentum provided by ESDP, in 2001 the Commission organized a conference on European defense procurement in the twenty-first century. The theme was that there needs to be a more coordinated and transparent standardization system, but again the Commission needs member state support.

Without moving to theoretical arguments about "who governs" in the European Union,[24] in the areas under discussion the role of the fifteen member states either unilaterally or intergovernmentally or in the EU Council is crucial. This is epitomized by the decisions at the Edinburgh European Council in December 1992 and in a protocol to the Amsterdam Treaty that made it clear that Denmark would "not participate in the elaboration and the implementation of decisions and actions . . . which have defense implications";[25] and in the Seville decision in June 2002 that Ireland had a policy of "military neutrality."[26] Both of these will have some impact on EU action on armaments procurement.

Legally the Council remains the relevant forum for policy, but it has restricted itself to political obligations only. It did set up in 1993 the Working Group on Exports of Conventional Arms (COARM) and in 1995 the Working Group on European Armaments Policy (POLARM). COARM concerns armaments exports to third countries, and has worked on the basis of eight export criteria determined by European Councils in Luxembourg in June 1991 and Lisbon in June 1992. These were adopted by the Council in June 1998 as the Code of Conduct on Arms Exports. Again these criteria are politically binding only.

The 1998 code was a Council "statement." It concerns cases where exports should be avoided and an agreement whereby if one state refuses to sell arms to a third country, another state will not step in and sell arms to it. The eight criteria are: respect for international commitments of member states; respect for human rights; having regard to the internal situation in the country; regional peace and stability; the national security of the state; the attitude of the buyer state; the risks of diversion to another state; and whether the exports conform to the technological capacity of the buyer.[27] As is usual in the EU, there can be many viewpoints as to what these criteria mean and how they can be applied.

Despite POLARM, like COARM, meeting six times a year and reporting to the Committee of Permanent Representatives (Coreper), it has found progress difficult to achieve because of fundamental differences between states over an intergovernmental versus a more Union role, the role of the state in the defense industry, and different conceptions of defense.

The European Parliament has long taken an interest in defense policy and armaments, but has no real power except for those competencies it shares with the Commission and its veto over the budget. One of the Parliament's first reports was prepared by Egon Klepsch in 1978. This was seen by many as a landmark in the evolution of European defense, although the actual report was careful to avoid grandiose claims, emphasizing instead the need to build on "existing institutions rather than to introduce a new one." It rehearsed what would become standard arguments—for example, that arms production was an important part of industrial policy, that only the Community would produce a structured market for procurement and sales, and the issue of competition with the United States. Klepsch also called for some rationalization of agencies.[28]

Since then the Parliament has issued a number of reports—for example, the 1997 report by Gary Titley on the Commission's proposals for European defense industries, and the 1998 report by Leo Tindemans on a EU common defense policy.[29] The real problems for the institutions are the different pillars of the EU, the nature of the treaty, the intransigence of governments, and the question of where defense and defense industries fit in.

OCCAR

Given the limitations of the European Union, it may be that initiatives outside the EU will be more promising with respect to European defense industries and armaments procurement. One such organization is OCCAR, which was established on November 12, 1996, by France, Germany, Italy, and Britain. It built upon emerging Franco-German cooperation on armaments and their agreement to establish an armaments agency to manage all their joint projects. They and other developments were frustrated by what had gone before. OCCAR is open to other states. Belgium and the Netherlands are the most interested, and Sweden has expressed some desire for membership. Newcomers have to accept the principles of OCCAR and take part in at least one of its programs. Interestingly, all OCCAR states are members of the EU. OCCAR is the first European program-management organization with integrated transnational teams (involving both governments and industry), but it can have broader missions.

In order to award contracts OCCAR has a legal personality and is based on the following five principles: (1) programs—obtain greater cost efficiency through new program management methods, more efficient procedures for letting contracts, and integrated industrial project management; (2) preparation for the future—coordination of long-term needs under joint policy for investment in technology; (3) procurement—improvement of the European defense industrial base, bringing companies closer together, developing identical rules for competitive tendering; (4) industrial cooperation—abandoning an analytical calculation of industrial *juste retour* on a program-by-program basis and replacing it with the pursuit of an overall multiprogram/multiyear balance; and (5) involvement of other partners—possible association of other European countries if all partners are agreed.[30]

In addition, OCCAR members have agreed to a European preference for equipment, or at least an OCCAR preference, although if there is reciprocity, competition can be extended. OCCAR is trying to achieve the consolidation of procurement efforts to give them more focus and to actually integrate some programs. It seeks complementary activity among its members. Most importantly, and practically, it has tried to break away from the principle of *juste retour* on particular programs, which often decreases efficiency. *Juste retour* and similar work-share arrangements mean that contracts are awarded on the basis of bargaining and not of competition, that the role of states remains too important compared to industry and the project, and that contracts take longer and involve duplication. If OCCAR can lead to management teams being held accountable for projects based on sound economic, technological, and management structures and can be given more programs, this would be an advance. How much is transferred to OCCAR will also tell a story, but it is an important beginning.

The Letter of Intent Framework

The Letter of Intent states are concerned with the supply side, namely industry. In July 1998, six defense ministers of the main European arms-producing states—France, Germany, Italy, Spain, Sweden, and the UK—signed a Letter of Intent specifying their objectives in encouraging the transnational restructuring of the defense industry in Europe. Ninety percent of the defense reorganization in Europe in the previous ten years had taken place in those six states. They accounted for 80 percent of armaments procurement in Europe and 90 percent of the armaments industrial capacity. They accepted that industrial restructuring would likely lead to the abandonment of some national capacity, and would involve mutual dependence.

The six states agreed six principles that would help industry by making it easier for companies to work together: (1) security of supply for the benefit of all signatories, no unfair practices or discrimination, and no unilateral prohibitions on exports; (2) agreement on basic principles governing exports, agreed by consensus; (3) the security of classified information on the basis of a "need to know"; (4) providing each other with information from their research and technology programs, their strategies, and their current and planned programs; (5) treating each other's technical information as it treated its own domestic industry; and (6) beginning to harmonize the military requirements of their armed forces by agreeing a common concept of force employment and a common understanding of corresponding military capabilities, and by developing harmonized force development and equipment acquisition planning.

In effect, this framework was about encouraging the creation and efficient working of transnational companies in the defense field, so that the companies could exploit their advantages. This was predicated upon the industry being primarily responsible for certain evolving structures and reorganization. It was hoped that lifting excessive constraints would help in building up new and powerful technological companies.

Some of the agreements were to be practical, legally binding measures. In July 2000 the six states signed an agreement establishing a restrictive legal framework fixing the above six principles. The aim again was to develop a more common approach between companies and states, and along with the development of OCCAR to provide the defense industry with a more favorable environment through a common framework.[31]

The six Letter of Intent states have demonstrated a will to succeed and the July 2000 agreement shows that they wish to move forward. However, there are still doubts about cooperation on research and technology and how far the harmonization requirements will go.

Defense Industry

With the help of governments, European firms have over forty years of experience with collaborative projects, some of which were successful and others not. For the most part, many of these schemes were government created, and were motivated by political rather than military or economic reasons. All of these projects operated on the principle of *juste retour,* and the key was the reality of a symbiotic relationship between the state and key defense industry companies—they needed each other. Things have now begun to change.

After the end of the Cold War, as seen above, defense spending dropped and the EU fifteen lost over 600,000 jobs in the defense industry. In the UK alone employment fell from over 600,000 jobs in the mid-1980s to 350,000 in the mid-1990s. National reactions in Europe were mixed, but it did lead to a greater consolidation of manufacturers within and between states, and an increasing number of joint ventures. For Europe there was the additional problem of fear of the consequences of the rapid and radical nature of the U.S. restructuring. Toward the end of the 1990s there were still ten European tank and armored vehicle manufacturers, ten helicopter producers, eleven missile companies, and fourteen warship yards. In each category, the United States fielded five companies or less.[32] The Europeans also had to come to terms, again, with the fact that the U.S. domestic defense market was much bigger than that of Europe (by about 100 percent), and that European NATO research and development at the end of 1990s was $9.7 billion (90 percent by Britain, Germany, and France) compared with $35.9 billion in the United States.[33] Not only did spending fall, but in the new environment of the 1990s Europeans had to cope with new types of conflict, which required equipment different from that which had protected the Central Front.

It came to be realized that national citadels were impossible to maintain, that national self-sufficiency was anachronistic, and that, like the momentum that led to and created the Single Market between 1985 and 1992, something needed to be done about the fragmented European market. The compartmentalization of the defense markets has been and remains a problem. As Christophe Cornu points out, "a European defence industry does not really exist, nor a homogeneous European market."[34]

Cornu argues that there are different categories of states in Europe when it comes to defense equipment needs: some have a good technological and industrial basis and are developed (for example, Britain and France), while others lag behind on technology, industrial basis, and development (for example, Greece and Portugal).[35] When NATO became involved in the former Yugoslavia (some fifty years after NATO was formed), it still found that the national equipment used in SFOR and KFOR by NATO members differed greatly.

Under President Chirac, even the French began to move on this issue and began to encourage mergers and more collaboration with Germany and others (see above). Increasingly, therefore, a more open defense market began to emerge, with further and faster creation of pan-European companies and the creation of a number of European firms that could compete in one particular defense industrial sector.

In 1999 the European Defense Industries Group (EDIG), a conglomerate of the national associations of defense companies in the former WEU, began to articulate their requirements for the future. In effect, they wanted governments to agree on common requirements and some common policies.[36] They wanted a European defense equipment market whose regulations would be competitive. They would accept interdependence and transnational budgetary measures as long as the markets were opened up on a reciprocal and equitable basis, although they preferred a "buy European" preference by governments. Most important, they sought the harmonization of military operational requirements. They also wanted increased spending for a comprehensive European research and development policy and a program of funded European demonstrator projects. In effect, they looked for the full political and military support of European governments, particularly with regard to exports.

Industry has begun to respond. In the late 1990s mergers began to take place: a new French grouping, Aerospatiale Matra Hautes Technologies (MHT)–Dassault Aviation, emerged in 1998; in 1999 the merger between British Aerospace (BAe) and the General Electric Company (GEC)–Marconi Group took place; and then there was Thales, the former Thomson-CSF group. In October 1999 the French prime minister, Lionel Jospin, and the German chancellor, Gerhard Schröder, announced the merger of Aerospatiale Matra and DaimlerChrysler to form the European Aeronautic, Defense, and Space Company (EADS). EADS became the third largest aerospace, missile, and satellite company in the world, behind Boeing and Lockheed, and had a turnover of £14 billion. Not far off is the new BAe Systems, which had a turnover of £11.5 billion. The two groups have also begun to work together on Airbus, missiles, Astrium in space, and the Eurofighter. Clearly in some industrial regroupings, there has been a marriage between political will and industrial logic. Europe, however, still has a long way to go before it matches the United States.

The question that emerges is how far such restructuring among small and medium-sized firms will go. What may make the process simpler is the political agreement of December 2000 by the EU governments to approve the European Company Statute, which makes restructuring across borders easier. Companies choosing to become Societies Europaea (SE) will be able to register themselves under a single model and under a uniform legal structure, while operating throughout the EU states. The new statutes will not be fully operational until 2004.

As can be seen, governments are involved in the restructuring of the armaments and defense industry and so are companies. As has become clear in this book, even if governments are the customers, regulators, and facilitators, the time scale for achieving some of these objectives is likely to be flexible. Some objectives may be impossible to achieve and changes can take a long time to implement. It is not governments who will determine the shape of the European industry or dictate who merges with whom, but industry itself.

The Transatlantic Dimension

As with many arguments about European defense, and accouterments surrounding ESDP, the relationship between Europe and the United States must be taken into account. On armaments procurement there has been a long history of Europeans buying U.S. equipment, initially because after 1945 the United States was unchallenged in both industrial and technological power. Many of the first initiatives were government led, but increasingly over the last ten years industry-led developments have taken over with alliances—for example, the April 2000 memorandum between EADS and Northrop Grumman to explore opportunities in the defense market, and an increased number of acquisitions by Europeans, especially the British, of smaller U.S. companies. It could be argued that companies are now more likely to be influenced by balance sheets, shareholders and stock markets, and business strategy than some of their traditional concerns about government policy, either domestically or internationally.

There are a number of reasons for transatlantic arrangements. There is a degree of interdependence politically, economically, and industrially across the Atlantic, as well as repeated NATO calls for rationalization, standardization, and interoperability. Both sides have resource problems with pressure on budgets and the resultant will to avoid duplication. Both sides hope that collaboration will ease access to markets and other programs. They hope that such arrangements will allow them to influence the future choices of governments and companies.

However, the difficulty until now has been the dominance of the U.S. market, industry, and technology, which has fueled claims of a "Fortress America." The United States has one enormous market, and for a long time exports were the icing on the cake. Recently, given the slide in defense spending, the U.S. government has become much hungrier for its defense industry to involve itself more forcefully in the competition for arms sales, and has promoted arms sales as a way to help. It has used its superpower status to secure advantages for its defense industry. The U.S. government, early after the Cold War, helped to stimulate restructuring and rationalization in the United States by easing antitrust laws and subsidizing contractors for the costs of consolidation, and by helping to create the conditions for horizontal and vertical mergers. As Gordon Adams points out, the result was "the fairly rapid emergence of four major aerospace firms: Northrop Grumman, Lockheed Martin, Boeing, and Raytheon. The aerospace/defence activities of the more diversified companies—General Electric, Ford, Texas Instruments and Hughes, among others—disappeared into these four firms."[37] These processes have continued.

A difficulty with such U.S. preponderance has been the questions the economic and technological imbalance raises in European minds, because the United States and Europe are not equal partners. Too often transatlantic projects have been very disadvantageous for European firms and governments. If a "Fortress America" exists, can Europe develop a common armaments policy—a "buy European" policy—in opposition to it, or will the Europeans always need to be subservient to U.S. objectives and equipment pressures, especially if the U.S. product is cheaper? Will the United States tolerate a "buy European" policy? A major question for the future is whether some in the United States want to prevent all potential rivals from emerging. It could be argued that the bottom-line issue is becoming "whether American government and industry will want to see the emergence of strong defence industrial businesses based within Western Europe, or whether the US body politic will prefer the prospect of weaker, nationally based European companies."[38]

Apart from history, this is a problem for Europeans because they still feel that there is a "Fortress America." Although the United States has begun to change the details of its laws, Europeans still complain about U.S. fears of foreign-owned firms not being loyal, or not making equipment available in time of war; of foreign takeovers or competition; of foreigners stealing technological secrets and classified information; and of exports going to countries that the United States has embargoes with.

Europeans are also aware that congressional votes on individual equipment acquisitions take place on the basis of the "pork barrel for their home states or districts rather than to acquire equipment on the basis of suitability."[39] Moreover, as Trevor Taylor says, "Washington constitutes not a single government but rather three sets of actors, each enjoying considerable independence [the administration, Congress, and (four) individual services]. . . . A successful collaborative project would require consistent, long-term support from all three of these governmental actors."[40] Indeed, even the administration can be at odds, given disputes between the Departments of Defense and State on easing some restrictions on collaboration. Some believe that there is a danger of a U.S. policy of divide and rule, particularly if the United States shows more regard to the British when it comes to technology, mergers, and the like, as was witnessed in the February 2000 Declaration of Principles for Equipment and Industrial Cooperation signed between the United States and Britain. There are continuing fears about the danger of U.S. money and technology dictating European military requirements and the danger of the United States becoming the monopoly supplier of certain types of equipment, especially in the high-tech area, or of Europeans becoming the "metal-bashers." Both the United States and Europe see these dangers, but seeing the dangers does not always mean that they will be confronted.

The Future

At the beginning of the 1990s, Keith Hartley argued that in "purchasing defence equipment nations have broad policy options. These range between the extremes of complete independence (nationalism) and buying everything from overseas, and the intermediate solutions of international collaboration involving joint development and production, or some variant of licensed production."[41] For Europeans, complete national independence is now regarded as too costly but perhaps given the EU Headline Goal there might be a greater likelihood of a more harmonized European policy. Given the rationales behind the Letter of Intent and OCCAR, a more explicit "buy European" policy may be emerging. Buying everything from overseas, that is, the United States, has all the costs identified above, partly in terms of sovereignty, prestige, and the freedom of decision and action; and partly in terms of industrial and technological competitiveness, that is, jobs. The intermediate collaborative solutions have some advantages, but again it looks more than ten years after the Cold War that there has "been an inclination towards European rather than transatlantic collaboration in procurement."[42]

A big question is whether the momentum established by the move to ESDP, the Letter of Intent, and OCCAR will be maintained. Another is whether Britain has finally come off the fence. Europe is unlikely to continue with the pre-1998 status quo, a path of irregular collaboration on specific projects. Yet Europe is not ready (and probably will not be ready for at least a generation) for a federalist model.

As Ian Gambles points out, this would "not only strip the states of one of the most important means of asserting separate, sovereign identities on the international stage, but also . . . bestow on the emergent European entity the advantages of powerful identity-forming devices such as martial symbols, military *esprit de corps* and shared exposure to casualty and risk."[43] Given the EU's temerity with defense (and the Danish and Irish positions), this seems unlikely. What is more likely is some variation of the Letter of Intent or OCCAR approach. The key armaments-producing states belong to both of them and the EU, and they are intergovernmental. Indeed, it may be that this will be an area where the "provisions on enhanced cooperation" come into play. The question will then be whether this "enhanced cooperation" matches other patterns that emerge.[44] In any case, progress in this area is likely to take time; indeed, William Walker and Philip Gummett have suggested that it could take twenty to thirty years to change armaments procurement systems in Europe.[45]

In armaments policy the EU member states still need to resolve several big issues: sovereignty, question marks over spillover, the lack of an agreed culture, and the nature of the institutional and industrial arrangements that might come about. Can the EU hope to resolve issues on a continental scale? There has to be some doubt. Despite the beginnings of ESDP, these issues are a long way from being resolved.

Notes

1. Pierre de Vestel, "The Future of Armaments Cooperation in NATO and the WEU," in K. Eliassen, ed., *Foreign and Security Policy in the European Union* (London: Sage, 1998), p. 197.

2. K. Krause, *Arms and the State: Patterns of Military Production and Trade* (Cambridge: Cambridge University Press, 1992).

3. Pierre de Vestel, *Defence Markets and Industries in Europe: Time for Political Decisions?* Chaillot Paper no. 21 (Paris: WEU Institute for Security Studies, 1995), p. 27. Vestel does observe that the sole exception was the placing of Germany's armed forces under NATO integrated command.

4. Ibid.

5. *Consolidated Version of The Treaty on European Union* (Luxembourg: Office for Official Publications of the European Communities, 1997), art. 23.

6. *EEC Treaty,* March 25, 1957.

7. *Consolidated Version of the Treaty on European Union,* art. 17.1.

8. Christophe Cornu, "Fortress Europe: Real or Virtual?" in Gordon Adams, Christophe Cornu, and Andrew D. James, *Between Cooperation and Competition: The Transatlantic Defence Market,* Chaillot Paper no. 44 (Paris: WEU Institute for Security Studies, 2001), p. 61.

9. Burkard Schmitt, conclusion to Adams, Cornu, and James, *Between Cooperation and Competition,* p. 127.

10. William Wallace, introduction to William Wallace, ed., *The Dynamics of European Integration* (London: Pinter, 1992), p. 9.

11. Leon Lindberg, *The Political Dynamics of European Economic Integration* (Stanford: Stanford University Press, 1963), p. 10.

12. Ernst Haas, "The European and the Universal Process," *International Organization* 15, no. 4 (1961): 363.

13. Leon Lindberg, "Integration as a Source of Stress on the European Community System," *International Organization* 20, no. 2 (1966): 228.

14. Werner J. Feld and John K. Wildgen, "National Administration Elites and European Integration Saboteurs at Work," *Journal of Common Market Studies* 13, no. 3 (1975): 255–256.

15. Alyson Bailes, "European Defence: What Are the 'Convergence Criteria'?" *RUSI Journal* (June 1999): 60–65.

16. *Treaty of Economic, Social, and Cultural Collaboration and Collective Self-Defence,* Brussels, 1948 and 1954, Command Papers 7599 and 9304 (London: HMSO, 1949 and 1954).

17. Jocelyn L. Mawdsley, *The Changing Face of European Armaments Cooperation: Continuity and Change in British, French, and German Armament Policy, 1990–2000,* Ph.D. diss., Newcastle upon Tyne, 2000, p. 24.

18. Jean Baptiste Colbert, French prime minister from 1670 to 1680, believed that prosperity depended upon self-sufficient, protected industry.

19. Prime Minister Tony Blair, "The New Challenge for Europe," speech presented in Aachen, Germany, May 14, 1999.

20. Keith Hartley, *The Economies of Defence Policy* (London: Brassey's, 1991), p. 144.

21. *Declaration on the Role of the Western European Union and Its Relations with the European Union and with the Atlantic Alliance,* Declaration 30, *Treaty on European Union,* December 10, 1991 (Luxembourg: Office for Official Publications of the European Communities, 1992).

22. *Armaments Cooperation in the Future Construction of Defence in Europe,* WEU Assembly Document 1671, November 10, 1999; and Cornu, "Fortress Europe," pp. 75–77.

23. COM(97)583 final of November 12, 1997.

24. See, for example, Ben Rosamond, *Theories of European Integration* (London: Macmillan, 2000).

25. European Policy Center, *Making Sense of the Amsterdam Treaty* (Brussels, 1997); see pp. 90–91 for the protocol.

26. Seville European Council, *Presidency Conclusions,* June 21–22, 2002, SN 200/02, *National Declaration by Ireland* and *Declaration of the European Council.*

27. Cornu, "Fortress Europe," p. 87.

28. Egon Klepsch, *Report on European Armaments Procurement Cooperation,* European Parliament Working Document no. 83/78, May 8, 1978.

29. European Parliament Committee Report, no. 219.812 of March 6, 1997, and European Parliament no. 224.862 of April 30, 1998.

30. *Armaments Cooperation in the Future Construction of Defence in Europe,* pp. 20–21.

31. "Outline Agreement for the Accompanying of the Industrial Restructuring Process in Europe," joint statement by the European ministers of defense on the A400M, Farnborough, July 27, 2000.

32. Tom Dodd, *European Defence Industrial and Armaments Cooperation,* House of Commons Library Research Paper no. 97/15, February 4, 1997.

33. Gordon Adams, "Fortress America in a Changing Transatlantic Defence Market," in Adams, Cornu, and James, *Between Cooperation and Competition,* p. 12.

34. Cornu, "Fortress Europe," p. 57.

35. Ibid., pp. 55–59.

36. *Armaments Cooperation in the Future Construction of Defence in Europe,* pp. 36–37.

37. Adams, "Fortress America," p. 17.

38. Trevor Taylor, "Transatlanticism Versus Regional Consolidation," in David G. Haglund and S. Neil MacFarlane, eds., *Security, Strategy, and the Global Economies of Defence Production* (Halifax: McGill-Queen's University Press, 1999), p. 68.

39. Dodd, *European Defence Industrial and Armaments Cooperation,* p. 14. He also notes that in Europe political pressure can influence procurement.

40. Taylor, "Transatlanticism Versus Regional Consolidation," p. 66.

41. Hartley, *The Economies of Defence Policy,* p. 107.

42. Mawdsley, *The Changing Face of European Armaments Cooperation,* p. 2.

43. I. Gambles, *European Security Integration in the 1990s,* Chaillot Paper no. 3 (Paris: WEU Institute for Security Studies, November 1991), p. 14.

44. See de Vestel, *Defence Markets and Industries in Europe,* pp. 33–40.

45. William Walker and Philip Gummett, *Nationalism, Internationalism, and the European Defence Market,* Chaillot Paper no. 9 (Paris: WEU Institute for Security Studies, September 1993), p. 28.

8

Concluding Themes

What Role for the European Union?

Regarding the term "European Union," in 1975 the European Court of Justice observed that "it is not yet clear what the expression imports."[1] Over twenty-five years later, the same might be said of the European Security and Defense Policy (ESDP). The voyage to ESDP is a "journey to an unknown destination."[2]

It is by no means clear that, apart from the rhetoric of Robert Schuman in 1950 about a "European Federation,"[3] the Treaty of Rome's 1957 emphasis on "an ever closer union among the peoples of Europe,"[4] and the 1992 Treaty on European Union (TEU) decision to "establish among themselves a European Union," what the Europeans actually meant to achieve by European integration.[5] The pizzazz, however, has now gone.

It is true that the nature of the EU cannot be understood by a formal, legalistic study of the provisions of the formal treaties alone. It must be located within a wider political environment. Full cognizance needs to be given to the political developments and aspirations, especially given the belief in spillover, that the economic integration was intimately related to political integration and would lead to common foreign and defense policies.

An obvious difficulty is that while many might agree with these broad objectives, all sorts of different means for achieving them have been pursued. The member states have different visions of the future of European integration. Some of these disputes have external repercussions—for example, is Europe progressing toward a federal system or retaining intergovernmentalism? The answer to that question contributes to a dispute about the European Rapid Reaction Force (ERRF)—if the EU is "just" an economic arrangement (customs union plus a monetary union), why does it need a defense force? On the other hand, if the member states are aiming at a federal union, then the EU needs a Common Foreign and Security Policy (CFSP) and an ESDP. Moreover, the EU fifteen have had very different ways of contributing to international security—neutrality, nonnuclear, nuclear, full Alliance membership, and so on—and have never really agreed which was best. This debate is still ongoing.

An equally important issue is whether Europe should go for the "Atlantic European" defense (predominantly dependent on the North Atlantic Treaty Organization [NATO] and the United States) or the "European Europe" defense as favored by the French. As Jacques Delors argued: "Should it be a forum for increased co-operation between the countries of Europe, a bridge to the Atlantic Alliance, or should it be a melting-pot for a European defence embedded in the Community, the second pillar of the Alliance?"[6] The United States, for one, would like to know the answer.

Just as the word "supranational" was once included in the Treaty of Paris of 1951 and the European Defense Treaty of 1952, it has now disappeared from the treaty lexicon. It has been replaced with the principles of subsidiarity and flexibility (provisions on closer cooperation). The first gives weight to the notion that decisions should be taken as low in the political hierarchy as is possible, and the second that some member states can establish closer cooperation between themselves without all of the EU partners. Few, if any, now advocate the creation of a federal system. In the debate between sovereignty and intergovernmental and supranationalism, the solution among the EU fifteen increasingly seems to be for the former, especially regarding defense. EU member states still have to resolve whether ESDP is going to be another variant of "closer cooperation," another directoire.

According to Article 3 the European Union is served by "a single institutional framework which shall ensure the consistency and the continuity of the activities . . . in particular the consistency of its external activities."[7] This and what has gone before raise the question of whether the EU can be an "international actor."[8] The EU does act in the international political system, mainly but not only through the Common Commercial Policy (CCP) and Association Agreements, and in the foreign policy areas through the CFSP. The international character of the EU can also arise from the natural evolution of policies within the treaties' economic framework, for example, the Common Agricultural Policy (CAP) and industrial policy, and the natural spillover of some of these policies into nontreaty areas, for example, the link between industrial policy and the arms industry. A problem for the EU is, while by treaty and formally they are separate categories, in the real world the relationship is not as clear.

According to Roy Ginsberg, action can be defined as a specific, conscious, goal-oriented undertaking putting forth a unified membership position toward nonmembers, international bodies, and international events and issues.[9] Action implies intervention or influence. But as Stanley Hoffman notes, "in the widest sense . . . every act of a state constitutes intervention . . . even non-acts."[10] Action leads to expectations. For example, in the case of the European involvement in Yugoslavia in 1991–1992, not only did the European Community (EC) become involved, but it was expected to become involved. Action itself creates customary patterns of behavior for the EU that are expected by the international system. However, an actor must possess a minimum amount of power.

Carol Cosgrove and Kenneth Twitchett see three points as necessary for considering an organization an incontestable actor in the international system: (1) the degree of autonomous decisionmaking power embodied in its institutions; (2) the extent to which it performs significant and continuing functions having an impact in interstate relations; and (3) the significance attached to it in the formation of the foreign policies of third states.[11] To these should be added power—the EU through the CCP and other policies has an economic impact. Now, as has been seen, it is trying to add some degree of military power.

But any categorization, however much it tries to quantify and measure the components of power, does not provide the ultimate answer to the question: Can A influence the behavior of B? Most researchers have placed military power at the apex of all other measurements, an instrument to which the EU is trying to evolve. Notwithstanding its lack of such an instrument until now, there can be little debate that the Union has evolved into an actor capable of statelike behavior on very many issues. However, there are tensions that spring from (1) the Union's institutional framework, (2) the origins and functioning of CFSP/ESDP, and (3) the perceptions of the outside world. The Union derives its ability to act cohesively and with a singularity of purpose toward third states when the friction between these opposing forces can be minimized. However, until the relationship between the High Representative and the Commissioner for External Relations is sorted out, and until the Member States are willing to surrender some sovereignty, there is a problem.

Whether the EU is an "actor" or a "presence" (as argued by David Allen and Michael Smith),[12] one issue traditionally has been whether the EC/EU has aspired to be a nonmilitary power or a superpower. François Duchêne argued:

> The European Community's interests as a civilian group of countries long on economic power and relatively short on armed force is as far as possible to *domesticate* relations between states. . . . This means trying to bring

to international problems the sense of common responsibility and structures of contractual politics which have in the past been associated almost exclusively with "home" and not foreign, that is *alien,* affairs.[13]

Johan Galtung had other ideas. In *The European Community: A Superpower in the Making* (no question mark), he argued that "a new superpower is emerging."[14] According to Galtung there was an effort to recreate (1) a Eurocentric world, a world with its center in Europe; and (2) a unicentric Europe, a Europe with its center in the West.[15] This is possible because the European Economic Community (EEC) had "resource power" and "structural power," and Galtung uses these to develop a structural analysis that puts most play on dominant classes or economic interests. In fact, neither then nor afterward did the EC/EU mood or predilections justify his claim.

Others argued perceptively against the view that "traditional military/ political power" was giving way to "civilian power." Hedley Bull argued:

> There is no supranational community in Western Europe but only a group of nation-states (moreover, if there *were* a supranational authority in Western Europe, this would be a source of weakness in defence policy rather than of strength; it is the nation-states of Western Europe—France, Germany, Britain—their capacity to inspire loyalty and to make war—that are the sources of its power). . . .
> What we have in Europe is a concert of states, whose basis is an area of perceived common interests among the major powers.[16]

It is also true that the EC/EU has long been guilty of the so-called capability-expectations gap.[17] Whether or not an actor or a presence, a civilian power or an embryonic superpower, the EC/EU faced a "serious challenge to the actual capabilities of the EC, in terms of its *ability to agree,* its *resources,* and the *instruments* at its disposal. . . . Not just in terms of substantial resources . . . but in terms of the *ability to take decisions and hold to them*—the EC is still far from being able to fulfil the hopes of those who want to see it in great power terms."[18]

This book has shown that these problems remain. The EU has not really confronted the issue of how to make decisions, nor does it have the necessary capabilities to implement all but the most basic military tasks. Even if ESDP is successful, the EU will become a regional player, but in this generation it will not become a superpower.

For forty years the EC/EU collectively failed to see the connection between foreign, security, and defense policy—or it considered that its primary security needs were taken care of by NATO and the United States. But despite wanting to restore European influence, the EC failed to see that the world situation required military power, and that diplomatic activity or economic activity without the potential to resort to military power could only be partially successful. Military power is the ultimate tool for protecting and promoting a state's vital interests. On occasion, force or the threat of force is the only means whereby a state may achieve its objectives. Thus while attention is rightly paid to the growing awareness of other dimensions of security, "the military one attracts disproportionate attention in thinking about security. . . . Mostly . . . because military means can still dominate outcomes in all other sectors. A state and its society can be, in their own terms, secure in the political, economic, societal and environmental dimensions, and yet all of these accomplishment can be undone by military failure."[19] Henry Kissinger was right when he said that, "in a society of sovereign states, a power can in the last resort indicate its interpretation of justice or defend its vital interests only by a willingness to employ force."[20] For too long the EC/EU forgot this, and did not really envisage the use of force until 1998–1999.

The Treaty on European Union not only created CFSP, but also made it clear that the discussion could "include all questions related to the security of Union, including the eventual framing of a common defence policy, which might in time lead to a common defence."[21] At Amsterdam (the treaty came into being on May 1, 1999) this was changed to the "progressive framing of a common defence policy," which now included the Petersberg tasks.[22]

However, given the position of Denmark and Ireland (and the 2002 Copenhagen decision on Cyprus and Malta), it is difficult to see how much movement there can be toward common defense. A further difficulty emerges since there is no definition of peacemaking, and there was a problem of whether peacekeeping and peacemaking could involve the actual physical enforcement of military cease-fires or indeed military action against those who violated them.

Armaments?

While arms decisions need long lead times, the EU has been slow to move in this direction. Indeed the NATO doctrine of rationalization, standardization, and interoperability has also been slow. In the EC/EU there have been two problems. There has been no "industrial policy" as such, partly because of fundamental national differences on the role of state and Union institutions (see Chapter 7) and partly because of the old Article 223.1(b) of the EEC Treaty. The EU still has to face old problems in this area. The question is whether there is now sufficient pressure to bring about a less restrictive policy than in the past.

A stronger orientation or a decisive opting for European collaboration will be crucial in the next few years. An alternative is that increasingly Europe will be forced to buy "off the shelf" from the United States, strengthening the economy of a major economic rival, especially when the United States is so protectionist about its own industry. To have a credible arms procurement policy would seem to be a sine qua non of a credible autonomous defense policy.

Divergences Within the EU?

It is especially important to remember that between 1973 and 1995, Ireland was the only "neutral" state in the EC, and even it bent the rules of neutrality. When negotiations started on February 1, 1993, for the 1995 enlargement, neutrality was a dog that did not bark, and Austria, Finland, and Sweden passively accepted the TEU's CFSP. In 1997 they accepted the amended version in the Amsterdam Treaty.

Austria, Finland, Ireland, and Sweden clearly have different views about the role of alliances, NATO, and the utility of the use of weapons, than the other eleven states of the EU (who were in NATO). In essence they were opposed to collective or territorial defense and instead preferred the notion of "soft security"—prevention and crisis management.[23] Ireland took comfort from Article 17 of the TEU, which states: "The policy of the Union . . . shall not prejudice the specific character of the security and defence policy of certain Member States."[24] Ireland read this article as alluding to its neutrality, nonparticipation in existing alliances, and nonassumption of mutual defense guarantees. As seen by the declaration Ireland made in Seville in June 2002, the Irish have asserted their "military neutrality."

Even those who have been in NATO since 1949 cannot always agree on defense policy: France withdrew from the integrated military structure in 1966; Denmark has national legislation that does not allow nuclear weapons or foreign troops to be stationed on its territory in peacetime; and Spain (a later member) did not participate in the integrated military structure until 1997. Given this, the question must be raised about how decisions can be made, and whether the EU will ever agree a strategic culture.

The treaties are clear that CFSP "shall respect the obligations of certain Member States which see their common defence realised in the North Atlantic Treaty" (Article 17).[25] Even if the EU fifteen have set up the machinery for situation monitoring and common analysis by creating, under the Treaty of Amsterdam, the Policy Planning and Early Warning Unit (PPEWU) and the High Representative for CFSP, the problem remains as to whether the analysis of the national interests of the member states has actually converged on significant issues. There is also the problem of how much trust and confidence there is among the fifteen. The UK does not share, for example, all of its intelligence secrets with all of its colleagues. Clearly trust and confidence have been a problem in the past, and given what has happened in other areas, like Justice and Home Affairs, they are likely to be a problem in CFSP/ESDP. There has been no learning curve in some of these areas. The nature of the European contribution has also come up in the "burden-sharing" argument over the years between the European members of NATO and the United States, but there is of course also the burden-sharing argument among the Europeans.

Whatever the definition of defense (global or European), the United States has spent much more on defense than the Europeans (see Table 8.1), but the gap between NATO Europe and the United States had become smaller until the recent Bush increases after September 11, 2001. Moreover, there is no "norm" of European defense spending. France and Britain have proportionally spent more than other Europeans, while Germany and Italy, two of the potential members of the directoire, have continually underspent. In most years, seven to ten member states fall

Table 8.1   Defense Expenditures as Percentage of GDP (current prices), 1990–1999 Averages

	1990–1994	1995–1998	1999
Belgium	2.0	1.5	1.4
Denmark	1.9	1.7	1.6
France	3.4	2.9	2.7
Germany	2.1	1.6	1.5
Greece	4.4	4.6	4.8
Italy	2.1	1.9	2.0
Luxembourg	0.9	0.8	0.8
Netherlands	2.3	1.8	1.8
Norway	2.8	2.2	2.2
Portugal	2.6	2.3	2.2
Spain	1.6	1.4	1.3
Turkey	3.8	4.4	5.4
United Kingdom	3.8	2.8	2.5
NATO			
Canada	1.9	1.4	1.3
Czech Republic	—	2.3	—
Europe (16)	2.6	2.2	2.1
Hungary	—	—	1.6
Poland	—	—	2.1
United States	4.7	3.3	3.0

Source: NATO Handbook 2001.

below the European NATO average. The figures for the European "neutrals" in the EC/EU from 1990 to 1999 are shown in Table 8.2.

With the exception of Sweden over the years, and Finland in the mid-1990s, the figures show that the EU "neutrals" have not taken defense seriously. They are nowhere near the NATO European average for most of the period, averaging only 50 percent of NATO European figures and further illustrating that there is some way to go for achieving a European "norm." Figures for armed forces manpower tell the same story.

Flexibility?

One solution to these problems is variable geometry, or enhanced cooperation or flexibility, whereby some member states might proceed with a measure ahead of, or without, the rest of the Union. Originally the principle of the six European Coal and Steel Community states was "all for one and one for all"—all going to the same destination at the same pace.[26]

By the 1990s the question of "ahead of or without" became a big issue and in the TEU it became official: not all would join the European Monetary Union (EMU) on day one, and some (Britain and Denmark) might never join. It was already clear that outside the European Community some member states wanted to collaborate more closely with, for example, the Schengen Agreement of 1989. In 1991, in another example of flexibility, François Mitterrand and Helmut Kohl announced that they proposed to form a Franco-German corps, which in 1992 they agreed should have 35,000 troops. This became the Eurocorps with the addition of new members Belgium, Luxembourg, and Spain.

Particularly given the prospect of enlargement, some felt that "there

Table 8.2   Neutral Spending on Defense as Percentage of GDP,
1990–1999

	1990	1995	1999
Austria	1.0	1.0	0.8
Ireland	1.1	1.4	0.9
Finland	1.4	2.0	1.4
Sweden	2.5	2.9	2.3
NATO Europe	2.6	2.2	2.1

Source: Military Balance (Oxford: Oxford University Press), 1991–1992, p. 212; 1996–1997, p. 306; 2000–2001, pp. 297–298.

may be some areas of integration that even in the long term will not be attractive or acceptable to a number of member States."[27] Others were keen that those who were "willing and able" to meet the requirements of closer cooperation and integration should be able to go ahead, without those who were not.[28]

In Amsterdam in 1997 it was agreed that a majority of member states could adopt measures and instruments that only applied to themselves, albeit within strict limits. Amsterdam did not provide enhanced cooperation for CFSP, but it did reconfirm the 1992 TEU provisions that:

> The policy of the Union . . . shall not prejudice the specific character of the security and defence policy of certain Member States and shall respect the obligations of certain Member States under the North Atlantic Treaty and be compatible with the common security and defence policy established within that framework.

and that:

> The provisions of this Article shall not prevent the development of closer cooperation between two or more Member States on a bilateral level, in the framework of the WEU [Western European Union] and the Atlantic Alliance, provided that such cooperation does not run counter to or impede that provided for in this Title.[29]

Nice amended the provisions on CFSP, on questions of foreign policy and security, and on "joint action or a common position," but not on "matters having military or defence implications."[30]

Flexibility can be seen in that eleven of the fifteen EU states are in NATO, ten are bound by Brussels Treaty arrangements of the former WEU (not Austria, Denmark, Finland, Ireland, and Sweden), and five are in the Eurocorps, as well as a host of other bilateral and multilateral defense arrangements. The real question for the future is whether there will be more "coalitions of the willing," WEU arrangements or Eurocorps outside the European Union framework. In the future, will it be the EU member states or fifteen minus Denmark and Ireland or "fifteen minus n"? This raises the question of whether it would be an EU force.

Frustration and Continental Drift?

For most of the postwar generation "the transatlantic relationship" was crucial for almost all international issues, but increasingly other powers, interests, and concerns have intruded into this framework. As Lawrence Freedman has said, "The increased diversity and complexity of the environment creates new interests and preoccupations, cuts across old ties and undermines old assumptions."[31]

While U.S. political and social institutions had fascinated Europeans in the 1940s and 1950s, because they seemed innovative and successful while European institutions had failed, this was increasingly not the case, a trend accelerated by Vietnam and Watergate. With the increasing disillusionment with the United States as the leader of the Western world came a growing call from some Europeans for autonomy from U.S. leadership.

Europeans became wary of what they see as a U.S. tendency to concentrate too narrowly on military responses to potential aggression, a trend exacerbated by the "decline in the ability of European countries to project significant military power outside the continent, although it is of note that since Vietnam, British and French forces have seen more action outside Europe than those of the US."[32]

However, the Europeans had to come to terms with the extent of European dependence on the United States. For example, in the Gulf in December 1990 the United States had 400,000 ground troops, 2,100 tanks, 1,900 combat aircraft, and over 50 warships. The only significant European forces were 35,000 British ground troops, 163 tanks, 96 combat aircraft, 26 warships and fleet auxiliaries, and 5 mine countermeasure vessels. France provided 5,500 ground troops, 72 tanks, 42 combat aircraft, and 8 warships.[33] In the Gulf War, of the twelve EC states only France, Italy, and the UK took part in offensive air operations; France and Britain in offensive land operations; and France, Italy, the Netherlands, and the UK in offensive naval operations. With the exception of German participation, operations in the last few years (in the former Republic of Yugoslavia) have shown that not much has changed.

Over the years there have been economic tensions between the United States and Europe. There have been numerous precedents in the history of the Alliance, often over the same issues—interest and exchange rates, protectionism, especially the EC CAP (after all, there was a "chicken war" in 1963) and the vexed question of European subsidies for agricultural production and steel. Europeans have periodically felt that the United States has been aggressively raising and pursuing trade disputes. Technology transfer has been another issue of long-term concern.

In 1973 President Nixon asked: "Can the principle of Atlantic unity in defense and security be reconciled with the European Community's increasingly regional economic policies?"[34] Have the aid, advice, and concern been to both sides' advantage, or increasingly has the United States felt that it has given but not received?

At the end of the Cold War, in November 1991 at the historic NATO summit in Rome, weeks before the Maastricht summit, some of the U.S. frustration came out, as President George Bush told his European partners:

"If, my friends, your ultimate aim is to provide individually for your own defence, the time to tell us is today."[35] That frustration was also evident in the so-called Bartholomew memorandum of February 1991. The question now is whether the current Bush administration feels the same way. How committed is it to Madeleine Albright's "three Ds" statement and how far has the administration come in reconciling it?

> First, we want to avoid decoupling. . . . European decision-making [should not be] unhooked from broader alliance decision-making. Secondly, we want to avoid duplication. . . . And third, we want to avoid any discrimination against NATO members who are not EU members.[36]

The Commitment?

Despite all of this, the United States has been tied to Europe by NATO, especially Article 5 of the North Atlantic Treaty.[37] That commitment is very limited, and has only been invoked once—after the September 11, 2001, terrorist attacks. States have considerable discretion in the commitment; there is no automatic declaration of war. The U.S. commitment has been made manifest by the physical presence of U.S. troops, from a high of 417,000 during the Berlin crisis of 1961 to a current number of below 100,000. The troops were in Europe to reaffirm the U.S. commitment and to make clear that any military action would bring the USSR inexorably into conflict with the United States. That presence was complemented for most of the period by the substantial numbers of U.S. nuclear weapons. Not everybody agreed about how committed the United States was, but then and now, the presence showed that the United States cared. Given that the United States now contributes less than 100,000 personnel to Europe, the new question is whether reduced expenditure and reduced physical commitment lead to a reduction in U.S. leadership and interest.

European Union and NATO Enlargements

Both the European Union and NATO face difficult choices and decisions about their future in terms of membership, their roles, and their vision. Quite apart from the issues previously discussed, both face compelling arguments for enlargement. By May 2004 the European Union plans to enlarge to twenty-five member states and also by 2004 NATO plans to have more than nineteen members after the decision at Prague in November 2002 to admit seven new states. This will have a major impact, given that both are "significant parts of the European security architecture."[38] Both the EU and NATO have enlarged on four occasions (the EU in 1973, 1981, 1986, and 1995 and NATO in 1952, 1955, 1982, and 1999).

As a consequence of changes in the environment, internal as well as external, both have changed their nature: the EU has broadened its areas of competence from the economic to the political and military, and since 1989 NATO has been seeking new roles with peacekeeping, new strategic concepts, and dialogue and cooperation with its former adversaries. The EU and NATO have found adapting difficult and have a mixed record in coping with changing membership and functions. However, the EU and NATO are each unique and that makes any talk of interface or linkages between their enlargements fanciful.

Indeed, the EU and NATO have differences in membership and differences in applicants for membership.[39] There will not be an identity of membership. Membership in one will not be offered as compensation for failure to attain membership in the other. There are enormous differences in the hurdles that each requires of new members.

For the EU, applicants have to accept the EU *acquis* and adjust to it. The EU member states also laid down additional criteria: stability of democracy and human rights, a functioning and competitive market economy, acceptance of all the obligations of membership (political, economic, and monetary), adjustment of administrative structures, and assurances that the *acquis* would actually be applied.[40] In addition, in Agenda 2000 and at the March 1999 Berlin European Council, the EU took key decisions about its own policies and budget.[41] These hurdles are much tougher than those of NATO, which focuses on the military elements and on the applicants' military spending. Indeed, to meet the EU entry requirements, they will have less to spend on the military.

In Brussels in December 1994 the ministerial meeting of the North Atlantic Council reiterated that NATO membership was "open" to other European countries, taking into account democracy and "political and security developments."[42] There was no list of criteria for inviting new members. Decisions are subjective, and in effect would be based upon whether membership would contribute to overall stability and security in Europe. NATO's decisions were *"ratio decidendi . . . political."*[43]

In 1999 in Washington the North Atlantic Council drew up the Membership Action Plan (MAP) to put into place a "programme of activities to assist aspiring countries in their preparations for possible membership."[44] The MAP sets out some aspects of such a program, but does not require the same restructuring of economics and society that admission to the EU does. This discrepancy between the two is likely to continue.

Having said that, most of the applicant states are predominantly small and poor and have little either economically or militarily to bring to the EU or NATO. This is why there are differences across the Atlantic and within

Europe over the scale and timetable of enlargement. President Bush, on his visit to Europe in June 2001, argued that no one should be excluded from NATO because of history or location or geography, and argued against the idea of a veto from outside.[45] However, the U.S. decision reflects U.S. domestic politics. History, geopolitics, and domestic politics have also influenced European governments on both enlargements. Indeed, that partly explains why some are keener on a wider EU enlargement than on a NATO enlargement; the UK, for example, wishes NATO's key attributes to be preserved.

Both the EU and NATO do face many of the same problems with enlargement. The EC was founded on six states and NATO on twelve. Many of their decisionmaking techniques reflect their origins. In defense the EU still relies on unanimity. NATO still relies on consensus—that is, extensive discussion leading to a common view or at least an acceptable view held by all. Given the exponential growth of member states, how long can either continue to make decisions? Heterogeneity in history, geopolitics, strategic culture, and military experiences will make it difficult in both to agree on when to use personnel and weapons, and how to conduct operations—something that NATO suffered from in 1999. There are and will be problems relating to managerial capacity, differing interpretations of the "vision thing," and the fundamental issue of limited resources, especially when membership enlarges. The EU thinks it has resolved the budgetary issue, but those decisions are only binding until 2006, when the enlarged EU will need to decide. European defense budgets are flat or declining. ESDP will require more spending. If there is no increase in spending, will this be another reason for increased recourse to "coalitions of the willing" or in a version of ESDP "enhanced cooperation"?

How Big Is the Question Mark?

The development of ESDP and, within that, the ERRF is well under way. Some political decisions have been taken and *rhetoric* suggests that the political will does exist to see that the goal of a European security and defense policy is achieved. This political commitment will now be truly tested by the financial and military issues that have to be confronted: investing in crucial capabilities and creating an effective level of interoperability. Some hope that the EU may well do this, if only because this project is almost too important for the EU to allow to fail, like the EMU. ESDP, if effective, will improve security directly for the EU states and indirectly for the EU candidates and other European states, providing both groups with another strong and capable option when seeking to prevent or manage crises.

If ESDP does bring added value to the EU's international role, it could be the final link in establishing peace and security across the European continent. However, if the financial, military, and to a lesser extent political challenges are not met, then the EU will have created another policy without substance and the credibility of the EU as an international actor will be severely damaged.

Notes

1. *Suggestions of the Court of Justice on European Union,* Bulletin of the European Communities Supplement 9-1975 (Luxembourg: Office for Official Publications of the European Union, 1975).

2. Andrew Shonfield, *Europe: Journey to an Unknown Destination* (Harmondsworth: Penguin, 1973).

3. Trevor Salmon and William Nicoll, eds., *Building European Union: A Documentary History and Analysis* (Manchester: Manchester University Press, 1997), p. 45.

4. *Treaty of Rome Establishing the European Economic Community,* March 1957, Command Paper 4864 (London: HMSO, 1972), preamble.

5. *Consolidated Version of the Treaty on European Union* (Luxembourg: Office for Official Publications of the European Communities, 1997), art. 1.

6. Jacques Delors, "Address to the International Institute of Strategic Studies," March 7, 1991, reproduced in *Survival* 33, no. 2 (March–April 1991): 107.

7. See *Consolidated Version of the Treaty on European Union.*

8. Gunnar Sjöstedt, *The External Role of the European Community* (Farnborough: Teakfield, 1977).

9. Roy Ginsberg, *Foreign Policy Actions of the European Community* (London: Adamantine Press, 1989), p. 2.

10. Stanley Hoffman, "The Problem of Intervention," in Hedley Bull, ed., *Intervention in World Politics* (Oxford: Clarendon Press, 1984), p. 8.

11. Carol Ann Cosgrove and Kenneth Twitchett, eds., *The New International Actors: The UN and the EEC* (London: Macmillan, 1970), p. 20.

12. Allen and Smith questioned the concept of "actor" and preferred to use the term "presence," noting that the EU has "variable and multi-dimensional presence, which plays an active role in some areas of international interaction and a less active one in others." David Allen and Michael Smith, "Western Europe's Presence in the Contemporary International Arena," *Review of International Studies* 16, no. 1 (January 1990): 20.

13. François Duchêne, "The European Community and the Uncertainties of Independence," in M. Kohnstamm and W. Hager, eds., *A Nation Writ Large? Foreign-Policy Problems Before the European Community* (London: Macmillan, 1973), pp. 19–20; and François Duchêne, "A New European Defence Community," *Foreign Affairs* 50, no. 1 (October 1971): 69–82.

14. Johan Galtung, *The European Community: A Superpower in the Making* (London: George Allen, 1981), p. 12.

15. Ibid.

16. Hedley Bull, "Civilian Power Europe: A Contradiction in Terms?" *Journal of Common Market Studies* 21, nos. 1–2 (1981): 149–164.

17. Christopher Hill, "The Capability-Expectations Gap, or Conceptualizing Europe's International Role," *Journal of Common Market Studies* 31, no. 3 (1993): 305–328.

18. Ibid., pp. 315–318.

19. Barry Buzan, "Is International Security Possible?' in K. Booth, ed., *New Thinking About Strategy and International Security* (London: HarperCollins, 1991), p. 35.

20. Henry Kissinger, *Nuclear Weapons and Foreign Policy* (New York: Harper and Row, 1957), p. 4.

21. *Treaty on European Union* (Luxembourg: Office for Official Publications of the European Communities, 1992), art. J.4.

22. *Consolidated Version of the Treaty on European Union,* arts. 17.1–17.2.

23. Patrick Keatinge, *European Security: Ireland's Choices* (Dublin: Institute of European Affairs, 1996), pp. 211–213.

24. *Consolidated Version of the Treaty on European Union,* art. 17.

25. Ibid.

26. Leo Tindemans, *Report on European Union* (December 1975), Bulletin of the European Communities Supplement 1/76.

27. Malcolm Rifkind, British foreign secretary, September 1995, quoted in Salmon and Nicoll, *Building European Union,* p. 277.

28. Wolfgang Schäuble and Karl Lammers, "Reflections on European Policy," in Salmon and Nicoll, *Building European Union,* p. 260.

29. *Treaty on European Union,* arts. J.4.4–J.4.5, and *Consolidated Version of the Treaty on European Union,* arts. 17.1, 17.4.

30. *Treaty of Nice,* 2001/C80/01, http://europa.eu.int/eur-lex/en/treaties/index.html.

31. Lawrence Freedman, "The Atlantic Crisis," *International Affairs* 58, no. 3 (1982): 398.

32. Ibid., p. 408.

33. Julian Thompson, "The Military Coalition," in James Gow, ed., *Iraq, the Gulf Conflict, and the World Community* (London: Brassey's, 1993), p. 140.

34. Richard Nixon, Chicago, March 15, 1973.

35. Agence Europe, 1746/7, November 20, 1991.

36. Maartje Rutten, ed., *From St. Malo to Nice: European Defence—Core Documents,* Chaillot Paper no. 47 (Paris: WEU Institute for Security Studies, 2001), pp. 11–12.

37. "The Parties agree that an armed attack against one or more of them in Europe or North America shall be considered an attack against them all; and consequently they agree that, if such an armed attack occurs, each of them . . . will assist the Party or Parties so attacked by taking forthwith, individually and in concert with the other Parties, such action as it deems necessary, including the use of armed force, to restore and maintain the security of the North Atlantic area."

38. William Hopkinson, *Enlargement: A New NATO,* Chaillot Paper no. 49 (Paris: WEU Institute for Security Studies, 2001), p. 57.

39. For the EU: Bulgaria, Cyprus, Czech Republic, Estonia, Hungary, Latvia, Lithuania, Malta, Poland, Romania, Slovenia, Slovakia, and Turkey. For NATO: Albania, Bulgaria, Estonia, Latvia, Lithuania, Macedonia, Romania, Slovenia, Slovakia, and possibly Croatia.

40. Council of the European Union, *Presidency Conclusions,* June 1993, December 1995, and December 1997, Bulletin of the European Communities/Union 6-1993, 12-1995, and 12-1997.

41. European Commission, *Agenda 2000: For a Stronger and Wider Europe,*

Bulletin of the European Communities Supplement 5/97; and Council of the European Union, *Presidency Conclusions,* March 1999, Bulletin of the European Communities 3-1999.

42. *Communiqué Issued by Ministerial Meeting of the North Atlantic Council,* December 1, 1994, *NATO Review* no. 6/1 (December 1994–January 1995): 26.

43. Hopkinson, *Enlargement,* p. 2.

44. *Membership Action Plan,* issued by North Atlantic Council, Washington, D.C., *NATO Review* no. 2 (Summer 1999): D13.

45. *New York Times,* June 16–17, 2001.

Acronyms

AFNORTH	Allied Forces Northern Europe
AFSOUTH	Allied Forces Southern Europe
ARRC	Allied Rapid Reaction Corps
ATARES	Air Transport and Air Refueling Exchange of Service
AWACS	Airborne Warning and Control System
BAe	British Aerospace
BTO	Brussels Treaty Organization
BVR	beyond visual range
C^3	command, control, and communications
C^3I	command, control, communications, and intelligence
CAP	Common Agricultural Policy
CCHQs	component command headquarters
CCP	Common Commercial Policy
CCT	Common Customs Tariff
CFSP	Common Foreign and Security Policy
CJTF	Combined Joint Task Force
COARM	EU Council Working Group on Exports of Conventional Arms
COPS	Comité Politique et de Sécurité
Coreper	Committee of Permanent Representatives
CPSU	Communist Party of the Soviet Union
CSCE	Conference on Security and Cooperation in Europe
DCI	Defense Capabilities Initiative
DGEUMS	Director-General of EUMS
DMC	Defense Ministers Council
DSACEUR	Deputy Supreme Allied Commander for Europe
EAA	European Armaments Agency

EADS	European Aeronautic, Defense, and Space Company
EC	European Community
ECAP	European Capability Action Plan
ECJ	European Court of Justice
ECR	electronic combat and reconnaissance
ECSC	European Coal and Steel Community
EDC	European Defense Community
EDIG	European Defense Industries Group
EEC (EC)	European Economic Community
EMU	Economic and Monetary Union
EPC	European Political Committee
ERRF	European Rapid Reaction Force
ESDI	European Security and Defense Identity
ESDP	European Security and Defense Policy
EU	European Union
EUMC	European Union Military Committee
EUMS	European Union Military Staff
EUPM	European Union Police Mission
Euratom	European Atomic Energy Community
FAWEU	forces answerable to the WEU
FHQs	force headquarters
FSTA	Future Strategic Tanker Aircraft
FYROM	Former Yugoslav Republic of Macedonia
GAC	General Affairs Council
GDP	gross domestic product
GEC	General Electric Company
GPS	global positioning satellite
HALE	high altitude long endurance
HTF	Headline Task Force
IEPG	Independent European Program Group
IFOR	Implementation Force
IGC	intergovernmental conference
IMS	International Military Staff
ISR	intelligence, surveillance, and reconnaissance
ISTAR	intelligence, surveillance, target acquisition, and reconnaissance
JDAM	joint direct attack munition
KFOR	Kosovo Force
KRK	Crisis Reaction Corps (Germany)
LOCE	Limited Operational Capability for Europe
LOI	Letter of Intent
LPD	landing platform dock
LPH	landing platform helicopter

LPM	Loi Programmation Militaire
MALE	medium altitude long endurance
MAP	Membership Action Plan
MAPE	Multinational Advisory Police Element
MHD	Matra Hautes Technologies–Dassault
MRP	Movement Républicain Populaire
NAC	North Atlantic Council
NAT	North Atlantic Treaty
NATO	North Atlantic Treaty Organization
NRF	NATO Response Force
OAF	Operation Allied Force
OCCAR	Organisme Conjoint de Coopération en Matière d'Armement (Organization for Joint Armament Cooperation)
OHQs	operational headquarters
OSCE	Organization for Security and Cooperation in Europe
PGM	precision-guided munition
PJHQ	Permanent Joint Headquarters (UK)
PoCo	Political Committee
POLARM	EU Council Working Group on European Armaments Policy
PPEWU	Policy Planning and Early Warning Unit
PSC	Political and Security Committee
RoRo	roll-on/roll-off
SACEUR	Supreme Allied Commander for Europe
SDR	Strategic Defense Review
SE	Societies Europaea
SEA	Single European Act
SEAD	suppression of enemy air defenses
SFOR	Stabilization Force
SHAPE	Supreme Headquarters Allied Powers Europe
STOVL	short takeoff vertical landing
TEU	Treaty on European Union
UAV	unmanned aerial vehicle
UK	United Kingdom
UN	United Nations
UNPROFOR	United Nations Protection Force
USEUCOM	U.S. European Command
USSR	Union of Soviet Socialist Republics
WEAG	Western European Armaments Group
WEAO	Western European Armaments Organization
WEU	Western European Union
WUDO	Western Union Defense Organization

Bibliography

Primary Sources

Europe

Armaments Cooperation in the Future Construction of Defence in Europe. WEU Assembly Document 1671. November 10, 1999.

COM(97)583 final of November 12, 1997.

Consolidated Version of the Treaty on European Union. Luxembourg: Office for Official Publications of the European Communities, 1997.

Council of the European Union. General Affairs. *Council Joint Action of 20 July 2001 on the Establishment of a European Union Institute for Security Studies.* 2001/554/CFSP.

———. General Affairs. *Council Joint Action of 20 July 2001 on the Establishment of a European Union Satellite Centre.* 2001/555/CFSP.

———. *Military Bodies in the European Union and the Planning and Conduct of EU-Led Military Operations.* Brussels, February 29, 2000. 6215/1/00.

———. *Presidency Conclusions.* Luxembourg: Office for Official Publications of the European Union, various years.

Cologne. Bulletin of the European Union 6-1999.
Copenhagen. Bulletin of the European Communities 6-1993.
Edinburgh. Bulletin of the European Communities 12-1992.
Feira. Bulletin of the European Union 6-2000.
Göteborg. Bulletin of the European Union 6-2001.
Helsinki. Bulletin of the European Union 12-1999.
Laeken. Bulletin of the European Union 12-2001.
Lisbon. Bulletin of the European Union 3-2000.
Nice. Bulletin of the European Union 12-2000.
Seville. Bulletin of the European Union 6-2002.
Vienna. Bulletin of the European Union 12-1998.

221

———. *Statement on Improving European Military Capabilities.* Brussels, November 19, 2001.

———. *2342nd Council Meeting, General Affairs.* Brussels, April 9, 2001. 7833/01, press release 141.

Declaration on the Establishment of a Policy Planning and Early Warning Unit. Luxembourg: Office for Official Publications of the European Communities, 1997.

Declaration on the Role of the Western European Union and Its Relations with the European Union and with the Atlantic Alliance. Declaration 30, *Treaty on European Union,* December 10, 1991. Luxembourg: Office for Official Publications of the European Communities, 1992.

European Commission. *Agenda 2000: For a Stronger and Wider Europe.* Bulletin of the European Communities Supplement 5/97. Luxembourg: Office for Official Publications of the European Communities, 1997.

———. *Communication from the Commission: A Project for the European Union.* Brussels, May 22, 2002.

The European Defence Community. Command Paper 9127. London: HMSO, 1954.

European Parliament. Committee of Institutional Affairs. *Selection of Texts Concerning Institutional Matters of the Community from 1950 to 1982.* Luxembourg, n.d.

European Parliament Committee Report. No. 219.812. March 6, 1998.

———. No. 224.862. April 30, 1998.

European Policy Center. *Making Sense of the Amsterdam Treaty.* Brussels, 1997.

Final Communiqué Issued by the Conference Chairman (Copenhagen, December 1973). Bulletin of the European Communities 12-1973. Luxembourg: Office for Official Publications of the European Communities, 1973.

Forcieri, L. *NATO Forces: Preparing for New Roles and Missions.* North Atlantic Assembly Committee Reports, Defense and Security Committee, Subcommittee on the Future of the Armed Forces. Brussels: North Atlantic Assembly, November 1998.

Irish Presidency. *A General Outline for a Draft Revision of the Treaties.* Dublin European Council, December 1996.

Klepsch, E. *Report on European Armaments Procurement Cooperation.* European Parliament Working Document no. 83/78, May 8, 1978.

Lemoine, G. *The New Challenges Facing European Intelligence: Reply to the Annual Report of the Council.* Paris: Assembly of the WEU, April 2002. C/1775.

NATO: Facts and Figures 1989. Brussels: NATO Information Services, 1989.

North Atlantic Council. Berlin, June 1996. *NATO Review* no. 4 (July 1996).

———. Brussels, January 1994. *NATO Review* no. 1 (February 1994).

———. Madrid, July 1997. *NATO Review* no. 4 (July–August 1997).

———. Washington, D.C., April 1999. *NATO Review* no. 2 (Summer 1999).

Protocol Modifying and Completing the Brussels Treaty. October 1954. Command Paper 9304. London: HMSO, 1954.

Report on European Institutions Presented by the Committee of Three to the European Council. Luxembourg, 1980. Council of the European Union, catalog no. BX-30-80-011-EN-C.

Report on European Political Cooperation. London, October 13, 1981. Bulletin of the European Communities Supplement no. 3/81. Luxembourg: Office for Official Publications of the European Communities, 1981.

Single European Act. Bulletin of the European Communities Supplement 2/86.

Luxembourg: Office for Official Publications of the European Communities, 1986.

Tindemans, L. *Report on European Union*. December 1975. Bulletin of the European Communities Supplement 1/76. Luxembourg: Office for Official Publications of the European Communities, 1976.

Treaty of Amsterdam. Luxembourg: Office for Official Publications of the European Communities, 1997.

Treaty of Economic, Social, and Cultural Collaboration and Collective Self-Defence. Brussels 1948 and 1954. Command Papers 7599 and 9304. London: HMSO, 1949 and 1954.

Treaty of Nice. 2001/C80/01. http://europa.eu.int/eur-lex/en/treaties/index.html.

Treaty of Rome Establishing the European Economic Community. March 1957. Command Paper 4864. London: HMSO, 1972.

Treaty on European Union. Luxembourg, Office for Official Publications of the European Communities, 1992.

Wilkinson, J. *European Strategic Lift Capabilities: Reply to the Annual Report of the Council*. Paris: Assembly of the WEU, Interim European Security and Defense Assembly, November 5, 2001.

Zierer, B. *A European Crisis Reaction Force: Reply to the Annual Report of the Council*. Document no. 1668. Paris: Defense Committee of the Assembly of the WEU, November 10, 1999.

Member States

Anglo-Italian Joint Declaration Launching European Defence Capabilities Initiative. Italy, July 19–20, 1999.

Department of Foreign Affairs (Ireland). *White Paper on Foreign Policy*. Dublin, 1996.

Dumoulin, A., R. Mathieu, and V. Metten. *Introduction to the Comparative Survey of the White Papers, Official Documents, and General Policy Papers Related to the Security and Defence Policy of the Fifteen Member States of the European Union*. Brussels: Royal Defence College, 2001.

Federal Ministry of Defense (Germany). *German Security Policy and the Bundeswehr*. Bonn: Press and Information Office of the Federal Government, October 1997.

Foreign and Commonwealth Office (UK). *Memorandum of the United Kingdom's Approach to the Treatment of European Defence Issues at the 1996 Inter-Governmental Conference*. London, 1995.

Government of Greece. *Memorandum of the Greek Government of 24 January 1996 on the IGC: Greece's Positions and Comments*. Athens, 1996.

House of Lords. European Union Select Committee. *Eleventh Report: The European Policy on Security and Defence*. London, January 29, 2002.

Joint Declaration on European Defence Issued at the British-French Summit. St. Malo, France, December 3–4, 1998.

Ministry of Defense (France). *Defense and the Armed Forces of France*. Paris: Service d'Information et de Relations Publiques des Armées, June 1998.

Ministry of Defense (Netherlands). *Framework Memorandum for the 2000 Defence White Paper*. The Hague, March 1999.

Ministry of Defense (UK). *Kosovo: NATO Forces: Fact and Figures—The Kosovo Peacekeeping Force, KFOR*. London, 1999.

————. *The Role of the Reserves in Home Defence and Security.* London, June 2002.

————. *The Strategic Defence Review.* London: HMSO, July 1998.

————. *The Strategic Defence Review: A New Chapter.* London, 2002.

Ministry of Foreign Affairs (Denmark). *The Agenda for Europe.* Copenhagen, June 1996.

————. *Basis for Negotiations Open Europe: The 1996 Intergovernmental Conference, Chief Task.* Copenhagen, 1995.

United States

Cohen, W., and H. Shelton. *Joint Statement of William Cohen, Secretary of Defense, and General Henry Shelton, Chairman of the Joint Chiefs of Staff, Senate Armed Services Committee Hearing on Kosovo After-Action Review.* Washington, D.C., October 14, 1999.

Hearing Before the Committee on International Relations. House of Representatives, 106th Congress, 1st sess. Washington, D.C., November 10, 1999.

Subcommittee on Europe of the Committee on International Relations. House of Representatives, 107th sess. Washington, D.C., April 25, 2001.

U.S. Department of Defense. *Report to Congress: Kosovo/Operation Allied Force After-Action Report.* Washington, D.C., January 31, 2000.

————. *Strengthening Transatlantic Security: U.S. Strategy for the Twenty-First Century.* Washington, D.C., December 2000.

U.S. Department of State bulletin. Washington, D.C., June 15, 1947.

U.S. General Accounting Office. *European Security: U.S. and European Contributions to Foster Stability and Security in Europe.* Washington, D.C., November 2001.

Websites

Annan, K. Press release, SG/SM/6598, June 15, 1998. www.un.org/news/press/docs/1998/19980615.sgsm6598.html. Accessed June 20, 2002.

"Appointment of the Head of the Military Experts Seconded by Member States to the EU Council Secretariat." March 8, 2000. http://ue.eu.int/newsroom. Accessed April 3, 2000.

Blair, T. Press conference at Portschach after the Austrian Presidency's informal summit, October 25, 1998. Cited in Information Centre Releases, www.number-10.gov.uk/publi...eech_display.asp?random=0&index=1. Accessed November 5, 1998.

Burns, N. "U.S.-European Capabilities Gap Must Be Narrowed." Press conference, Ljubljana, Slovenia, February 28, 2002. www.useu.be/categories/defense/feb2802burnsuseucapabilities.html. Accessed May 13, 2002.

Council of the European Union. General Affairs. "Military Capabilities Commitment Declaration." Brussels, November 20, 2000. Press release, 13427/2/00.http://ue.eu.int/newsroom/oaddoc.cfm?ma...doc=!!!&bid=75&did=63995&grp=2957&lang=1. Accessed November 23, 2000.

Eurocorps. *History.* www.eurocorps.org. Accessed April 13, 2002.

European Parliament. *White Paper on the 1996 Intergovernmental Conference.* Vol.

2, *Summary of Positions of the Member States of the European Union with a View to the 1996 Intergovernmental Conference.* 1996. www.europa.eu.int/en/agenda/igc-home/eu-doc/parlment/peen2.htm. Accessed January 25, 2000.

Eyskens, M. 1991. www.wsws.org/articles/1999/sep1999/belg-s13.shtml. Accessed March 27, 2002.

Federal Ministry of Defense (Germany). *The Bundeswehr and Its Mission.* October 1997. www.bundesregierung.de/english/02/0205/index12.html. Accessed May 18, 1999.

Franco-German Summit. Defense and Security Council. *Toulouse Declaration.* May 29, 1999. www.ambafrance.org.uk/db.phtml?id=2842. Accessed June 7, 1999.

Ministry of Defense (UK). *Kosovo: Lessons from the Crisis.* London, June 2000. www.mod.uk/news/kosovo/lessons/chapter8.htm. Accessed June 13, 2000.

———. "Outcome of the Strategic Sealift (RoRo) and Alternative Landing Ships Logistics (ALSLs) Competitions." Press release, October 26, 2000. www.mod.uk/index.php3?page=2&nid=1059&view=724&cat=0. Accessed October 27, 2000.

———. "Short Term Strategic Airlift Contract Announced." Press release, 221/00, September 4, 2000. www.mod.uk/index.php3?page=2&nid=1059&view=724&cat=0. Accessed September 21, 2000.

North Atlantic Treaty Organization. "Financial and Economic Data Relating to NATO Defence: Defence Expenditures of NATO Countries (1980–2001)." Press release, M-DPC-2(2001)156, December 18, 2001. www.nato.int/docu/pr/1998/p98-147e.htm. Accessed February 25, 2002.

"Remarks by Dr. Javier Solana, High Representative of the EU for CFSP at the Inaugural Meeting of the Interim Military Body." March 7, 2000. http://ue.eu.int/newsroom. Accessed April 3, 2000.

"Remarks by Dr. Javier Solana, High Representative of the EU for CFSP on the Occasion of the Official Launching of the Political and Security Committee." March 1, 2000. http://ue.eu.int/newsroom. Accessed March 2, 2000.

Robertson, G. "Defence in Europe." Presentation to the Assembly of the Western European Union, December 1, 1998. www.mod.uk/news/speeches/sofs/98–12–01.htm. Accessed June 7, 1999.

Royal Navy. "Future Ships." www.royal-navy.mod.uk/rn/print.php3?page=1969. Accessed April 12, 2002.

Straw, J. "EU-U.S. Relations: The Myths and the Reality." Speech to the Brookings Institution, May 8, 2002. www.fco.gov.uk. Accessed May 13, 2002.

Western European Union. Council of Ministers. *Audit of Assets and Capabilities for European Crisis Management Operations: Recommendations for Strengthening European Capabilities for Crisis Management Operations.* Luxembourg, November 23, 1999. www.weu.int/eng/mini/99luxembourg/recommendations.htm. Accessed November 24, 1999.

———. *Multinational Forces Answerable to WEU.* www.weu.int/eng/info/faweu.htm. Accessed October 2, 2000.

Secondary Sources

Adams, G. "Fortress America in a Changing Transatlantic Defence Market." In G. Adams, C. Cornu, and A. D. James, *Between Cooperation and Competition: The Transatlantic Defence Market.* Chaillot Paper no. 44. Paris: WEU Institute for Security Studies, 2001.

Akehurst, M. *A Modern Introduction to International Law.* London: Allen and Unwin, 1984.

Allen, D., and M. Smith. "Western Europe's Presence in the Contemporary International Arena." *Review of International Studies* 16, no. 1 (January 1990).

Andréani, G., C. Bertram, and C. Grant. *Europe's Military Revolution.* London: Center for European Reform, 2001.

Bailes, A. "European Defence: What Are the 'Convergence Criteria'?" *RUSI Journal* (June 1999).

Bayliss, J. "French Defence Policy." In J. Bayliss, K. Booth, J. Garnett, and P. Williams. *Contemporary Strategy: Theories and Policies.* London: Croon Helm, 1975.

Bull, H. "Civilian Power Europe: A Contradiction in Terms?" *Journal of Common Market Studies* 21, nos. 1–2 (1981).

Burrows, B., and G. Edwards. *The Defence of Western Europe.* London: Butterworths European Studies, 1982.

Buzan, B. "Is International Security Possible?" In K. Booth, ed., *New Thinking About Strategy and International Security.* London: HarperCollins, 1991.

Camps, M. *Britain and the European Community.* London: Oxford University Press, 1964.

Cawley, A. *De Gaulle.* London: Collins, 1969.

Center for Defense Studies. *Achieving the Helsinki Headline Goals.* London: Center for Defense Studies, 2001.

Churchill, R., ed. *The Sinews of Peace.* London: Cassell, 1948.

Cornu, C. "Fortress Europe: Real or Virtual?" In G. Adams, C. Cornu, and A. D. James, *Between Cooperation and Competition: The Transatlantic Defence Market.* Chaillot Paper no. 44. Paris: WEU Institute for Security Studies, 2001.

Cosgrove, C. A., and K. Twitchett, eds. *The New International Actors: The UN and the EEC.* London: Macmillan, 1970.

Croft, S., J. Howorth, T. Terriff, and M. Webber. "NATO's Triple Challenge." *International Affairs* 76, no. 3 (July 2000).

Dahrendorf, R. "A New Goal for Europe." In M. Hodges, ed., *European Integration.* Harmondsworth: Penguin, 1972.

de Vestel, P. *Defence Markets and Industries in Europe: Time for Political Decisions?* Chaillot Paper no. 21. Paris: WEU Institute for Security Studies, 1995.

———. "The Future of Armaments Cooperation in NATO and the WEU." In K. Eliassen, ed., *Foreign and Security Policy in the European Union.* London: Sage, 1998.

Delors, J. "Address to the International Institute for Strategic Studies." March 7, 1991. Reproduced in *Survival* 33, no. 2 (March–April 1991).

Dodd, T. *European Defence Industrial and Armaments Cooperation.* House of Commons Library Research Paper no. 97/15. London: House of Commons Library, February 4, 1997.

Donfried, K., and P. Gallis. *European Security: The Debate in NATO and the European Union.* CRS report to Congress, April 25, 2000.

Duchêne, F. "The European Community and the Uncertainties of Independence." In M. Kohnstamm and W. Hager, eds., *A Nation Writ Large? Foreign-Policy Problems Before the European Community.* London: Macmillan, 1973.

———. "A New European Defence Community." *Foreign Affairs* 50, no. 1 (1971).

Duff, A., ed. *The Treaty of Amsterdam: Text and Commentary.* London: Federal Trust, 1997.

Duke, S. *The Elusive Quest for European Security.* London: Macmillan, 2000.

Edwards, G. *Politics of European Treaty Reform.* London: Pinter, 1997.

Eichler, W., ed. *Europe Speaks.* London: Militant Socialist International, 1944.

Feld, W. J., and J. K. Wildgen. "National Administration Elites and European Integration Saboteurs at Work." *Journal of Common Market Studies* 13, no. 3 (1975).

Freedman, L. "The Atlantic Crisis." *International Affairs* 58, no. 3 (1982).

———. *Britain and Nuclear Weapons.* London: Macmillan, 1980.

———. *The Evolution of Nuclear Strategy.* 2nd ed. London: Macmillan, 1989.

Fursdon, E. *The European Defence Community.* New York: St. Martin's Press, 1980.

Galambos, L., ed. *Papers of Dwight David Eisenhower.* Vol. 12, *NATO and the Campaign of 1952.* Baltimore: Johns Hopkins University Press, 1989.

Galtung, J. *The European Community: A Superpower in the Making.* London: George Allen, 1981.

Gambles, I. *European Security Integration in the 1990s.* Chaillot Paper no. 3. Paris: WEU Institute for Security Studies, November 1991.

Gerbet, P. *La Construction de l'Europe.* Paris: Imprimerie Nationale, 1983.

Ginsberg, R. *Foreign Policy Actions of the European Community.* London, Adamantine Press, 1989.

Guicherd, C. *A European Defense Identity: Challenge and Opportunity for NATO.* CRS report to Congress, June 12, 1991.

Haas, E. "The European and the Universal Process." *International Organization* 15, no. 4 (1961).

Haas, R. *The Reluctant Sheriff: The United States After the Cold War.* New York: Council on Foreign Relations Press, 1997.

Hartley, K. *The Economies of Defence Policy.* London: Brassey's, 1991.

Healey, D. *The Time of My Life.* London: Michael Joseph, 1989.

Heath, E. *Old World, New Horizons: Britain, the Common Market, and Atlantic Alliance.* London: Oxford University Press, 1970.

Heisbourg, F. "Europe's Strategic Ambitions: The Limits of Ambiguity." *Survival* 42, no. 2 (Summer 2000).

Heisbourg, F., et al. *European Defence: Making It Work.* Chaillot Paper no. 42. Paris: WEU Institute for Security Studies, September 2000.

Hill, C. "The Capability-Expectations Gap, or Conceptualising Europe's International Role." *Journal of Common Market Studies* 31, no. 3 (1993).

———. ed. *National Foreign Policies and European Political Cooperation.* London: Allen and Unwin, 1983.

Hill, L. "EU Military Staff Goes Operational." *European Voice* 35, no. 25 (June 20, 2001).

Hix, S. *The Political System of the European Union.* Houndmills: Macmillan, 1999.

Hoffman, S. "The Problem of Intervention." in H. Bull, ed., *Intervention in World Politics.* Oxford: Clarendon Press, 1984.

Hopkinson, W. *Enlargement: A New NATO.* Chaillot Paper no. 49. Paris, WEU Institute for Security Studies, 2001.

Howorth, J. *European Integration and Defence.* Chaillot Paper no. 43. Paris, WEU Institute for Security Studies, 2000.

Howorth, J., and A. Menon, eds. *The European Union and National Defence Policy.* London: Routledge, 1997.

Hoyle, C., R. Scott, and C. Foss. "The Long Haul." *Jane's Defence Weekly,* February 6, 2002.

International Institute for Strategic Studies. *The Military Balance 2001–2002.* Oxford: Oxford University Press, October 2001.

Keatinge, P. *European Security: Ireland's Choices.* Dublin: Institute of European Affairs, 1996.

Kissinger, H. *Nuclear Weapons and Foreign Policy.* New York: Harper and Row, 1957.

———. *The Troubled Partnership: A Re-appraisal of the Atlantic Alliance.* New York: McGraw Hill, 1965.

Krause, K. *Arms and the State: Patterns of Military Production and Trade.* Cambridge: Cambridge University Press, 1992.

Kupchan, C. A. "In Defence of European Defence: An American Perspective." *Survival* 42, no. 2 (2000).

Laursen, F., and S. Vanhoonacker. *The Intergovernmental Conference on Political Union: Institutional Reforms, New Policies, and International Identity of the European Community.* Dordrecht: Martinus Nijhoff, 1992.

Layne, C. "Death Knell for NATO?" *Policy Analysis* no. 394 (April 4, 2001).

Lindberg, L. "Integration as a Source of Stress on the European Community System." *International Organization* 20, no. 2 (1966).

———. *The Political Dynamics of European Economic Integration.* Stanford: Stanford University Press, 1963.

Lutz, R. A. *Military Capabilities for a European Defence.* Copenhagen: Danish Institute of International Affairs, 2001.

Mansergh, N. *Documents and Speeches on British Government Affairs, 1931–1952.* London: Oxford University Press, 1953.

Mawdsley, J. L. *The Changing Face of European Armaments Cooperation: Continuity and Change in British, French, and German Armament Policy, 1990–2000.* Ph.D. diss., Newcastle upon Tyne, 2000.

Mayne, R. *The Recovery of Europe.* London: Weidenfeld and Nicolson, 1970.

Monnet, J. *Memoirs.* Trans. Richard Mayne. London: Collins, 1978.

Moravcsik, A., and K. Nicolaidis. "Explaining the Treaty of Amsterdam." *Journal of Common Market Studies* 37 (1999).

Morgan, R. *High Politics, Low Politics: Towards a Foreign Policy for Western Europe.* Washington Papers no. 11. London: Sage, 1973.

Nicoll, W., and T. C. Salmon. *Understanding the European Union.* Harlow: Pearson Education, 2001.

O' Hanlon, M. "Transforming NATO: The Role of European Forces." *Survival* 39, no. 3 (Autumn 1997).

Peters, J. E., et al. *European Contributions to Operation Allied Force.* Santa Monica, Calif.: RAND, 2001.

Rice, C. "Promoting the National Interest." *Foreign Affairs* 79, no. 1 (January–February 2000).

Riggle, S. "The Fuss About Turkey." *European Security Review* no. 5 (April 2001).

Robertson, A. H. *The Council of Europe.* 2nd ed. London: Stevens and Sons, 1961.

Rosamond, B. *Theories of European Integration.* London: Macmillan, 2000.

Rutten, M., ed. *From St. Malo to Nice: European Defence—Core Documents.* Chaillot Paper no. 47. Paris: WEU Institute for Security Studies, 2001.

Salmon, T., and W. Nicoll, eds. *Building European Union: A Documentary History and Analysis.* Manchester: Manchester University Press, 1997.

Schake, K. *Constructive Duplication: Reducing the EU Reliance on U.S. Military Assets.* London: Center for European Reform, 2002.

Schmitt, B. Conclusion to G. Adams, C. Cornu, and A. D. James, *Between*

Cooperation and Competition: The Transatlantic Defence Market. Chaillot Paper no. 44. Paris: WEU Institute for Security Studies, 2001.

Sheehan, M., and J. Wyllie. *Pocket Guide to Defence.* Oxford: Blackwell and Economist, 1986.

Shonfield, A. *Europe: Journey to an Unknown Destination.* Harmondsworth: Penguin, 1973.

Silj, A. *Europe's Political Puzzle: A Study of the Fouchet Negotiations and the 1963 Veto.* Occasional Papers in International Affairs no. 17. Harvard: Harvard Center for International Affairs, 1967.

Sjöstedt, G. *The External Role of the European Community.* Farnborough: Teakfield, 1977.

Skold, T. "States Pledge Resources for Crisis Management." *European Security Review* no. 3 (December 2000).

Sloan, S. "French Defence Policy: Gaullism Meets the Post Cold War World." *Arms Control Today,* April 1997.

———. *The United States and European Defence.* Chaillot Paper no. 39. Paris: WEU Institute for Security Studies, 2000.

Soetendorp, B. *Foreign Policy in the European Union.* London: Pearson Education, 1999.

Taylor, T. *European Defence Cooperation.* London: Routledge and Kegan Paul, 1984.

———. "Transatlanticism Versus Regional Consolidation." In D. G. Haglund and S. N. MacFarlane, eds., *Security, Strategy, and the Global Economies of Defence Production.* Halifax: McGill-Queen's University Press, 1999.

Terriff, T., M. Webber, S. Croft, and J. Howorth. *European Security and Defence Policy After Nice.* Briefing paper, New Series no. 20. London: Royal Institute of International Affairs, April 2001.

Thompson, J. "The Military Coalition." In J. Gow, ed., *Iraq, the Gulf Conflict, and the World Community.* London: Brassey's, 1993.

Truscott, P. *European Defence: Meeting the Strategic Challenge.* London: Institute for Public Policy Research, 2000.

van Eekelen, W. *Debating European Security, 1948–98.* The Hague: Sdu, 1998.

Vaughan, R. *Post-War Integration in Europe.* London: Edward Arnold, 1976.

Walker, W., and P. Gummett. *Nationalism, Internationalism, and the European Defence Market.* Chaillot Paper no. 9. Paris: WEU Institute for Security Studies, September 1993.

Wallace, H., and W. Wallace. *Policy-Making in the European Union.* 4th ed. Oxford: Oxford University Press, 2000.

Wallace, W. "Cooperation and Convergence in European Foreign Policy." In W. Wallace, ed., *The Dynamics of European Integration.* London: Pinter, 1992.

"X." "The Sources of Soviet Conduct." *Foreign Affairs* 25 (July 1947).

Youngs, T., M. Oakes, P. Bowers, and M. Hillyard. *Kosovo: Operation Allied Force.* House of Commons Library Research Paper no. 99/48. London: House of Commons Library, April 29, 1999.

Index

About the Book

The European Union's ineffectual actions during the Balkan wars of the 1990s have led to increasingly loud calls for this political and economic giant to develop an effective military arm—an integrated force capable of dealing with conflict in Europe's backyard and projecting military power globally. *Toward a European Army* offers a comprehensive analysis of this European defense project: its origins, purpose, and goals.

The authors ask whether a powerful European army should replace U.S. military involvement in Europe and discuss how the respective roles of the various EU countries—especially France, Germany, and Britain—should be defined. They also explore the institutional, military, industrial, and especially political practicalities of defense integration. Throughout, the issue of relations between the EU and NATO looms large.

Should a new European security system linked to the EU replace the status quo? This book equips the reader to thoroughly engage this question.

Trevor Salmon is professor of international relations at the University of Aberdeen and for many years a professor at the College of Europe. **Alistair Shepherd** is lecturer in contemporary European security at the University of Wales, Aberystwyth.